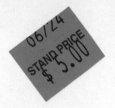

HEINRICH HEINE

PARADOX AND POET

THE POEMS

HEINRICH HEINE. From the plaque modeled from life by David d'Angers. Heine's sister, Charlotte, considered this his best likeness.

HEINRICH HEINE

PARADOX AND POET

BY

LOUIS UNTERMEYER

The Poems

HARCOURT, BRACE AND COMPANY

NEW YORK

Typography by Robert Josephy

PRINTED IN THE UNITED STATES OF AMERICA
BY QUINN & BODEN COMPANY, INC., RAHWAY, N. J.

FOR

ESTHER

Wenn ich in deine Augen seh',
So schwindet all mein Leid und Weh';
Und wenn ich küsse deinen Mund,
So werd' ich ganz und gar gesund.

CONTENTS

CONTENTS

CONTENTS

THE HOME-COMING

CONTENTS xiii

THE NORTH SEA—SECOND CYCLE

NEW POEMS

NEW SPRING

BALLADS

POEMS FOR THE TIMES

CONTENTS

ROMANCERO

NARRATIVES

LAMENTATIONS AND LAZARUS

HEBREW MELODIES

LAST POEMS—POSTHUMOUS POEMS

MISCELLANEOUS LYRICS

xxiv CONTENTS

FOREWORD

❧ 1 ❧

EVERY translator, it seems, begins his preface in an apologetic tone, proceeds to self-justification, and ends on a note of deprecating triumph. This foreword will not attempt to disturb the tradition, although the apology, the deprecation, and the defense may be somewhat mixed.

At the beginning it should be reiterated (repeated from the original and revised editions of *Poems of Heinrich Heine,* 1917 and 1923) that this translation is little more than the libretto, the "book" of the opera, and that Heine's music can be heard only in the original German. This is true of any translation; for the combination of music and meaning which is poetry—the metamorphosis into a new thing complete in itself, final and self-defining—cannot be paraphrased. The translator can only hope to render the meaning of the poem at a sacrifice of its music, or attempt, by writing an entirely new poem, to suggest the music at the expense of meaning. The versions in this volume represent a continual compromise. Where the translator deals with description, narration, wit, satire, effects of sense—fairly simple devices which can be brought over into another language—he is most nearly successful. Where he deals with the sheer songs and lyrics, with poetry as poetry, he fails flatly and inevitably. How is one to translate the tonal beauty of *Im wunderschönen Monat Mai,* which is literally the platitudinous "In the miraculously lovely month of May," or the alliterative and intricate delicacy of *Leise zieht durch mein Gemüt liebliche Geläute* which in its prose equivalent baldly says that the sweet sound of bells is softly drawing through my heart. One can as easily describe a perfume or explain a color.

Apart from the verbal melodies, which cannot be expressed in any but their own terms, the words themselves present sufficient problems. It is a curious linguistic phenomenon that most of the abstractions, e.g., Love, Faith, Truth, Joy, Grief, Life—those so-convenient English monosyllables—become *"Liebe,"* *"Glaube,"* *"Wahrheit,"* *"Freude,"* *"Kummer,"* *"Leben"* in the dissyllabic German. This basic difference has necessitated a continual recasting of the simplest lines, for Heine, though a rebel in many ways, including experiments in poetic speech, was fond of the traditional abstractions. Another difficulty which confronts the translator is the German employment of *"du"* and *"sie."* To use "thou" for *"du"* without deviation is likely to give a stilted and, often, falsely archaic ring to a poem otherwise direct, while rendering *"du"* consistently as "you" is sometimes too cool and inappropriately colloquial. In Heine, the problem is complicated, for he himself uses the more intimate personal pronoun ironically or, for certain willful effects, archaically. I have ventured to employ both pronouns without any fixed program, using "thou" and "you" wherever it seemed to fit the context, and Heine's purpose, best. We have in English no method of showing the shades of difference between the German two, and it is because of this (and incidentally because of an astonishing misconception of the poems themselves) that so many of Heine's translators have missed the point of several poems, poems which bear a subtle reminder or a sarcasm more stinging than a column of invectives. Examine the lyric Number 28 from "The Home-Coming" (see page 124) beginning *Die Jahre kommen und gehen.* The last quatrain runs:

> *Nur einmal möcht ich dich sehen,*
> *Und sinken vor dir aufs Knie;*
> *Und sterbend zu dir sprechen:*
> *"Madam, ich liebe sie!"*

"Madam, I love but you," Todhunter ineffectually concludes. Even Mrs. Browning, possibly due to her ignorance of German, rendered it, "Lady, I love but thee." And another translator, surpassing them all in incomprehension of the last line and its startling use of *"sie,"* turns Heine's bitterest irony into maudlin sentiment. Thus Robert Levy:

> Oh, that I once might see you,
> Kneel to you! Then would I
> Say: "Lady mine, I love you!"
> And, speaking so, would die.

In this lyric, as in two or three others where Heine depends on a pun for his satire, I have dared to reconstruct the lines and use a phrase totally unlike the German to indicate the strange juxtaposition, the peculiar turn of language, and the sudden twist of purpose. This is also half-true of the puzzling Number 30 in the "Lyrical Intermezzo." Here Heine, in an effort to achieve a light ironic emphasis, employs a series of French derivatives with a single rhyme-scheme. As embodying these intact would leave part of the verses untranslated without even approximating Heine's purpose (for the use of French is not, as it was with the German writers, a superelegance of language), I have paraphrased them all, depending on a series of the same double-rhymes for a similar half-satirical end.

Heine has suffered most from those who, appreciating only the superficial charm of his verse, have been repelled by the spirit behind the words. Unable, or unwilling, to see what seemed petty, painful, or, worst of all, vulgar in Heine, they have attempted to turn the rude outcries and impolite laughter into refined badinage; they have tried to prettify him into a typically sentimental minor poet.

This refusal to accept Heine as he was, with his mockery, his outspokenness, his bursts of coarseness and pain interrupting his most ecstatic moments, is the reason why many versions are, even when readable, unreliable. Some translators have taken up the work in a curiously academic manner. Here and there, a kindly professor has blinked an eye rather than witness an undignified prank; another has closed his ears to episodes too bitter or racy for the class-room. Their attitude has usually been that of smiling-superior disapproval or condescension toward a talented but badly behaved undergraduate. Either they condemned Heine's own utterances with silence or spoiled them with explanations and apologies. Charles Godfrey Leland almost negated the value of his work by inserting irrelevant, patronizing, and often admonitory footnotes throughout the volumes. Attempting to "purify" Heine, Leland not only corrected and "edited" the prose, but bowdlerized the poetry. In a posthumous poem *Ich mache die kleinen Lieder* (see page 410), obviously intended for Amalie, Heine compares his creation with hers: his songs and her children. The lyric begins with a pretty appeal and ends in a bawdy double entendre. When he came to these stanzas Leland was shocked; he dutifully translated the first three quatrains, but calmly omitted the fourth and final verse, which is the whole point of the poem. Here, and elsewhere, Leland ruined Heine as effectually as Quiller-Couch ruined Donne when he printed "The Ecstasy" in *The Oxford Book of English Verse* and deleted not only the largest part of the selection but the very lines which make the poem clear.

Heine has been violated not only by those who have endeavored to purify him, but by those who tried to prettify him. The stripped simplicity, the direct parlance, the very forthrightness seem to have been a challenge to other poets—a challenge not to render Heine's inspired colloquialisms as vividly as possible, but to change them into hyper-elegances, rhetorical flourishes, and elaborate inversions. This, for example, is the way Louise Chandler Moulton (in *At the Wind's Will*) begins her translation of *Wie dunkle Träume stehen* from *Die Heimkehr*:

> Like dark dreams stand the houses,
>   Stretched out in lengthened row;
> And shrouded close in my mantle
>   I silently by them go.

> The bell of the Cathedral
> Chimes midnight from above;
> I know, with charms and kisses,
> Now waits for me my Love.

And these are the first two incredible stanzas from the re-
nowned Havelock Ellis's translation of *Du schönes Fischermädchen* from the same cycle:

> You lovely fishermaiden,
> Push off the boat from land,
> And come and sit beside me,
> And we'll chatter hand in hand.
>
> Lay your small head on my bosom,
> And do not fear so much;
> Do you not trust you daily
> Into the ocean's clutch!

Nothing could be more ridiculous than such awkward simpers,
such stilted inversions and ludicrous stylisms; nothing could be
further from Heine's simple address and his fresh and vigorous
idiom. Heine could be humorous enough, even broadly farcical
on occasion; but he was never absurd, never unconsciously comic.

꣠ 2 ꣠

Heine has been insufficiently considered as a writer of dexter-
ous, even light, verse. In the midst of withering irony and brutal
cynicism there suddenly appear stanzas of gossamer texture and
unexpected fastidiousness. "A Miscellany" is especially rich with
these surprises. Heine carries his technique to the very limit of
prestidigitation; the lyricist who can be as naïve as Burns becomes the designer of *vers de société* to outdazzle Dobson, Praed,
and Locker-Lampson. Even Browning, with his "fabric-dab
brick," "mark ace-cigar-case," "jasmine-alas, mine," "failure-pale
lure," and "loosened-dew send" scarcely surpasses Heine with
his less frequent but equally astonishing *"Hochzeit-Ehejoch seit,"*

"Vorgestellt sein-Held sein," "Satyr-naht dir," and *"Pastor-ver-hasst Thor!"*

Besides such tricky matching of sounds, Heine often experimented in assonance, in dissonance, and in such "slant" or "suspended" rhymes as *"Käuen-speien," "glühn-Melodien," "Träume-reime," "freu'n-schein," "Lied-Gemüt,"* and others which the purist might find equally suspect. In his technical effects, as in his subject-matter, Heine continually employed new devices to vivify old themes and revitalize old patterns. His very shifting music, his fluent gravity and light diablerie is a kind of triumph over the language in which it was framed. German, with its harshly accumulating gutturals and its palatal *chs*, is anything but a liquid tongue. Yet Heine perfected a melodic speech and composed countless songs which even the Italian language for all its limpidity, has never surpassed.

It is true that Heine often echoed himself, that he luxuriated in emotion, and that his lyrics were sometimes not the result of reflection, but a reaction. Yet Heine knew how to vary his echoes and make the most of a ready response. Even his repetitions have the charm of music often heard, but no less persuasive after repeated re-hearings. The range is not extraordinary; after the initial shock the themes are not surprising; few of the ideas are new. But they are individualized by Heine's mastery of touch and effect. Never has there been a more incongruous but successful combination of sophistication and spontaneity, of grace and daring, of folk-craftsmanship and that rare art which conceals its artfulness.

To suggest the resourcefulness of Heine's technique, I have followed Heine's structures, his meters, even his rhyme-schemes throughout. With a few exceptions I have reproduced the single and double rhymes as they appear in the original. The masculine rhyme has more weight in English, the feminine is usually employed for speed and humor, while in German the reverse is true. Yet, although the single rhyme is the more natural and frequent in English poetry while it is almost the opposite in German, I felt it imperative to preserve Heine's own form in an attempt to echo some of the music. In a few instances I have departed from the pattern, though not the rhythm, where the differences in language demanded a different treatment; but such departures are exceptional.

I regret that in many cases, particularly in the very simplest of the lyrics, the exquisite and fragile music has been broken. Many of Heine's poems, wholly colloquial in speech and casual, even trite in idea, are transmuted into magic by their word-music and the perfection of vowel and consonant sound. Such properties cannot be transplanted; the sense can be captured, the magic inevitably escapes. I would suggest that, having ascertained the meaning, the reader take up the German and read the original for the virgin beauty, the intrinsic color and cadence of the melodic line.

ξα 3 ɒξ

Poems of Heinrich Heine, Selected and Translated by Louis Untermeyer, was first published in 1917; it contained 325 poems, chiefly short verses. The present volume represents, first of all, a more scrupulous revision than the preceding collection. But its principal distinction is its amplification; to the original 325 poems more than half as many again have been added, so that there are now some 500 translations. Moreover, instead of consisting almost wholly of brief lyrics, this volume includes several poems of considerable length, such as "For La Mouche," "The God Apollo," "Jehuda ben Halevy," which, with its 600 lines, is almost a book in itself, and more of the ballads, the political, and the posthumous poems. Thus, with the exception of the book-length "Germany" and "Atta Troll," which are represented in this volume only by a selection or two, no important poem of Heine has been omitted. The two chief sequences from

the "Book of Songs" ("Lyrical Intermezzo" and "The Home-
Coming") have been translated in their entirety, as well as prac-
tically all of the early "Dream Pictures," the two "North Sea
Cycles," the "New Poems," the later "Romancero" and the final
"Lazarus." Several of the poems appear in English, for (as far as
I have been able to ascertain) the first time, and, as mentioned
before, all the translations are unexpurgated.

A few changes have been made in the conventional arrange-
ment of the poems. The main groups are printed as they appear
in most of the German editions, but I have rearranged the
posthumous work, printing it in what seems to be the natural
sequence. It is impossible to speak definitely about the date of
composition of all the posthumous poems; and if here and there
I have erred on the side of arbitrariness, it is because I prefer an
order which is poetically logical rather than strictly chrono-
logical. For the most part, however, I have followed the order in
which the verses appeared in the collections printed by Hoff-
mann and Campe, Heine's original publishers.

                                                    L. U.

Elizabethtown, N. Y.
1937.

THE BOOK OF SONGS

PREFACE TO THE THIRD EDITION
OF THE "BOOK OF SONGS"

Das ist der alte Märchenwald

It was the old, enchanted wood;
    The linden was in flower.
The cold, white magic of the moon
    Inflamed me with its power. . . .

I wandered on, and as I went
    I heard the heavens ringing;
Of love and the keen ache of love
    The nightingale was singing.

Of love and the keen ache of love
    She sang; of tears and laughter—
So sad her mirth, so sweet her sobs,
    That dead dreams followed after.

I wandered on, and as I went
    A wide space lay before me.
And there, with towering spires, there rose
    A castle huge and stormy.

Barred were its windows; over all
    Lay grief and silence, giving
The sense that in these wasted walls
    Nothing but Death was living.

Before the door there lay a Sphinx,
    Half-horrible, half-human;
A lion's form in body and claws,
    The forehead and breast a woman.

3

A woman fair! Her marble gaze
Was sensuous and commanding.
Her dumb lips curved into a smile
Of secret understanding.

The nightingale so sweetly sang,
What use was my resistance—
I kissed her radiant face, and that
Transformed my whole existence.

For lo, the marble statue woke;
The stone was touched with fire;
She drank the fervor of my kiss
With an unslaked desire.

She drank my very breath from me
And then, with lustful ardor,
Her lion's claws sank in my flesh,
Holding me closer, harder.

O exquisite torture, rapturous wounds!
O pain and pleasure unending!
For while I drank the kiss of her mouth
The claws were tearing and rending.

The nightingale sang, "O wondrous Sphinx,
O Love, why this always distressing
Mingling of death-like agony
With every balm and blessing?

"O lovely Sphinx! Explain to me
This riddle that puzzles sages.
I've pondered on it hopelessly,
Alas, for many ages."

.   .   .   .   .

—I could have said all this just as well in decent prose. . . . But when one reads over one's old poems, freshening a phrase here and there, and touching them up for a new printing, the tinkling habit of rhyme and rhythm steals over one imperceptibly—and lo! it is with verse that I open this third edition of the "Book of Songs."

O Phoebus Apollo! if these verses be bad thou wilt surely forgive me. For thou art an all-wise god, and thou knowest well enough why it was that many years have passed since I have busied myself exclusively with the measuring and harmonizing of words. . . . Thou knowest why the flame which once delighted the world with its brilliant display of fireworks was suddenly turned to a more serious blaze. . . . Thou knowest why this silently glowing fire is now consuming my heart. Thou dost understand me, great and glorious god; for even so didst thou exchange, now and again, the golden lyre for the mighty bow and the death-dealing arrows. . . . Dost thou not still remember Marsyas, whom thou didst flay alive? That was long ago, and a similar example may be necessary. . . . Thou smilest, O my eternal Father!

Heinrich Heine

Written in Paris, February 20, 1839.

YOUNG SORROWS
(1817-1821)

DREAM PICTURES

Mir träumte einst von wildem Liebesglühn

I used to dream of love's perennial pains,
  Of myrtle, mignonette, and maiden's tress,
  Of lips turned bitter and of lips that bless,
Of doleful lyrics set to dirge-like strains.

Those dreams have perished with the changing times,
  Their very pattern vanished; all that last
  Are the old pains and passions which I cast
Into the soft and sentimental rhymes.

Only the song persists! . . . You, too, should fade,
  Tracking a vision that I used to know;
  And should you find the dream of long ago,
This empty breath salutes that breathless shade.

Ein Traum, gar seltsam schauerlich

A strange dream shuddering through the night
Brought me half fear and half delight;
The scenes still play before my eyes
And clutch my heart with cold surprise.

There was a garden good to see,
In which my whole soul longed to be;
Flowers there were, a jeweled lawn;
It was a joy to look upon.

Birds twittered happily and sang
Of love until the twilight rang;

9

The setting sun in red and gold
Made every color twice as bold.

Light odors flung their snares aloft;
The evening airs were sweet and soft;
And all was friendly, all was fair,
Spreading its magic everywhere.

Among the flowers that edged the wood,
A massive marble fountain stood,
And there a maid bedecked in light
Busily washed a garment white.

Pale cheeks, mild eyes, demeanor quaint,
The very portrait of a saint;
And as I gazed, I saw that she
Was strange yet, somehow, known to me.

There, within that flowery ring,
Over her task, I heard her sing:
"Water, work your crystal spell;
Wash my linen—wash it well!"

Closer I crept; I felt no dread
Until she saw me. Then I said,
"Tell me, you lovely child of light,
For whom do you wash that garment white?"

Her words came swift, her voice was sweet:
"This garment is your winding-sheet—
Your winding sheet!" And as she spoke
The dream, like some great bubble, broke.

Then the scene shifted and I stood
Within a gaunt and gloomy wood.
Dark trees shot, towering, to the skies;
I stood, and stared, and rubbed my eyes.

Hark! A dull echo beat, as though
A distant ax struck blow on blow.
Swiftly I tore through tangled space
Until I reached an open place.

There, in that spot, that green escape,
An oak upreared its noble shape;
And, with an ax upon that oak,
The maid—my maid—laid stroke on stroke.

Stroke upon stroke, nor stop nor stay;
And as she swung I heard her say:
"Iron, iron, hew to the line;
Hurry and hew me an oaken shrine."

Closer I crept; I felt no dread
Until she saw me. Then I said,
"Tell me, child of the shining cloak,
For whom do you make this house of oak?"

Her words came swift: "Your hours are few;
It is your coffin that I hew.
The time is short!" And as she spoke
The dream, like some great bubble, broke.

Now all lay waste, leafless and dour;
Nothing but black and barren moor.
How I came there I did not know;
I only shuddered that it was so.

And as, with aimless feet, I strayed
I saw a glow, a glimmering shade;
I hurried, stumbling through a glen,
And lo—it was the maid again!

There, in that wide and lifeless waste,
She dug earth deep, she dug with haste.

She was so fearsome, yet so fair,
I scarcely dared to look at her.

Steel upon stone—I felt it ring—
And over her task, I heard her sing:
"Shovel, plow from side to side;
Plow me a pit that is deep and wide."

Closer I crept; I felt no dread
Until she saw me. Then I said,
"Tell me, child with brow severe,
What should a pit be doing here?"

Her words came swift: "Be still! Be brave!
This is your cool and quiet grave."
And, as she spoke, the air grew chill,
And the wide pit yawned wider still.

Spite of myself, I peered below;
Black horror shook me, throe on throe.
The grave gaped wider; the ground broke,
Plunging me down.—And I awoke.

Im nächt'gen Traum hab' ich mich selbst geschaut

I dreamed I saw myself puffed out with pride,
    From head to foot, elaborately dressed
    As for a festival: black coat, silk vest:
And my dear love was standing at my side.
I bowed to her and said, "Are you the bride?
    Congratulations—ah—my very best!"
    Yet something clutched my quivering throat, repressed
The formal sounds until they choked and died.

And then the sound of weeping filled my ears;
    It was my love—her pale, unhappy face

Almost dissolved in a great wave of tears.
Oh, innocent eyes, love's holy stars, deceive
   Me once again; whate'er the time or place,
Sleeping or waking. I would still believe!

Im Traum sah ich ein Männchen, klein und putzig

   I dreamed I saw a dwarf in dapper clothing,
      Who walked on stilts, each step an ell or more.
      Sported white linen—but the stuff he wore
   Was black inside: one saw the dirt with loathing.
   Within he was all sham; a fuss and frothing
      To draw attention from the rotting core.
      He talked of being brave, and was a bore.
   His courage was all cant, and came to nothing.

   "And do you know that man, or can you guess?"
      The Dream-god asked me; and he showed me then
      A picture of a church. . . . And of all men
   The dwarf was at the altar, nothing less,
   My love beside him; both were saying "Yes!"
      And twice a thousand devils laughed "Amen!"

   Was treibt und tobt mein tolles Blut?

   Why is my mad blood rushing so?
   Why is my heart in such a glow?
   My blood speeds like an angry dart,
   And seething fires consume my heart.

   My blood is boiling, foaming, mad,
   Because of an evil dream I've had. . . .
   He came, the shadowy son of Night,
   And bore me, gasping, in his flight.

He brought me to a brilliant house
Where harps and lights and gay carouse
And revelers raised a merry din.
I reached the hall; I entered in.

It was a wedding revelry;
The guests were mingling merrily;
And when the happy pair I spied—
Alas! My darling was the bride.

It was my love in all her pride,
A smiling stranger at her side.
I crept up close behind their chair,
And silently I waited there.

The music grew; I stood quite still;
The happy clamor made me ill.
The bride, with ecstasy possessed,
Folded the bridegroom to her breast.

I saw the bridegroom fill his glass
And drink and with a gesture pass
The wine to her. She drank and laughed.—
And, woe! It was my blood they quaffed.

The bride then took an apple, and
Put it into the bridegroom's hand.
He took a knife and cut it straight.—
And, woe! It was my heart they ate.

Their looks were long, their glances blazed;
He held her lovingly embraced,
Kissing her hot cheeks passionately.—
And, woe! 'Twas Death's cold lips on me.

My tongue lay in my mouth like lead—
I could not speak, the words fell dead.
And then—the music through the hall,
The bridal couple leading all!

I stood there, lost to all the world;
The dancers round about me swirled.
His words grew warm, his whispers bold:
She reddened, but she did not scold. . . .

Im süssen Traum bei stiller Nacht

In a sweet dream one silent night
Magic declared its secret might:
My love, a flower of magic bloom,
Came without warning to my room.

I gazed at her, that lovely child;
I gazed at her; she smiled and smiled,
Until my anguished heart found tongue
In words impassioned and unstrung.

"Take all, take everything I own;
Grant me one thing, one thing alone:
Be mine, completely mine, and stay
From midnight till the break of day."

She eyed me long and curiously,
With a strange look. And then said she,
"Give me your hope of heaven, give me
Your soul for all eternity."

"My youth's hot blood, my life distraught,
I'd give without another thought;
Whate'er you ask is gladly given—
But not, oh love, my hope of heaven."

The wild words poured out passionately.
She merely stood and smiled at me,
Lovelier still, and shook her head:
"Give me your hope of heaven instead."

The words fell on me heavily;
A flood, like a foreboding sea,
Swept o'er my spirit, evil-starred;
My breath came slow, my breath came hard.

There had been angels here that shed
Glory about each golden head;
But now a horde of loathsome, black
Goblins were swarming to attack.

They battled with the sons of light,
Driving them out into the night;
And then the loathly crew likewise
Vanished like mist before my eyes.

Meanwhile, I held her close to me,
Dying, it seemed, of ecstasy;
She nestled softly, like a roe,
Yet weeping with a nameless woe.

I kissed her mouth, suspecting why
She wept. "Be still, my love," said I,
"Fear nothing now; all will be well.
Come, yield yourself to love's sweet spell."

"Come, yield yourself to love's sweet spell"—
Suddenly all the heavens fell;
My blood turned ice; the wild air beat;
And the earth yawned beneath my feet.

Out of that black, abhorrent vale
The black crew swarmed—my love turned pale!
Out of my arms she slid, my own,
Leaving me utterly alone.

About me all the goblins danced,
In narrowing circles, then advanced
And seized me, held me prisoner there,
While mocking laughs rang everywhere.

Narrower still the circle grew
And louder laughed the hideous crew:
"He gave his hope of heaven, he
Is ours for all eternity."

Ich kam von meiner Herrin Haus

I came from my love's house and stood,
Wrapped in a dark and midnight mood,
Within a lonely churchyard, where
The tombstones glistened bright and bare.

It was the glimmering moon that shone
Still brighter on the Minstrel's stone.
I heard, "Wait, brother—the hour flies."
And, pale as the mist, I saw him rise.

It was the Minstrel, bone for bone,
Who rose and sat on his crumbling stone;
He grasped his zither and sang this song
In a voice that was hollow and harsh and strong:

"Ha! do ye know the old refrain,
Ye strings, that echo with its pain?

> Know ye the name thereof?
> The angels call it Heaven's desire,
> The devils call it Hell's own fire,
>   And man, he calls it—Love!"

Scarce had he shouted the final word
When all the buried people stirred.
Up from their graves they rose, and sprang
About the Minstrel as they sang:

> "Love, oh, Love, your power has led
> Us to this, our final bed.
> Eyes are closed in a quiet head—
> Why do you call and rouse the dead?"

And loudly they rattled and whimpered and wailed,
They chattered and clattered and rumbled and railed;
And madly the swarm ran round and about,
While the Minstrel played, and sang with a shout:

> "Bravo! Bravo! Madmen still!
> Welcome, madmen,
> Good and bad men,
> That my magic words could thrill!
> Ye who lie, year in, year out,
> In a dark and dusty drought,
> Let this be a merry rout!
> But look first
> If there's anyone about.
> Fools we were when we were living,
> While our burning blood was giving
> Us a mad and passionate thirst.
> Now, for pastime and for glory,
> Everyone shall tell his story;

Tell what brought him to this place;
   How he fared
   And was snared
In Love's mad and furious chase."

And then from the circle, as light as the wind,
There hopped a lean phantom who hummed as he grinned:

"A tailor's lad was I, sirs,
   (With needle and with shears,)
I was so slick and spry, sirs,
   (With needle and with shears.)
My master's daughter tricked me
   (With needle and with shears,)
And to the heart she pricked me
   (With needle and with shears.")

The spirits all laughed till their skeletons shook;
And a second stepped forth with a serious look:

"O, Rinaldo Rinaldini,
Robin Hood and Orlandini,
And Carl Moor (the best of those)
Were the models that I chose.

"I, too, in a milder fashion,
Like these brigands, tasted passion;
While a certain lady's face
Haunted me from place to place.

"All my hopes were crushed and saddened;
And, when Love at last grew maddened,
My mad fingers, growing rash,
Dipped into my neighbor's cash.

"But a watchman who was jealous
Said my mourning was too zealous;
Said I tried to dry my griefs
In my neighbor's handkerchiefs.

"Then the old policemen caught me;
To the station-house they brought me;
And the great, gray prison pressed
Me to its maternal breast.

"Thoughts of love (I could not choke 'em)
Plagued me still while picking oakum;
Till Rinaldo's shadow passed
And released my soul at last."

The spirits all laughed with a boisterous shout;
And powdered and perfumed, a third stepped out:

"As king of the boards I had striven
    To play every amorous rôle;
How often I ranted, 'Oh heaven!'
    And whispered a wild, 'Ah, my soul.'

"As Romeo none could do better;
    (My Juliet was always so fair!)
Though I acted my lines to the letter
    She never would answer my prayer.

"One night, as I started to stagger
    At the end, and as 'Juliet!' I cried,
I stuck the sharp point of the dagger
    A little too deep in my side."

The spirits all laughed with a boisterous shout;
And, clad in a white cloth, a fourth stepped out:

"The professor talked of the spirit and letter.
  He talked, and he talked—and I slept right well.
But one thing of his I enjoyed far better:
  His daughter, more lovely than words could tell.

"For me were her eyes and the smiles that she lavished,
  My flower of flowers, my Love's own light!
But my flower of flowers was stolen and ravished
  By a sour Philistine, a wealthy old blight.

"Then I cursed all rich scoundrels and women together;
  The devil's own brew I prepared at the end.
I drank with Lord Satan (two birds of a feather),
  Who hiccuped '*Fiducit*, old Death is your friend.' "

The spirits all laughed with a boisterous shout;
And, a rope 'round his neck, a fifth stepped out:

"The Count, he boasted and bragged at his wine
Of his daughters divine and his jewel so fine.
Your jewel, dear Count, may be ever so fine,
But, truly, I'd rather your daughter were mine.

"The Count kept them both under lock, bolt, and key;
And a houseful of servants to guard them had he.
What mattered his locks and his servants to me—
I got me a ladder and mounted with glee.

"I stood at her window with ardor and joy,
When I heard a voice calling beneath me, 'Ho, boy!
Fine doings, my lad, but give me my share—
I'm also in love with the jewel that's there.'

"And thus the Count jeered at and mocked me, the while
His servants flocked 'round, with a sinister smile.

'The devil!' I cried. 'Do you think I would thieve?
I came for my love, which I'll take by your leave.'

"But anger availed not, nor pleadings nor prayers;
And they marched in a solemn parade down the stairs.
When the sun rose, she started, astonished to see
The gallows so shining and heavy—with me."

The spirits all laughed in a boisterous shout;
With his head in his hand, a sixth stepped out:

"Love drove me to the poacher's trade,
And, musket on my arm, I strayed
Beneath the trees where ravens scoff
And croak and cough: 'Heads—off! Heads—off!'

"Oh, if I only saw a dove
I'd bring it home to my true love;
And, so determined, every tree
Received my hunter's scrutiny.

"What do I hear? What billing's that?
Two turtle-doves! I've got 'em pat.
I crept up close; I caught the pair—
And lo! I found my own love there!

"It was my nestling dove, my bride;
A strange man snuggling at her side.
Now, you old marksman, aim; aim well!
There, in his blood, the stranger fell.

"Soon, through the woods, the hangman's crew,
With me, chief actor, in review
Passed the same trees where ravens scoff
And croak and cough: 'Heads—off! Heads—off.' "

The spirits all laughed in a boisterous chorus;
Until the Minstrel himself stepped before us:

"I once had a song that I cherished,
　But that sweet song is gone.
When the heart has loved and perished
　Then all of the singing is done."

And the crazy laughter grew twice as loud,
As the circle swayed wide with its ghostly crowd,
The bells struck "One" . . . and, to a man,
Howling into their graves they ran.

Ich lag und schlief, und schlief recht mild

I lay and slept, and slept right well,
　Free of the old despair;
When in my deepest dream there fell
　The vision, fond and fair.

Her face was like a marble girl's,
　But lovelier with the change;
Her eyes had the cold sheen of pearls,
　And her bright hair was strange.

And softly, without stir or start,
　That maiden, marble-pale,
Came and lay down upon my heart,
　Mutely and marble-pale. . . .

I throb and thrill with hot unrest,
　The maddest fevers rise;
No throb nor thrill shakes her fair breast
　That is as cold as ice.

"No throb nor thrill can stir my breast
    That is as cold as ice.
Yet I know Love's eternal quest,
    Its pain and paradise.

"My mouth and heart's unwarmed with blood,
    No red stream courses through.
But do not shudder—think how good
    And kind I am to you."

She held me tight until the dawn,
    Struggling to no avail.
A cock crowed once . . . and she was gone,
    Mutely and marble-pale.

Da hab' ich viel blasse Leichen

My rhythmic conjurations
    Have called up phantoms and ghosts,
Who scorn my supplications
    To join the spectral hosts.

The spell that should make them obey me
    I've forgotten in anguish and fright.
Now it is they who gainsay me;
    'Tis I who am ruled by their might.

Ye demons hateful and hellish,
    Begone, and let me be!
There's many a joy to relish
    Still on this earth for me.

Desperate, glad or grieving,
    For one fair flower I pine;
Life is not worth the living
    Unless her love is mine.

If only once I might press her
  Lips, her heart, and her hair!
Completely to possess her,
  What torments would I not bear!

If only her mouth would turn kindly
  With one loving word or a kiss,
I'd follow you, phantoms, blindly
  Down to your darkest abyss.

The phantoms have heard, they press near me;
  Grinning, they grapple and shove.
My love, I implore you, hear me!
  My love, I implore you for love!

          Einsam klag' ich meine Leiden

  Lonely now, I pour my sadness
    In the intimate lap of night,
  Far from every human gladness,
    Far from men and their delight.

  All alone, my tears are flowing,
    Flowing softly, flowing still;
  But my heart's too-fiery glowing
    No amount of tears can chill.

  As a boy, a merry, thieving
    Youngster playing games alone,
  Care-free with the joy of living,
    Sorrow was a thing unknown.

  Then the world was one great garden
    Made for me, whate'er I chose;

And my work was but as warden
  Of the violet and the rose.

Golden skies and emerald grasses,
  And the sapphire brook flowed by . . .
Now, although the same brook passes,
  Pale's the picture meets my eye.

Pale am I, too, so they tell me,
  Since she wrought the deadly change.
Secret sorrows overwhelm me;
  Everything is sad and strange.

Once I felt a hushed assembling
  As of angels in my heart;
Now there's turbulence and, trembling,
  All the wings of peace depart.

Night, a blacker night, is falling;
  Shadows threaten, monstrous grown;
In my breast a voice is calling—
  And the voice is not my own.

Flames too frightful to believe in
  Shoot through veins like evil wine,
And my very bowels are riven
  With a fire that is not mine.

The dark voice, the unresting fire,
  These unholy flames that run
Through my heart till I expire—
  This, my love, this you have done!

SONGS

Wenn ich bei meiner Liebsten bin

When I am with my own adored,
  Oh, then my heart beats high;
I am as rich as any lord,
  The world is mine to buy!

But every time I leave her, then
  My wealth, that seemed secure,
Is spent; and I am once again
  The poorcst of the poor.

Morgens steh' ich auf und frage

Mornings I arise and wonder
  Will she come today?
Evening passes, still I ponder;
  Still she stays away.

In the night with heavy cumber
  Sleeplessly I lie;
And half dreaming, half in slumber,
  All my days go by.

Es treibt mich hin, es treibt mich her!

It drives me here, it drives me there;
  Soon, in an hour or two, I shall meet her,
  Yes, she herself, and what else could be sweeter—
Heart of mine, why are you throbbing with care?

The hours are such a lazy lot!
  Creeping along with one foot dragging,
  Going the rounds, yawning and lagging—
Come, stir yourselves, you lazy-bones!

Now I am seized with the madness of speed.
  Oh, but they never were lovers, these hours;
  Banded together with hideous powers
They mock at the lover's unrest and his need.

Ich wandelte unter den Bäumen

Wandering under dark branches,
  Alone with my despair,
Touched with a host of memories
  I started dreaming there.

"Who taught you that word, oh, you songsters,
  You linnets that circle and soar?
Oh, cease, for whenever I hear it
  My heart is tormented once more."

"A girl came singing it always;
  From her own lips we heard,
And all of us birds recaptured
  That lovely, golden word."

"Oh, how can you tell such a story,
  You birds, so sagacious and sly;
You also would capture my sorrows—
  But I will trust no one, not I."

Lieb Liebchen, leg's Händchen aufs Herze mein

Beloved, lay your hand on my heart in its gloom.
Do you hear that! Like tapping inside of a room?

A carpenter lives there. With malice and glee
He's building a coffin, a coffin for me.

He hammers and pounds with such fiendish delight
I never can sleep, neither daytime nor night.
Oh, carpenter, hurry the hours that creep;
Come, finish your labors—and then I can sleep.

Ich wollte, meine Lieder

I wish that all my love-songs
    Were flowers bright and rare;
I'd send them to my dearest
    And she might find them fair.

I wish that all my love-songs
    Were kisses that could speak;
I'd send them to my dearest
    To hang about her cheek.

I wish that these, my love-songs,
    Were peas, so firm and fat;
I'd make a nice, rich pea-soup—
    And she would relish *that!*

In Vaters Garten heimlich steht

In father's garden there stands apart
    A flower, unhappy and pale.
Winter has gone, Spring fervors start,
    But the flower still remains pale.
The flower looks hollow-eyed,
Like a too delicate bride.

The pale flower saw me; softly she said,
    "Pluck me and joy will be ours."

"Not I," I answered, shaking my head,
  "I pluck no pallid flowers;
I look to find instead
A blossom burning red."

Pale flower said, "Seek here, seek there,
  Seek on till you are dead,
You seek in vain; you'll find nowhere
  Your blossom burning red.
But pluck me, wanderer, do—
I am as sick as you."

Thus whispered pale flower and pleaded so,
  I plucked it in haste and fear,
And the blood that was bitter ceased to flow,
  And the eyes of my spirit grew clear,
And in my wounded breast
Peace came to rest.

Schöne Wiege meiner Leiden

Lovely cradle of my sorrow,   ·
  Lovely tomb where peace might dwell,
Smiling town, we part tomorrow.
  I must leave; and so farewell.

Farewell, threshold, where still slowly
  Her belovèd footstep stirs;
Farewell to that hushed and holy
  Spot where first my eyes met hers.

Had you never caught or claimed me,
  Fairest, heart's elected queen,
Wretchedness would not have maimed me
  In its toils, as you have seen.

Never have you found me grieving
   For your love with anxious prayer;
All I asked was quiet living,
   Quietly to breathe your air.

But you drove me forth with scourging
   Bitter words and lashing scorn;
Madness in my soul is surging,
   And my heart is flayed and torn.

And I take my staff and stumble
   On a journey, far from brave;
Till my head droops, and I tumble
   In some cool and kindly grave.

Warte, warte, wilder Schiffsmann

Wait, oh, wait, impatient pilot;
   First, before the boat can stir,
There must be a double parting
   Both from Europe and from her.

Blood, break from my broken body,
   Blood, flow from my eyes like rain;
So, with blood that's bright and burning,
   I can write down all my pain.

Ah, my love, why should you shudder
   Just today to watch me bleed?
Many a year you've seen me wounded,
   Many a year, and paid no heed.

You recall the ancient legend
   Of the serpent's subtle lies,

How his apples plunged our parents
Headlong out of Paradise.

Apples always spread misfortune!
    With them Eve brought death with shame.
Flame was brought to Troy by Eris.
    You—you brought both death and flame.

Berg' und Burgen schaun herunter

Hill and hall are mirrored brightly
    In the clear glass of the Rhine;
And my little ship sails lightly
    Where the sunlit waters shine.

Quietly I watch the shaken,
    Golden billows at their play;
And the thought still comes to waken
    What I hoped was laid away.

For the stream leaps to enamor
    With its warm and laughing light;
Yet I know, for all its glamor,
    Death is in its heart—and night.

Stream, you are her own reflection:
    She can also smile and sin;
She, like you, is all affection—
    Fair outside, and false within.

Anfangs wollt' ich fast verzagen

I despaired at first, declaring
    It could not be borne; and now—
Now I bear it, still despairing.
    Only never ask me how!

Oben wo die Sterne glühen

Overhead, where stars are glowing,
Surely there we will be knowing
   All the joys denied us here.
Life itself in the enormous
Arms of death at last will warm us,
   And the endless night will clear.

Mit Rosen, Cypressen und Flittergold

With rose and with cypress, with tinsel and gold,
This book I'd embellish, brilliant and bold,
Like a royal casket to make men stare,
And all my songs would be buried there.

Could I bury my love, ah, that would be best!
On the grave of love grows the flower of rest.
Others may gather the blossom, not I.
'Twill bloom for me only when buried I lie.

Here, then, are the poems, impulsive and hot
As the lava-streams which from Aetna shot,
Hurled from the depths, leaving many a gash,
With the livid flame of a lightning-flash.

Now, cold as corpses, they lie on their bier,
With fixed, hollow eyes, lackluster, here.
Yet swiftly the blood would leap and flow
If love were to breathe on them, set them aglow.

Now in my heart there are whispers that pray
Love will weep over these songs some day.
Some day this book will come to your hand,
My own dear love, in a distant land.

And on that day love will break the spell;
The cold, dead letters will live and be well.
Your eyes will revive them; the words will move
With the breath and the pain and the longing of love.

Die du bist so schön und rein

Thou who art so fair and fine,
Lovely little lady mine,
All myself, bad or benign,
To thy service I'd consign.

Those sweet eyes retain a shine
Softer than when moonbeams twine;
On thy cheeks appears the sign
Of a rose-bud dipped in wine.

And thy mouth reveals a line
Of fairer pearls than crown the Nine.
Yet the jewel most divine
Lies within thy bosom's shrine.

May our love ne'er be malign,
Ne'er disturb the soul or spine;
Thou art pure, and I am thine,
Lovely little lady mine.

Wenn junge Herzen brechen

When young hearts break with passion
  The stars break into laughter,
They laugh and, in their fashion,
  Gossip a long time after:

"Poor souls, those mortals languish
  With Love; 'tis all they cherish.

It pays them back with anguish
  And pain until they perish.

"We never can discover
  This Love, so brief and breathless,
So fatal to each lover—
  And hence we stars are deathless."

Die Wälder und Felder grünen

There's green on meadow and river;
  The lark seeks a loftier height;
And Spring has come in with a quiver
  Of perfume and color and light.

The lark's song has opened the prison
  Of winter-moods, stubborn and strong;
Yet out of my heart has arisen
  A fragment of sorrowful song.

The lark's all a-twitter and cheery:
  "Oh, what makes your singing so drear?"
The song is an old one, my dearie,
  I've sung it for many a year.

'Tis the same ballad, no other,
  With its burden of sorrowful rhymes—
Why, darling, your own grandmother
  Has heard it a score of times!

Ich dacht an Sie den ganzen Tag

I thought about her all the day,
  I thought about her half the night,
And then, while fast asleep I lay,
  A dream disclosed her to my sight.

Like a young rose her color came,
   Sitting so quietly at peace;
She held a small embroidery frame
   Worked in young lambs with virgin fleece.

She looked at me to no avail;
   Why I was there she did not know.
"What makes your face so drawn and pale?
   Heinrich, tell me, what hurts you so?"

She looked so tenderly that I
   Trembled; the tears began to flow.
"Why do you weep so hard? And why
   Are you in pain? Who hurts you so?"

She looked so mild, so much at rest,
   My words leaped like an angry blow:
"The pain, my dear, is in my breast;
   You are the one who hurts me so."

Then she stood up and laid her hand
   Upon my heart; like a release
The suffering ceased at her command,
   And once again I was at peace.

Ich will mich im grünen Wald ergehn

I shall go and walk in the woods a space,
Where flowers are gay and birds are singing;
For when I am once laid six feet under,
With eyes and ears that are closed to wonder,
I shall not see one flower lift its face
Nor hear one bird's song set the silence ringing.

Tag und Nachts hab' ich gedichtet

I have written daily, nightly;
Still I have done nothing rightly.
Lyric fret, melodic frothing—
And it all has come to nothing.

Dass ich dich liebe, o Möpschen

That I must love you, Mopser,
  You surely understand;
For when I feed you sugar
  You always lick my hand.

You're nothing but a doggie
  And only pose as such.
All of my other friends, alas,
  Disguise themselves too much.

Gewiss, gewiss, der Rath wär gut

Certainly the advice was good—
But ours was young and eager blood.
We poured, we drank till we were dumb;
We knocked, and someone answered "Come!"

If, here and there, a fair one frowned,
We knew where kisses could be found.
And when the glass was drained of wine,
Well—grapes still grow along the Rhine.

Lieben und Hassen, Hassen und Lieben

Loving and hating, hating and loving,
Life has swept over me, recklessly moving;

I have tasted it all to the bitter core—
Yet I am the same as I was before.

Du warst ein blondes Jungfräulein, so artig

You were a maiden, blonde, without a flaw,
Perfect and prim. I stayed, but never saw
The hour when you (fond, foolish expectation!)
Opened your heart to any inspiration—

To inspiration for one noble thing
Of which not only poets dare to sing,
But simple certainties the whole world yearns for,
And mankind somehow suffers, bleeds, and burns for.

There was a day I won't forget along the Rhine:
The hills were heavy with the terraced vine.
We walked. The sun laughed; gulls were soaring;
Out of each flower's heart warm scent was pouring.

Roses and pinks, confessing their desire,
Sent forth red kisses, little jets of fire;
Even the daisy's gold held brighter plunder,
And every wayside weed was touched with wonder.

But you, in your white dress, walked on with me,
So careful of yourself, so properly;
Neat as a Netcher painting, pink and nice—
Beneath your stays, a little heart of ice.

THE NUPTIAL EVE

1

Mit deinen grossen allwissenden Augen

Yes, you are right. Your all-wise glances
  Brim with a truth that makes me sad.
How could we two have met life's chances—
  You are so good, and I so bad.

I am so bitter and malicious;
  Even my gifts bear wry respect
To you, who are so sweet and gracious
  And, oh, so righteously correct.

2

O, du kanntest Koch und Küche

Oh, you knew the cook and kitchen,
  Every turn and nook and bin;
In our childhood plays and struggles
  You would be the one to win.

Now you've won my own belovéd,
  That is droll; but, truth to tell,
This, my friend, is even droller:
  I must smile and wish you well!

3

O, die Liebe macht uns selig

"Oh, 'tis Love that makes us grateful,
  Oh, 'tis Love that makes us rich!"
So sings man, and every fateful
  Echo bears his amorous speech.

You, you know the song's own spirit
  And its inner meaning, too;
Joyfully you wait and hear it
  Till the great day dawns for you.

Till the bride, with a caressing
  Smile is yours, from head to feet,
And her father gives his blessing—
  And a few things more concrete.

Linen, silver by the crateful,
  Silks with many a costly stitch. . . .
Oh, 'tis Love that makes us grateful,
  Oh, 'tis Love that makes us rich!

4

Der weite Boden ist überzogen

The ground is carpeted with flowers,
  The woods are a triumphal arch;
And songsters in a thousand bowers
  Strike up a glad and welcoming march.

It is the Spring who enters, spreading
  Joy from his gay and sparkling eyes. . . .
You should have asked him to your wedding,
  For he goes gladly where true love lies!

ROMANCES

THE STRICKEN ONE

Allen thut es weh im Herzen

Every heart is moved to sorrow
  When they see this pale young swain,
Whose pale face bears many a furrow
  Printed deep by living pain.

Winds compassionately stealing
  Cool his brow, but he goes by;
Girls would gladly furnish healing,
  Maidens circumspect and shy.

From the city's wild upheaval
  Toward the wood he goes, and grieves,
Though he knows the gay, primeval
  Song of birds and laugh of leaves.

But whene'er he nears the forest
  Laughter ceases, leaves hang still.
Hushed are all the birds that chorused;
  And the wood grows sadly chill.

THE MOUNTAIN ECHO

Ein Reiter durch das Bergthal zieht

A horseman through a valley rode
  Singing a solemn stave:

"Am I nearer now to my true love's arms,
   Or am I nearer the grave?"
      There was no answer, save
      "Nearer the grave."

And farther still the horseman rode,
   And a sigh broke from his breast:
"Though I must pass to my last abode,
   Perhaps the grave brings rest."
      And echo half-expressed
      "The grave brings rest."

The sorrowful horseman wept a tear,
   And from his cheek it fell,
"And if in the grave there's rest for me
   Then all in the grave is well."
      And echo rose to tell
      "The grave is well."

TWO BROTHERS

Oben auf der Bergesspitze

On the summit stands a palace
   Wrapped in night and gloomy shades;
In the deepest of the valleys
   Comes the lightning-clash of blades.

They are brothers who, contending
   Furiously for love and land,
Fight on to a tragic ending.
   Brothers! Each with sword in hand!

Countess Laura's glance of fire
   Burned them till they were undone;

Drunk with love, their one desire
  Is for her, the peerless one.

Which of them has won her favor?
  Which will make the maid his bride?
Who can say which is the braver?
  Out, then, sword! Let death decide!

Oh, that men should act so towards men!
  Blow meets blow with reckless might!
Watch yourselves, you savage swordsmen;
  Evil is abroad tonight.

Woe! O woe! O bloody brothers!
  Woe! O woe! O bloody heath!
Each contender on the other's
  Sword has fallen, done to death.

.   .   .   .   .

Dust now many a generation;
  Many a century has gone;
Gloomy on its lordly station,
  The old castle still looks down.

But each midnight something happens:
  On that terror-haunted plain
There's the ghostly flash of weapons,
  And the brothers fight again.

POOR PETER

1

Der Hans und die Grete tanzen herum

Oh, Hansel and Gretel are dancing around,
There's shouting and clapping of hands there.

But Peter looks on with never a sound,
And, paler than chalk, he stands there.

For Hansel and Gretel are bridegroom and bride,
Around them the radiance lingers.
But Peter, in workaday clothes, turns aside;
He mutters, and bites his fingers.

Poor Peter still gazes; his grief is intense;
And, watching the pair, he starts sighing:
"Oh, were it not for my good, common sense
I'd end all my sorrows by dying."

2

"In meiner Brust, da sitzt ein Weh"

"Within my breast there's such a woe
      That I am torn asunder.
It stirs, and though I stay or go
      It drives me always yonder.

"It drives me to my love, it cries
      As though she still could heal me.
Alas, one look from Gretel's eyes
      And I must fly, conceal me.

"I climb the mountain's highest peak:
      Man is, at least, alone there;
Where all is still and none may seek
      My heart may weep and moan there."

3

Der arme Peter wankt vorbei

Poor Peter, he goes stumbling by
As pale as lead, ashamed and shy.

And all the people stand and stare
Whenever Peter passes there.

The girls all whisper, "Give him room,
He must have risen from the tomb."
Ah, no, my dears, your pity save;
He's only going to his grave.

He's lost his love, his future's dim,
And so the grave's the place for him;
For there his tortured spirit may
Await in peace the Judgment Day.

THE PRISONER'S SONG

Als meine Grossmutter die Liese behext

When grandma bewitched little Lisa, 'twas rich,
　For magic was just her obsession;
Though everyone cried, "Let's burn the old witch!"
　She never would make a confession.

Yet when the flames leaped and the caldron was hot,
　She screamed and she yelled bloody murder;
Then she turned to a raven right there on the spot,
　And croaked, although nobody heard her.

Come back, little black-feathered grandmother dear,
　Come, visit me down in this dungeon.
Come, fly through the grating that keeps me in here,
　And bring cheese and cake for my luncheon.

Come back, little black-feathered grandmother! Rise
　And save me from more than my sorrow.
Let none of your relatives pick out my eyes
　When I swing on the gallows tomorrow.

THE GRENADIERS

Nach Frankreich zogen zwei Grenadier'

Toward France there wandered two grenadiers;
In Russia they had been taken.
And as they reached the German frontiers,
Body and spirit were shaken.

For there they learned the tragic tale
That France had been lost and forsaken;
The Army had suffered to no avail,
And the Emperor, the Emperor was taken!

They wept together, those two grenadiers;
To one thing their thoughts kept returning.
"Alas," said one, half choked with tears,
"That old wound of mine keeps burning."

The other said, "This is the end;
With you I'd gladly perish.
But there's the homeland to defend,
And wife and child to cherish."

"What matters wife? What matters child?
With far greater cares I am shaken.
Let them go and beg with hunger wild
My Emperor, my Emperor is taken!

"And, brother, this my only prayer,
Now I am dying, grant me:
You'll bear my body to France, and there
In the soil of France you'll plant me.

"The cross of honor with crimson band
Lay on my heart that bound me;

Then put the musket in my hand
  And strap my saber round me.

"So I will lie and listen and wait,
  A sentinel, down in the grass there,
Till I hear the roar of the guns and the great
  Thunder of hoofs as they pass there.

"The Emperor will come and the columns will wave;
  The swords will be flashing and rending;
And I will arise, full-armed, from the grave,
  My Emperor, my Emperor defending!"

THE MESSAGE

Mein Knecht! steh auf und sattle schnell

My page! arise and quickly mount
  The horse of swiftest stride;
And breathlessly, through wood and field,
  To Duncan's palace ride.

Wait softly in the stable there
  Until you are espied;
Then ask, "Which one of Duncan's girls
  Is going to be a bride?"

And if they say "The dark-haired one"
  Then rush home like the blast.
But if they say "The light-haired one"
  You need not ride so fast.

But in the village buy a rope,
  A rope with toughened strands.
Then ride back slowly, speak no word,
  And place it in my hands.

BRINGING HOME THE BRIDE

Ich geh' nicht allein, mein feines Lieb

I'll not go alone, my lovely love,
  For thou must go thither
To the dear, old, lawn-like part of the glen
And the drear, cold, yawning heart of the fen,
Where Mother keeps watch and cowers outside
Until her poor son brings home his bride.

"Oh! touch me not, thou fearful man!
  Who summoned thee thither!
Thy hand is ice, though thy breath is bold;
Bright are thine eyes, but thy cheek is cold;
And I have a right to be free, to run
Where the roses breathe in the light of the sun."

Let the roses breathe, let the sun shine on,
  My best belovéd!
Put on your white veil and your bridal attire,
Pluck every string of the sounding lyre,
And sing the words of a wedding-song
The night-wind knows. We must get along.

DON RAMIRO

Donna Clara! Donna Clara!

"Donna Clara! Donna Clara!
Loved for years and loved with sorrow!
You have caused my utter ruin,
Caused it without grief or pity.

"Donna Clara! Donna Clara!
Life has gifts of joy and splendor;
In the earth it's cold and gruesome,
And the grave's the last surrender.

"Donna Clara! Life laughs with you!
Don Fernando on the morrow
Guides you to the happy altar.—
Will you ask me to your wedding?"

"Don Ramiro! Don Ramiro!
Those words wound me; they are bitter,
Bitter as the stars' cold sentence,
Menacing my fixed intention.

"Don Ramiro! Don Ramiro!
Rouse yourself from morbid fancies.
Earth is full of willing maidens.
God has made our parting final.

"Don Ramiro! You who bravely
Overcame the Moorish armies,
Overcome yourself. Take courage.
Come tomorrow to my wedding."

"Donna Clara! Donna Clara!
I will be there—yes, I swear it!
We will dance there, never fear it.
So farewell until tomorrow.

"So farewell." The window clatters.
Don Ramiro stands there sighing;
As though turned to stone he stands there.
Then he disappears in darkness.

Darkness also disappears
As the long night yields to morning,
And the fair town of Toledo
Glows like some great flower-garden.

Palaces and precious buildings
Glitter in the growing sunshine,
And the towering domes of churches
Glisten as though newly gilded.

As if iron bees were swarming
Distant chimes increase their humming;
Prayers and psalms are rising sweetly
From God's consecrated houses.

But below them! There! Look yonder!
With a surge and restless uproar,
See, the festive crowd is coming
From the market-place cathedral.

Shining knights and shimmering ladies,
Even gaily tricked-out servants—
And the great bells peal their loudest,
And the organ-tones grow fervent.

Suddenly the horde of people
Makes a passage, rapt and reverent,
For the radiant bridal couple,
Donna Clara, Don Fernando.

Thousands of glad eyes caress them,
Thousands of glad voices praise them:
"Hail, Castile's fair maid of maidens!
Hail, fair flower of Castile's knighthood!"

And the jubilant procession
Brings them to the bridegroom's palace;
And the ancient ceremonies
Are begun in proper fashion.

Games, and bouts, and banquet tables—
All is mirthful merry-making;
Heedlessly the hours are flying
While the light of day is dying.

Now the wedding-guests assemble
In the great hall for the dancing;
Every costume is a jewel
Suddenly illuminated.

Bride and bridegroom have been seated
On an almost regal dais;
Donna Clara, Don Fernando.
Hold a smiling conversation.

In the hall the happy dancers
Move to laughing waves of music;
While the drums declare their summons
And the horns blare out the answer.

"But, my lovely lady, tell me,"
Pleads the knight, perplexed and anxious,
"Why your gaze is so intently
Fixed upon that one far corner."

"Do you not see, Don Fernando,
That strange figure darkly mantled?"
And the knight smiles reassurance:
"That? 'Tis nothing but a shadow."

But the shadow, drawing nearer,
Is a man completely shrouded.
Donna Clara, trembling, flushing,
Recognizes Don Ramiro.

Now the dance begins, the dancers
Whirl and whisper, interweaving
In a waltz's circling measure,
While the floor throbs with their pleasure.

"Gladly I will tread this measure
Hand in hand with you, Ramiro;
But 'twas hardly kind to come here
Clad in such funereal garments."

Fixed his eyes are, fixed and piercing,
As he looks on his belovéd;
Then, a muffled drum, he answers,
"It was you who bade me come here."

Whereupon the two are swallowed
In the whirlpool of the dancers,
While the drums declare their summons,
And the horns blare out the answer.

"Ah! Your cheeks are white and ghastly!"
Whispers Clara, terror-stricken.
"It was you who bade me come here."
And they waltz into the whirlpool.

"Leave me! Leave me! Don Ramiro!
For your breath recalls the graveyard!"
Once again the words fall darkly:
"It was you who bade me come here."

Smoke coils from the glowing dance-floor;
Gayer sweeps the fiddle-music;
Everything is swiftly circling
In a web of mad enchantment.

"Leave me! Leave me! Don Ramiro!"
Like a whimper in a wind-storm.
And her lover always answers,
"It was you who bade me come here."

"Go, then, go! Depart in God's name!"
Clara cries in mortal anguish.
And the words are scarcely spoken
When she sees Ramiro vanish.

There she totters, night-enveloped,
While an icy hand benumbs her;
Then, with death in every feature,
Utter darkness overcomes her.

Gradually the mists of slumber
Leave her, and she lifts her eyelids;
But amazement swiftly follows
Till she fears to keep them open.

For, through all the din and dancing,
She has never left the dais;
She is still beside her bridegroom,
As the anxious knight inquires:

"Tell me why your cheek grows pallid?
What should make your bright eyes darken?"
"But Ramiro—?" stammers Clara,
And her tongue is stiff with horror.

Deeper still the questioning furrows
Gather on the bridegroom's forehead.
"Darling, why seek tragic tidings?
Don Ramiro died this noonday."

BELSHAZZAR

Die Mitternacht zog näher schon

The noon of night was drawing on;
Dark silence lay on Babylon.

But in the castle of the King
Were flaring lights and reveling;

There, in the royal banquet hall,
Belshazzar held high festival.

He saw his brilliant court recline
And empty bowl on bowl of wine.

He heard cups ring and vassals sing,
And all the brawling pleased the King.

The wine awoke and made him bold;
He flushed; his words grew uncontrolled.

Wine was his passion, wine his prod;
With obscene oaths he mocked at God.

He blasphemed Heaven and all its laws;
The wild court echoed with applause.

The King commanded, his brow was black;
The servant vanished, but hurried back,

Carrying treasures, rich and rare.
The spoil of Jehovah's Temple was there.

The King laid hands on a sacred cup;
With a lewd laugh he filled it up.

He drained the goblet in one quick draught,
And then, with slobbering lips, he laughed:

"Jehovah! I drink to your greatness gone;
I am the King of Babylon!"

The blasphemous words had scarce been said
When something struck the King with dread.

The ribald laugh died in the hall;
Silence fell like a deathly pall,

While on the white wall there appeared
A human hand, abrupt and weird,

And wrote, and wrote, in letters of flame,
And wrote, and vanished the way it came.

The King's pale features seemed to freeze;
He could not quiet his knocking knees.

Stone-cold about him his courtiers were;
They gave no sound, they made no stir.

Magicians came, yet none of all
Could read that writing upon the wall.

And in the night death came to one
Belshazzar, King of Babylon.

THE MINNESINGERS

Zu dem Wettgesange schreiten

Come the minnesingers, raising
　　Dust and laughter and lament.
Here's a contest that's amazing;
　　Here's a curious tournament.

Wild and ever restless Fancy
　　Is the minnesinger's horse,
Art his shield, the Word his lance; he
　　Bears them lightly round the course.

Many women pleased and pleasant,
　　Smile and drop a flower down;
But the right one's never present
　　With the rightful laurel-crown.

Other fighters nimbly canter
　　To the lists, care-free and whole;
But we minnesingers enter
　　With a death-wound in our soul.

And the one who wrings the inmost
　　Song-blood from his burning breast,
He's the victor; he shall win most
　　Praise and smiles and all the rest.

THE WOUNDED KNIGHT

Ich weiss eine alte Kunde

I know an old, old story;
　　Sad is the sound thereof:

A knight lies worn and wounded
  With grief for a faithless love.

He knows her faithless and scorns her,
  Yet hangs on her wretchedly;
He knows his passion is shameful,
  Yet knows it is stronger than he.

He longs to ride to the tourney
  And shout with a challenging stir,
"Let him prepare for the death-blow
  Who finds a blemish in her!"

But well he knows there'd be silence
  From all save his own unrest;
And his own lance would have to be leveled
  At his loud and accusing breast.

SEA-VOYAGE

Ich stand gelehnet an den Mast

I looked and counted every wave,
  Propped by the mast for pillows.
Farewell, belovéd fatherland;
  My ship plows through the billows.

We sailed past the belovéd's house,
  The windows were aflame there;
I watched each window, heart in mouth,
  Yet no one waved or came there.

Tears, do not blind my straining eyes;
  Leave me the pain of seeing.
And you, sick heart, break not with this
  New agony of being.

TO A SINGER

HEARING HER SING AN OLD BALLAD

Ich denke noch der Zaubervollen

She lives as clearly, that enchantress,
  As when she came into my ken.
Her voice was soft yet, somehow, ringing;
Each note a miracle of singing
That caught my heart and held it, clinging.
  I scarcely knew what happened then.

I dreamed, I sank into a vision:
  It seemed I was a child again
Deep in a fairy-tale; a glowing
Lamp showed the room; a fire was going.
Outside a bitter wind was blowing—
  It was a night of autumn rain.

And then life blew into the legends:
  Knights rose up, shining, from the grave;
As a fierce cavalcade came riding,
Roland himself swept out of hiding,
And at his heels, a black snake gliding,
  Came crafty Ganelon, the knave.

How shamefully is Roland bedded;
  Breathless and drowned in blood he lies.
Great Charles will never hear one flying
Blast from the horn beside him lying;
Roland, heroic heart, is dying,
  And with his death the vision dies.

But what unwelcome summons snatched me
  Out of my dream, brusque as a blow.

Gone were the legend and the glamor;
Hand upon hand began to hammer;
"Bravos" arose above the clamor—
 And the fair singer curtsied low.

THE LESSON

Mutter zum Bienelein

"Little bee, little bee,
Careful—stay close to me."
But what a bee should hear
Falls on a heedless ear.

Soon to the light he flies,
Deaf to his mother's cries
Calling him tremblingly:
"Little bee! Little bee!"

Blood of youth, never tame,
Seeks the eternal flame,
Where it burns fierce and free.
"Little bee—little bee."

Now with a mighty breath
Flame seeks a flaming death . . .
"Careful—beware of joy—
Oh, my boy! Little boy!"

THE SONG OF THE DUCATS

Meine güldenen Dukaten

O my golden ducats, say
Whither have you flown away?

Are you with the golden fishes
Flashing, floating, in the nooks I'd
See in every silver brookside?

Are you with the gilded blossoms
Scattered through the dewy meadow,
Sparkling in the shine and shadow?

Are you with the birds up yonder,
Stars of day, whose wings enliven
With their flight the daylit heaven?

Are you with the stars that glisten
In the deeper heavens nightly,
Smiling fixedly but brightly?

Ah, my little golden ducats,
Brooks and such are not for you;
Not for you the heavens blue,
Not for you the meadows fair,
Not for you the upper air.
Creditors—a word that awes!—
Hold you in their horrid claws.

DIALOG ON PADERBORN HEATH

Hörst du nicht die fernen Töne

Do you hear the dim and sprightly
Sounds of double-bass and fiddle?
Fair ones must be dancing, lightly
Swinging up and down the middle.

"My poor friend, you are mistaken.
Fiddles? Fiddlesticks! The squeaking

Comes from living pork and bacon;
   Piglings grunting, sows a-shrieking."

Did you hear that bugle blazing
   As the hunt swept through the forest?
Did you see the lambkins grazing
   While the shepherds' wood-winds chorused?

"Bugles? Wood-winds? These are words, man!
   Neither shepherds roamed, nor hunters.
It was nothing but the herdsman
   Driving home his pack of grunters."

Do you hear far spirits voicing
   Beauty unsurpassed, inspiring?
Angels clap their wings, rejoicing
   To applaud such heavenly choiring.

"Spirits? Angels? What's the use, boy,
   Of such fancies? Far from pious,
That was just a singing goose-boy
   And his geese that wandered by us."

Surely bells are now in motion;
   And from acres green with tillage
People walk in strict devotion
   To the chapel in the village.

"Nonsense, man! Those are the lowing
   Oxen and the bells of cattle
Plodding through the darkness, going
   To their stalls of mud and wattle."

And that veil, those soft, commanding
   Gestures—say, are those not real?

There my own true love is standing;
   There she waits, the lone ideal.

"She who teases you so much is
   None else but that poor old shadow,
Lisa, on her worn-out crutches,
   Limping slowly through the meadow."

Well then, friend, continue chaffing;
   I confess to the confusion.
Take my dreams; destroy them, laughing.
   Is my heart, too, an illusion?

ABSOLUTELY!

Wenn der Frühling kommt mit dem Sonnenschein

When the Spring comes in and the sun is bright
Then every small blossom beckons and blows.
When the moon on her shining journey goes
Then stars swim after her through the night.
When the singer looks into two clear eyes
Then something is stirred and lyrics arise . . .
But flowers and stars and songs just begun,
And moonbeams and eyes and the light of the sun,
No matter how much such stuff may please,
One can't keep living on things like these.

SONNET: TO MY MOTHER

Ich bin's gewohnt den Kopf recht hoch zu tragen

Stubborn and proud, I carry my head high;
Haughty by birth, inflexible by mood,
I would not bow to any king, I would
Not even veil my candid gaze, not I.

But, mother, never let me dare deny
How soon my pride, my boastful hardihood,
Shamed by your presence and solicitude,
Leaves me, without one small departing sigh.

Is it your spirit that o'ermasters me,
Your lofty, penetrating soul that clears
The earth, and cleaves to heaven, flying free?
Memory burns and rankles, for I know
How often I have brought your heart to tears,
The soft and suffering heart that loved me so.

FRESCO SONNET TO CHRISTIAN S(ETHE)

Ich lache ob den abgeschmackten Laffen

I laugh at all the puppies, fops, and dandies
    Who stare at me with such a goatish mien;
I laugh at every fox who can command his
    Nostrils to sniff at everything that's clean;
I laugh at monkeys who delight to tell us
    How wise they are, how proud of all their arts;
I laugh at all the cool and cowardly fellows
    Who hide and threaten us with poisoned darts.

For when Good Fortune suddenly has halfed her
    Donations or withdrawn her gifts in scorn,
    When beauty lies forgotten or forlorn,
And all is hurt and hopeless—even after
    The heart is broken, cut apart, and torn,
We still can laugh, a high and bitter laughter.

LYRICAL INTERMEZZO
(1821-1823)

LYRICAL INTERMEZZO

Meine Qual und meine Klagen

All my anguish, all my rages,
  I have poured and nought concealed here;
And, if you should turn these pages,
  You will find my heart revealed here.

PROLOG

Es war mal ein Ritter, trübselig und stumm

There once was a knight full of sorrow and doubt,
  With cheeks white as snow; indecision
Would lead him to stumble and stagger about
  As though he were trailing a vision.
And he was so wooden, so awkward and dumb
That flowers and maidens, whene'er he would come,
  Would watch him, and laugh in derision.

And often he'd sit in his gloom-shrouded place
  (From men and their joys he had broken)
Stretching thin arms in a yearning embrace,
  Though never a word would be spoken . . .
But just as the hours to midnight now ran,
A marvelous singing and ringing began,
  With a knock at his door for a token.

And lo, his love enters—a zephyr that blows;
  Of shimmering sea-foam her dress is.
She glows till she grows like the bud of a rose,
  Her veil gleams with gems; and her tresses
Fall to her feet in a golden array;

67

Her eyes are impassioned. The lovers give way
And yield to each other's caresses.

He holds her so close that his heart almost breaks.
The wooden one now is afire;
The pallid one reddens, the dreamer awakes,
The bashful is bold with desire.
But she, she coquettes and she teases, and then
With her magical veil she must blind him again,
Who blindly does nought but admire.

In a watery palace of crystalline light
She has 'witched him, and all that was bitter
Turns golden and fair, all is suddenly bright;
His eyes are bemused with the glitter.
The nixie still presses him close to her side;
The knight is the bridegroom, the nixie the bride—
Her maidens keep playing the zither.

Oh, sweetly they sing and sweetly they play;
Fair feet in the dances are shown there;
The knight in his ardor is swooning away
And tighter he clasps her, his own there . . .
Then all in an instant is plunged into gloom,
And our hero is sitting once more in his room.
In his poet's dim garret—alone there!

1

Im wunderschönen Monat Mai

All in the magic month of May
When every bud was springing,
My heart was filled with fervors,
With dreams of young love clinging . . .

All in the magic month of May
  When every bird was singing,
I poured out all the rapture
  With which my heart was ringing.

2

Aus meinen Thränen spriessen

Out of my tears and sorrows
  The blossoming flowers arise,
And nightingales in choir
  Are born of all my sighs.

Dear child, if you would love me
  Those flowers to you I bring—
And here before your window
  The nightingales would sing.

3

Die Rose, die Lilje, die Taube, die Sonne

The rose and the lily, the dove and the sun,
I loved them all once—before love had begun.
I love them no more. I worship now solely
The one and the only most holy and lowly.
She herself is the spirit of all these in one;
Being Rose and the Lily, the Dove and the Sun.

4

Wenn ich in deine Augen seh'

Whene'er I look into your eyes
Then all my grief and sorrow flies;

And when I kiss your mouth, oh, then
I am made well and strong again.

And when I lean upon your breast
My soul is soothed with godlike rest;
But when you say, "I love you!" See
How I must weep, how bitterly!

5

Dein Angesicht, so lieb und schön

Your face has grown so dear, it seems
A vision only seen in dreams;
So seraph-like, so mild and frail,
And still so pale, so sadly pale.

Only your lips are red, and they
Soon kissed by death turn cold and gray;
And dimmed will be the azure skies
That lie within those candid eyes.

6

Lehn' deine Wang' an meine Wang'

Oh, lean your cheek against my cheek,
  Our tears thus shall mingle and flow, love.
And to my heart press close your heart,
  The flames beating so, love, shall glow, love.

And when the leaping radiance glows
  With tears like torrents thronging,
And when my arms are enfolding you close,
  I die of Love—and longing.

7

Ich will meine Seele tauchen

I will baptize my spirit
  In the lily's glowing core;
The lily shall tremble and hear it,
  A song of the one I adore.

That song shall live and have me
  Thrilled with a subtle power,
Like the kiss that once she gave me
  In a sweet and poignant hour.

8

Es stehen unbeweglich

Immovable for ages
  The stars are set above;
They look upon each other
  With all the pain of Love.

And, oh, they speak a language,
  So wondrous, each to each,
That not the wisest scholar
  Can understand their speech.

But I have learned it, and never
  Can I hear it again unmoved;
For lo, I used as a grammar
  The face of my beloved!

9

Auf Flügeln des Gesanges

On the wings of song, my dearest,
  I will carry you off, and go
To where the Ganges is clearest;
  There is a haven I know.

In the moonlight's glow and glister
  Fair gardens radiate;
Eager to greet their sister
  The lotus-flowers wait.

Violets tease one another
  And gaze at the stars from the vales;
Roses are telling each other,
  Secretly, sweet-scented tales.

And lightly, trespassing slowly,
  Come the placid, timid gazelles;
Far in the distance, the holy
  River rises and swells.

Oh, that we two were by it!
  Beneath a palm by the stream.
To drink in love and quiet,
  And dream a peaceful dream.

10

Die Lotosblume ängstigt

The lotus-blossom cowers
  Under the sun's bright beams;
Her forehead drooping for hours,
  She waits for the night among dreams.

The Moon, he is her lover,
  He wakes her with his gaze;
To him alone she uncovers
  The fair flower of her face.

She glows and grows more radiant,
  And gazes mutely above;
Breathing and weeping and trembling
  With love—and the pain of love.

11

Im Rhein, im schönen Strome

In the Rhine, that stream of wonder,
  The great, the holy Cologne
Is mirrored, and there under
  The waves the Cathedral is shown.

The Cathedral has within it
  A portrait done in gold;
And, in my wild life's sin, it
  Has taken a wondrous hold.

Mid flowers and angels she stands there
  Our Lady we bow before.
But the eyes and the lips and the hands there
  Are those of the one I adore!

12

Du liebst mich nicht, du liebst mich nicht

You love me not—you love me not.
  Oh, that's a trivial thing.
For when I see your face, my lot
  Is that of any king.

You hate me, hate me—even this.
Your red lips dare declare it!
Well, let me have those lips to kiss,
And I, my child, can bear it.

13

Du sollst mich liebend umschliessen

O come, love—now I resign me,
  I yield myself to your charms;
O come, that you may intertwine me
  With the tenderest, supplest of arms.

And winding thus and wounding,
  Embracing and crushing, is shown
The fairest of serpents surrounding
  The happiest Laocoon.

14

O schwöre nicht und küsse nur

O kiss me, love, and never swear,
For women's oaths are light as air!
Your speech is sweet, but sweeter is
The perfect silence of your kiss!
'Tis this alone that has my faith—
The word is but a perfumed breath.

.   .   .   .   .

Well, swear then, love; oh, swear away;
I will believe each word you say!
And as I sink upon your breast
I will believe that I am blessed;
I will believe your love of me
Stretches beyond eternity.

15

Auf meiner Herzliebsten Äugelein

Upon my dearest's little eyes
  I make the best *canzoni*.
Upon her mouth, so small in size,
  The best of *terza rima*.
Upon my darling's cheeks, likewise
  I make the loveliest stanzas . . .
And if she had a heart, upon it
I'd make a really charming sonnet.

16

Die Welt ist dumm, die Welt ist blind

The world is dull, the world is blind.
  Each day more of a mad one!
It says, my dear, that, to its mind,
  Your character's a bad one.

The world is dull, the world is blind.
  Its dullness is really distressing;
It does not know how your kisses are kind,
  And how they can burn with their blessing.

17

Liebste, sollst mir heute sagen:

Come, and you shall tell me, dearest,
  Are you not a thing of dreams,
Such as, when the summer's clearest,
  From the poet's fancy streams?

Ah, but no, a mien so mild, dear,
  Such a mouth and eyes that wait,

Such a loving, lovely child, dear,
   Not a poet could create.

Basilisks whose glances freeze or
   Hippogriffs and dragons dire;
Horrid, fabled things like these are
   Fashioned in the poet's fire.

But yourself and your pretenses,
   And those eyes that could not hate—
And those false and fervent glances
   Not a poet could create.

18

Wie die Wellenschaumgeborene

Like the Foam-born, my love glows in
   Splendor and her beauty's pride,
For she is the happy chosen
   One to be a stranger's bride.

Though this treason may be hard on
   You, my heart, poor patient one;
Bear it, bear it still, and pardon
   What the pretty fool has done.

19

Ich grolle nicht, und wenn das Herz auch bricht

I will not mourn although my heart is torn,
Oh, love forever lost! I will not mourn.
Although tricked out in white and diamond light,
No single ray falls in thy heart's deep night.

I know this well. . . . I saw thee in a dream
And saw the night within thy heart supreme;
And saw the snake that gnawed upon thy heart.
I saw how wretched, oh, my love, thou art.

20

Ja, du bist elend, und ich grolle nicht

Yes, you are wretched, and I do not mourn—
   Wretched, my love, it seems we both must be.
Until in death the weary heart is torn
   Wretched, my love, it seems we both must be.

I see the twisted, scornful mouth; the wide
   Defiance in the sudden-blazing eye;
I see the bosom heave with angry pride.
   Yes, you are wretched, wretched even as I.

Your lips contract with unseen thrusts of pain;
   The tears are hidden; but adversity
Stabs the proud breast again and yet again—
   Wretched, my love, it seems we both must be.

21

Das ist ein Flöten und Geigen

The violins are shrilling;
   The trumpets blaze and blare;
The wedding-music is thrilling;
   My love is dancing there.

With what a droning and groaning
   The drums and reeds are rent;
While, sobbing and bemoaning,
   The cherubim lament.

22

So hast du ganz und gar vergessen

So now you have forgotten wholly
How once your heart was mine, mine solely;
Your heart had so sweet and so false a glow,
Nothing is sweeter or falser, I know.

So the love and the pain is forgotten wholly
That tortured my heart and made it lowly,
But whether the pain was as great as my love,
I know not. I know they were both great enough.

23

Und wüssten's die Blumen, die kleinen

And were it known to the flowers
    How wounded my heart must be,
Their tears would fall in showers
    To heal my agony.

If nightingale and linnet
    Knew of my sadness and pain,
Their singing would have in it
    A far more joyful strain.

If sorrow's tearful traces
    The golden stars could see,
They would come down from their places
    And try to comfort me.

But they cannot comprehend it—
    One, only, knows my pain;
She took my heart to rend it
    Again and yet again.

24

Warum sind denn die Rosen so blass

Oh, why are all the roses so pale,
  My love, come tell me why?
Oh, why, in fields that could not fail,
  Do violets droop and die?

Oh, why, to the sound of so doleful a lute,
  Do linnets lift their wings?
Oh, why does there spring from each fragrant root
  The odor of dead things?

Oh, why does the sun send so dreary a ray
  Over fields where he shone so brave?
Oh, why is all of the earth as gray
  And desolate as a grave?

And I, myself, am so troubled and weak;
  My love, why should this be?
Answer, my own; my lost darling, speak—
  Why have you done this to me?

25

Sie haben dir viel erzählet

They have told you many stories
  And made a great to-do;
But why my spirit worries
  Has not been told to you.

They made a stir and pother,
  Complaining and shaking the head,

"A devil!" they said to each other;
And you believed all they said.

And yet the very worst thing
They never have even guessed;
For the worst and most accurst thing,
I carry hid in my breast.

26

Die Linde blühte, die Nachtigall sang

The linden blossomed, the nightingale sang,
The great sun laughed with a friendly light;
You kissed me, my love, and the while my heart sprang,
To your palpitant bosom you folded me tight.

The raven screamed harshly, the withered leaves fell,
The sun's cold greeting was sharpened with spite;
We beckoned each other a frosty farewell,
And politely you curtsied a curtsey polite.

27

Wir haben viel für einander gefühlt

How deep we were wrapped in each other's life,
How well we behaved (and how bitter the moral);
How often we played at man and wife,
With never a blow or the sign of a quarrel.
We sported together in joy and in jest
And tenderly kissed and sweetly caressed;
And finally playing, like children that go
At hide and seek in the woodland together,
We managed to stray and hide ourselves so
That each of us now is lost to the other.

28

Ich glaub' nicht an den Himmel

I have no faith in Heaven
  Of which the preachers write;
Your eyes I do believe in—
  They are my Heaven's light.

I have no faith in Godhead
  Of which the preachers read;
Your heart I do believe in—
  No other God I need.

I have no faith in Satan,
  In Hell and Hell's fierce smart;
Your eyes I do believe in—
  And in your wicked heart.

29

Du bleibest mir treu am längsten

You were steadfast and true the longest;
  Your care you always gave me,
  Your thought would cheer and save me
When fear and need were strongest.

A gift of gold would not grieve you,
  And food you ne'er denied me;
  With linen you supplied me
Whene'er I had to leave you.

And for this great amount, He,
  The Lord, I pray will be tender
  To you and reward the splendor
Of your amazing bounty.

30

Die Erde war so lange geizig

The earth kept hoarding up its treasure;
  May spent it to a mighty babel
Of all that laughed and voiced its pleasure—
  But I, I find I am not able.

The bells' and flowers' speech reprove me,
  The birds converse as in the fable;
But all these wonders do not move me,
  For life is sad, and joy unstable.

Man bores me, even as the merest
  Gossip of friends about the table—
Because she is no longer "dearest,"
  But "Madam" . . . Hence my soul wears sable.

31

Und als ich so lange, so lange gesäumt

And thus, as I wasted many a day
In wandering and dreaming the hours away,
My love found the waiting too long a recess,
She started to sew on her wedding-dress;
And caught in her arms (oh, deluded and dupèd)
As husband, the stupidest one of the stupid.

My loved one is so mild and fair
Her likeness haunts me everywhere;
The rose-cheeks and the violet-eyes
Year in, year out, their ghosts arise.
And that I should lose a love so dear,
Was the stupidest act of my stupid career.

32

Die blauen Veilchen der Äugelein

The violets blue which are her eyes,
The crimson rose which her cheek outvies,
The lilies white which her hands disguise,
These blossom and glow; they never fade.
It's only the heart that has decayed.

33

Die Welt ist so schön und der Himmel so blau

The world is so fair and the heaven so blue
And the breezes so mild that come whispering through,
And the flowers arise on the roadside anew,
And glisten and gleam in the morning dew,
And mankind is happy, whatever the view—
And yet I would lie in the grave uncherished
With only the ghost of a love that has perished.

34

Mein süsses Lieb, wenn du im Grab

Love, when you sink where darkness lies
    Before you and behind you,
I shall go down with all that dies
    And seek you out—and find you.

I'll clasp you with kisses, burning and wild,
    So pale, so unmoved, and so cold there.
Trembling and weeping, rejoicing and mild
    I will grow like a corpse and mold there . . .

The dead stand up as midnight calls,
    They dance thro' airy spaces.

We two remain, wrapped in our palls;
  I lie in your embraces.

The dead stand up; the Judgment Day
  Calls them to pain or pleasure.
But we will dream the hours away
  Together at our leisure.

35

Ein Fichtenbaum steht einsam

A lonely pine is standing
  In the North where high winds blow.
He sleeps; and the whitest blanket
  Wraps him in ice and snow.

He dreams—dreams of a palm-tree
  That far in an Orient land
Languishes, lonely and drooping,
  Upon the burning sand.

36

Schöne, helle, goldne Sterne

Stars, with fair and golden ray,
Greet my loved one far away;
Say that I still wear the rue,
Sick at heart and pale—and true.

37

Ach, wenn ich nur der Schemel wär'

The Head Speaks:
Oh, were I but the stool that she

Uses to rest her feet from pain;
Yes, though she stamped and trod on me,
I would not murmur or complain.

The Heart Speaks:
Oh, were I but the cushion, too,
That holds the needle she employs;
Yes, though she pierced me through and through,
Each stab would wake the wildest joys.

The Song Speaks:
Oh, were I but the least—the mere
Paper with which she curls her hair!
Then would I whisper in her ear
What stirs in me, and all I dare.

38

Seit die Liebste war entfernt

Since, my love, we had to part
Laughter died within my heart.
Many jesters quip and quaff;
But I cannot hope to laugh.

Since my love was lost to me
Weeping also ceased to be.
Broken, tortured, robbed of sleep—
But I cannot even weep.

39

Aus meinen grossen Schmerzen

From my great grief, I fashion
The little songs I utter;

They lift bright wings, and flutter
Off to her heart with passion.

Over her bosom they hover—
  But soon they fly homeward complaining;
  Complaining but never explaining
What, in her heart, they discover.

40

Ich kann es nicht vergessen

It will not die, but solely
  This thought comes to condole,
How once I had you wholly;
  Your body and your soul.

Your body still I crave for,
  Your body's lovely growth.
Your soul you may dig a grave for;
  I've soul enough for us both!

I'll cut my spirit in two, dear,
  And breathe in you half of the whole
And clasp you—thus forming anew, dear,
  One perfect body and soul.

41

Philister in Sonntagsröcklein

Smug burghers and tradesmen are tripping
  Through woods in the smartest style;
Like goats they are hopping and skipping,
  Admiring 'fair Nature' the while.

In eyes that are bleary and blinking
A ray of romance springs;
And great, long ears are drinking
The song the sparrow sings.

But I am beclouding and shrouding
My windows with curtains of gray;
For a host of specters are crowding
To pay me a visit today.

The old love comes in, creeping
From death's immense domain;
She sits by my side, and, weeping,
She melts my heart again.

42

Manch Bild vergessener Zeiten

From graves of times forgotten
Old visions come to me
Revealing what, when near you,
My life once used to be.

By day I wandered dreaming
Through streets and alleys until
The people looked at me wondering;
I was so gloomy and still.

By night it was somewhat better—
The streets were an empty rout;
And I and my shadow together
Went staggering blindly about.

With ever-echoing footsteps
I crossed the bridge by chance;
The moon broke through the darkness
And shot me an earnest glance.

I stood there, before your dwelling,
And gazed into the night;
Gazing up at your window
My heart was torn at the sight . . .

I know that, from the window,
Those lonely streets you scanned,
And saw me in the moonbeams,
Like some white pillar stand.

43

Ein Jüngling liebt ein Mädchen

A young man loves a maiden
Whose heart for another has yearned;
This other loves another
By whom his love is returned.

The maiden weds in anger
The first good man she spies
Who runs into her pathway;
The youth grows bitter and wise.

It is an old, old story
But one that's always new;
And every time it happens
It breaks a heart in two.

44

Freundschaft, Liebe, Stein der Weisen

Friendship, Love, the Philosopher's stone,
These three things are ranked alone;
These I sought from sun to sun,
And I found—not even one!

45

Hör' ich das Liedchen klingen

I hear an echo singing
  The song she sang for me;
And a fresh grief is wringing
  My heart's old agony.

A wild unrest is sweeping
  Me where the high woods grow;
There I shall lose, through weeping,
  My overburdening woe.

46

Es schauen die Blumen alle

Now all the flowers are gazing
  At the glowing and radiant sun,
And all of the brooks are seeking
  The heart of the sea as they run.

And all of the songs are flying
  To the most desired and dear—
Take with you my tears and my sorrows,
  Ye songs that are saddened and drear.

47

Mir träumte von einem Königskind

I dreamed of the daughter of a king;
    With teary, weary faces
We sat beneath a linden's wing,
    Wrapt in each other's embraces.

"I do not want thy father's throne,
    His scepter with gold o'erladen,
I do not want his brilliant crown,
    I want but thee, dear maiden."

"That cannot be," she said to me,
    "For in the grave I am lying,
And only at night I come to thee,
    Because my love is undying."

48

Mein Liebchen, wir sassen beisammen

My dearest, we nestled devoted,
    Alone in a fairy-like bark.
The night was still; and we floated
    Out on the watery dark.

A Spirit-Isle we discovered
    In the moonlight's vague expanse;
Where airy music hovered
    And wove with a misty dance.

The sounds were sweet, and gladdened
    The night with their magicry.
But we—we passed it, saddened
    And worn on a widening sea.

49

Aus alten Märchen winkt es

From ancient fairy-stories
  Beckons an airy hand;
A voice, with hints of glories,
  Sings of a magic land,

Where flowers have fairer blossoms
  In a golden evening's grace,
And bare their fragrant bosoms,
  Lifting a bridelike face.

Where all the trees are voicing
  Their songs, as in a choir;
Where rivers dance, rejoicing,
  And every wind's a lyre.

Where wilder passions quicken,
  Where wilder beauty throngs,
Till you are wonder-stricken
  With wonder-striking songs!

Ah, to be taken yonder
  To let my heart go free;
There in a land of wonder
  How blesséd it would be . . .

Ah, Land of Pleasant Places,
  Land of a dreamer's dream—
Alas, like foam it passes,
  Swept by a hurrying stream.

50

Ich hab' dich geliebet und liebe dich noch!

I loved thee once—and I love thee now.
Though the stars in a golden shower
Should fall, above the chaos and glow
The flame of my love would tower.

51

Am leuchtenden Sommermorgen

On a radiant summer morning
Into the garden I stray;
The flowers rustle and whisper,
But I have nothing to say.

The flowers whisper and murmur,
Pleading as only they can:
"Oh, be not wroth with our sister,
Thou bitter and sorrowful man."

52

Es leuchtet meine Liebe

My love and its dark magic
Troubles me with its might,
Like a story, tender and tragic,
Told on a summer night:

"In an enchanted bower
Two lovers walk, half-awake;
The moon, like a great white flower,
Lies on the breast of a lake.

"A picture: the maid almost pliant,
   And on his knees, the knight.
When lo, from the shadows a giant
   Springs, and the maid takes flight.

"The knight sinks bleeding and dying,
   The giant tramps back to his hold" . . .
When in the grave I am lying
   The rest of the tale will be told.

53

Sie haben mich gequälet

Many have made me wretched,
   Made mine an evil fate;
Some of them with their loving,
   Some of them with their hate.

My cup has been filled with poisons,
   They poisoned the bread I ate;
Some of them with their loving,
   Some of them with their hate.

Yet she, whose poison made me
   Wretched all men above,
Gave me no word of hatred—
   And not a spark of love.

54

Es liegt der heisse Sommer

The golden flame of summer
   Burns in your glowing cheek;
But in your heart lies winter,
   Barren and cold and bleak.

Soon it will change, my darling,
    Far sooner than you seek;
Your heart will harbor summer,
    While winter lines your cheek.

55

Wenn zwei von einander scheiden

When two who love are parted,
    They talk, as friend to friend,
Clasp hands and weep a little,
    And sigh without an end.

We did not weep, my darling,
    Nor sigh "Why must this be!"
The tears, the sighs, the anguish
    Came later—and to me.

56

Sie sassen und tranken am Theetisch

'Twas tea-time; the mildly aesthetic
    Ensemble took *"Love"* as their theme.
The mood of the guests was "poetic";
    They gushed like a lyrical stream.

"True love must be always platonic,"
    A hardened old councilor cried.
With a laugh that was almost ironic
    His wife looked upward and sighed.

A canon spoke, "We must resist 'em,
    These pleasures that rouse and harass,
Or else they will ruin the system."
    And a pretty young thing lisped, "Alas."

The countess, drooping and yearning,
   Said, "Love must sweep on like the sea!"
As, elegantly turning,
   She handed the baron his tea.

Still, it was not quite complete, dear;
   Your place stood empty above.
And, oh, it would have been sweet, dear,
   To hear *you* prattle of love.

57

Vergiftet sind meine Lieder

My songs, you say, are poisoned.
   How else, love, could it be?
You have, with deadly magic,
   Poured poison into me.

My songs, you say, are poisoned.
   And well I know it, too.
I carry a thousand serpents
   And, love, among them—you.

58

Mir träumte wieder der alte Traum

Again the old dream came to me:
   'Twas May; the world was vernal;
We sat beneath the linden tree
   And pledged a faith eternal.

Great love and a deathless oath we swore.
   And that I might ne'er forget it,

With a passionate kiss and a thousand more
   You took my hand, and bit it.

Oh, sweetheart with the lips that cling,
   With eyes so clear and merry,
The oath was quite the proper thing—
   The bite, unnecessary.

59

Ich steh' auf des Berges Spitze

I stand on the mountain's summit
   Emotional and absurd.
Sighing these maudlin verses:
   "Would that I were a bird!"

Oh, if I were a swallow
   I'd fly to you for rest,
And, underneath your window,
   I'd build my little nest.

And if I were, oh, dearest,
   A splendid nightingale,
All night you'd hear me singing
   From many a verdant vale.

And if I were a jay-bird
   My hopes to you I'd raise;
For you are kind to jay-birds
   And to the woes of jays! [1]

---

[1] In this verse Heine puns satirically on the word *Gimpel*, which can mean either "a bullfinch" or "a fool." Since there is no exact equivalent in English ornithology, I have been compelled to substitute another sort of bird.

60

Mein Wagen rollet langsam

My carriage rolls on slowly;
  Woods are a cheerful green;
Valleys exult with flowers;
  The world's a magic scene.

I sit and think of my loved one,
  And dream she might be here;
And lo, at my side three phantoms
  Curtsey, and grin, and leer.

They bow, and bob, and caper,
  Mocking, yet bashful and kind.
And then, like an eddy of vapor,
  They titter and pass with the wind.

61

Ich hab' im Traum geweinet

I wept as I lay dreaming,
  I dreamed that you had died.
And, when I woke, the tear-drops
  Clung to my cheeks undried.

I wept as I lay dreaming,
  I dreamed you were false to me.
I woke, and for many hours
  Lay weeping bitterly.

I wept as I lay dreaming,
  I dreamed that your love was true.

I woke, to an endless weeping,
    And the endless thought of you.

62

Allnächtlich im Traume seh' ich dich

Beloved, in dreams we often meet,
    And lo, your voice is kindly.
I fling myself at your gracious feet,
    And weep there, long and blindly.

You shake your fair head, sunbeam-swept,
    Reproachful yet appealing,
As out of eyes that never wept
    The blesséd tears come stealing.

You whisper a word for me alone
    And give me a wreath, dream-begotten . . .
I wake. The cypress-wreath is gone,
    And the word is quite forgotten!

63

Das ist ein Brausen und Heulen

A howling storm is brewing,
    The wind and rain are wild;
And what can my love be doing,
    That pale and frightened child?

There at the window dreaming,
    I see her, worn and white;
With eyes no longer beaming,
    She stares into the night.

64

Der Herbstwind rüttelt die Bäume

Wild autumn shakes the branches,
  The night is damp and cold;
I ride through a lonely forest,
  Wrapped in my mantle's fold.

And, as I ride, my fancies
  Fly faster along the road;
They bear me, light and eager,
  To her beloved abode.

The dogs awake; the torches
  Flare, and the whole house stirs;
I storm the spiral staircase
  And mount, with a clatter of spurs.

Lo, in her own soft chamber,
  Warm with its fragrant charms,
My love awaits me, smiling—
  I fly to her open arms . . .

I hear the oak-tree speaking;
  The wind, in the branches, screams:
"What would you, O wild horseman—
  You and your wilder dreams!"

65

Es fällt ein Stern herunter

A star, a star is falling
  Out of the glittering sky.
The star of love! I watch it
  Sink in the depths and die.

The leaves and buds are falling
From many an apple-tree;
I watch the mirthful breezes
Embrace them wantonly.

A swan, a swan is singing;
I watch it floating by,
As, drooping low and lower,
The song and singer die.

It is so dark and silent!
The star that burned so long
Is dust; the leaves are ashes;
Hushed is the swan's last song.

66

Der Traumgott bracht' mich in ein Riesenschloss

The Dream-God led me to a castle grim
Full of strange lights, strange scents and stranger glamor;
And through great labyrinths there seemed to swim
Wild multitudes whom nothing could enamor.
Onward they swept, through halls and portals dim,
Wringing pale hands with an incessant clamor.
Maidens and knights I saw among the throng,
And, with the torrent, I was borne along.

When suddenly I am alone—and lo,
I cannot find a single face whatever.
Through frowning aisles and winding rooms I go;
Fiercely impelled by one intense endeavor.
But oh, my feet are lead, my footsteps slow . . .
To find the gate, and leave this place forever!
At last, I gain the portals with a prayer,
Fling wide the door and leap . . . *O God, who's there!*

My love! Beside that door I saw her stand,
  Pain on her lips and sorrow's crown above her.
Then back she turned me with a waving hand,
  Threatening or warning, I could not discover . . .
Yet, from her eyes, sprang, like a sweet command,
  A fire that made me once again her lover.
Tender and strong, her very glances spoke
The flaming speech of love—and I awoke.

67

Die Mitternacht war kalt und stumm

'Twas midnight, still and very cold;
Through the dark woods I sang and strolled.
I shook the trees with my doleful ditty;
They only nodded their heads in pity.

68

Am Kreuzweg wird begraben

They buried him at the cross-roads,
  Whose own hand wrought his doom;
And over him grow blue flowers
  Called the Poor-Sinner's-Bloom.

I stand at the cross-roads sighing,
  Wrapped in a cloak of gloom,
And watch the moonlight trembling
  On the Poor-Sinner's-Bloom.

69

Wo ich bin, mich rings umdunkelt

Now the night grows deeper, stronger;
  Darkness dense about me lies,

Since the stars died; since no longer,
  Love, I can behold your eyes.

Dimmed, forgotten is the dawning
  Of that great and golden light;
At my feet the pit is yawning.
  Take me—stark, eternal Night.

70

Nacht lag auf meinen Augen

Night lay upon my eyelids,
  Upon my mouth lay lead;
My heart and brain were barren;
  I lay with all the dead.

How long I lay there sleeping
  I know not; but I gave
A start and turned, for knocking
  Sounded above my grave.

"Rise up, rise up, O Heinrich,
  The dawn eternal breaks,
When all the dead are risen
  And deathless joy awakes."

I cannot rise, my dearest;
  Your face I cannot find.
I've wept until my sorrows
  And tears have made me blind.

"From your dear eyes, O Heinrich,
  I'll kiss the night away;
And you shall see the angels,
  And Heaven's bright array."

I cannot rise, my dearest,
  Bleeding I lie, unstirred;
Since, to the heart, you stabbed me
  With one short, bitter word.

"Softly I'll lay, O Heinrich,
  My hand upon your heart,
And it will bleed no longer,
  And I will soothe the smart."

I cannot rise, my dearest,
  My head is bleeding too;
'Tis there I fired the pistol
  The day that I lost you!

"With my own hair, O Heinrich,
  I'll stop the gaping wound,
Press back the streaming torrent,
  And make you strong and sound."

So soft her call, so tender,
  She could not be denied;
I strove to rend my coffin
  And struggle to her side.

Then all my wounds burst open;
  I felt the torrent break
From head and burning bosom . . .
  And lo, I was awake!

71

Die alten bösen Lieder

The songs, so old and bitter,
  The dreams so wild and drear,

Let's bury them together.
What ho! A coffin here!

I have so much to bury
It never will be done,
Unless the coffin's larger
Than Heidelberg's great Tun.

And bring a bier to match it
Of stoutest oaks and pines;
It must be even longer
Than the long bridge at Mainz.

And also bring twelve giants
Of mightier brawn and bone
Than Christopher, the sainted,
Whose shrine is in Cologne.

And in the great sea sink it
Beneath the proudest wave;
For such a mighty coffin
Should have a mighty grave.

You know what makes my coffin
So great, so hard to bear?
It holds my love within it,
And my too heavy care.

THE HOME-COMING
(1823-1824)

1

In mein gar zu dunkles Leben

In my life's too constant darkness
Once a vision shed its light;
Now, the phantom radiance vanished,
I am wrapped again in night.

Children, when oppressed by darkness,
When their happy hearts are cowed,
To allay their fears and trembling
Sing a song—and sing too loud.

I, a child half-crazed, am singing,
Singing in the darkness here.
If my song is loud and raucous,
It, at least, has soothed my fear.

2

(THE LORELEY)

Ich weiss nicht, was soll es bedeuten

I cannot tell why this imagined
Despair has fallen on me;
The ghost of an ancient legend
That will not let me be:

The air is cool, and twilight
Flows down the quiet Rhine;
A mountain alone in the high light
Still holds the faltering shine.

The last peak rosily gleaming
　Reveals, enthroned in air,
A maiden, lost in dreaming,
　Who combs her golden hair.

Combing her hair with a golden
　Comb in her rocky bower,
She sings the tune of an olden
　Song that has magical power.

The boatman has heard; it has bound him
　In throes of a strange, wild love;
Blind to the reefs that surround him,
　He sees but the vision above.

And lo, hungry waters are springing—
　Boat and boatman are gone. . . .
Then silence. And this, with her singing,
　The Loreley has done.

3

Mein Herz, mein Herz ist traurig

My heart is full of sorrow
　Though May is full of cheer;
I stand beside the linden,
　High on the bastion here.

I watch the blue moat idly;
　Gently it flows along.
A boy in a drifting rowboat
　Angles, and whistles a song.

Beyond, like a quaint, toy village,
　Tiny and many-hued,

Are houses, gardens and people,
  Oxen, meadow, and wood.

Bleaching their piles of linen
  The girls are frolicsome.
The millwheel spatters diamonds;
  I hear its distant hum.

Upon the old, gray tower
  A sentry-box stands low;
And there a chap in scarlet
  Is pacing to and fro.

He practices with his rifle
  That catches the sunset's red;
He shoulders it and presents it—
  Would that he shot me dead!

4

Im Walde wandl' ich und weine

I pace the greenwood, bitter
  With tears, and as I go
A thrush begins to twitter,
  "Why are you sorrowing so?"

Ask of your sisters, the swallows;
  They know, though none of them tells.
They nest in the eaves and hollows
  Where the belovèd dwells.

5

Die Nacht ist feucht und stürmisch

The night is wet and stormy,
  No stars are in the sky;

The boughs in the forest whisper.
I wander slowly by.

Far off a candle glimmers
From the forester's lonely room;
But there the light shall not lure me,
It is too wrapped in gloom.

The sightless grandmother's sitting
In the high-backed, leather chair;
She listens, stiff as a statue,
Uncanny and silent there.

Cursing and pacing in anger,
The forester's red-headed son
Laughs in a burst of fury,
And throws aside his gun.

The girl weeps at her spinning,
And moistens the flax with her tears.
While at her feet, the dachshund
Trembles with unknown fears.

6

Als ich auf der Reise zufällig

By chance I met on the journey
My dear one's family,
Sister and mother and father;
Smiling, they greeted me.

How was my health? My spirits?
They? . . . Oh, the same old tale.
I hadn't changed much, they told me;
Only a trifle pale.

I asked about aunts and cousins
  With interest (save the mark!),
And other such pleasing people,
  And the dog, with his gentle bark.

How was my married sweetheart
  Whom they had left behind?
And smilingly they told me
  That she had just been confined.

I coughed congratulations,
  And, stammering wretchedly,
I asked them all to greet her
  A thousand times for me.

Then spoke the little sister:
  "That puppy pet of mine
Grew up so big and horrid
  We drowned him in the Rhine."

The child resembles her sister,
  Sometimes remarkably so;
Those eyes and that way of laughing
  That brought me so much woe.

7

Wir sassen am Fischerhause

We sat by the hut of the fisher
  And idly watched the sea,
While in the hush of evening
  The mists rose silently.

The yellow lights in the lighthouse
  Shone like a burnished bell,

And in the hazy distance
One ship still rose and fell.

We spoke of storm and shipwreck,
Of sailors and their life,
Pulled between sky and water,
Fierce joy and lusty strife.

We gossiped of distant places,
Of North and of South we spoke,
Of wild and curious customs,
And wild and curious folk.

Of how the Ganges sparkles;
Of great exotic trees;
Of folk who worship the lotus
Silently, on their knees.

Of Lapland; its slovenly people,
Flat-headed, broad-featured and small,
That do little else but bake fishes
And squat by the fire and squall. . . .

The girls all listened breathless;
Then silence, like a spell.
The ship could be seen no longer—
Swiftly the darkness fell.

8

Du schönes Fischermädchen

Oh, lovely fishermaiden,
Come, bring your boat to land;
And we will sit together
And whisper, hand in hand.

Oh, rest upon my bosom,
  And fear no harm from me.
You give your body daily,
  Unfearing to the sea.

My heart is like the ocean
  With storm and ebb and flow;
And many a pearly treasure
  Burns in the depths below.

9

Der Mond ist aufgegangen

The yellow moon has risen,
  It slants upon the sea;
And in my arms' soft prison
  My love leans close to me.

Warm with her gentle clinging,
  I lie on the sands, half awake.
"Oh, what do you hear in the swinging
  Of the winds, and why do you shake?"

"That's never the wind that is swinging,
  This murmur that troubles me;
It is the mermaidens singing—
  My sisters drowned in the sea."

10

Auf den Wolken ruht der Mond

The moon is lying on the clouds,
  A giant orange, strangely beaming;
Stretched upon the harsh gray sea
  Long and broadening stripes are gleaming.

Alone I wander by the shore
  Where the waters break and whiten,
And I hear a watery voice,
  And my pulses leap and tighten.

Oh, the night is far too long
  And I cannot bear this quiet.
Come, ye lovely water-sprites,
  Dance and rouse the magic riot.

With my head upon your lap,
  Hold me close and never wake me.
Sing me dead and kiss me dead;
  Heart and soul and body—take me!

11

Eingehüllt in graue Wolken

Wrapped in clouds, as in a mantle,
  Now the great gods sleep together
And I hear them bravely snoring,
  And we're having awful weather.

It grows wilder; winds are howling,
  And the masts are bent like willows.
Who can curb the lordly tempest?
  Put a bridle on the billows?

I can't stop it, let it come then;
  Storms and terrors without number.
I will wrap my mantle round me,
  And, like any god, I'll slumber.

12

Der Wind zieht seine Hosen an

The wind pulls up his water-spouts
His white and foaming breeches; [1]
He whips the waves; he storms and shouts.
The whole sea heaves and pitches!

From the black skies, a furious might
Impels the rain's commotion;
It seems as though the ancient night
Had come to drown the ocean.

To the mast a vagrant sea-gull clings
With a hoarse shrilling and crying.
As though in despair she flaps her wings;
An evil prophesying.

13

Der Sturm spielt auf zum Tanze

The storm tunes up for dancing,
It yells and shrieks away;
Huzzah, how the old ship waltzes!
The night is wild and gay.

A riot of tossing mountains,
Thus seems the sea tonight.
Here, yawns a sinking chasm;
There, looms a wall of white.

[1] The original of the first two lines:

> *Der Wind zieht seine Hosen an,*
> *Die weissen Wasserhosen!*

There is an untranslatable play upon words here: "*Hosen*" being 'breeches'
and "*Wasserhosen*" 'water-spouts.'

The sound of prayers and puking
  And oaths from the cabin come;
I cling to the mast with a vengeance,
  And wish that I were home!

14

Der Abend kommt gezogen

Over the sea's vast acres
  The misty night lay warm;
Secretly up from the breakers
  A white spray grew into form.

Out of the waves a mermaid
  Came without beckon or call;
We sat, and some inner stir made
  Her white breasts heave and fall.

She clasped me and caressed me;
  More anguish than delight.
"Too closely hast thou pressed me,
  O lovely water-sprite."

"Though my embrace is stormy
  I am not rude nor bold;
It's you who must hold and warm me,
  For the night is far too cold."

"The moon has reached its nadir;
  Low clouds conceal its light.
Thine eyes grow wetter and sadder,
  O lovely water-sprite."

"Grieve not for Neptune's daughter;
  My eyes are sad and wet

For I came from depths of water
    And the salt is in them yet."

"I hear mad waters sounding;
    I see the gulls take flight;
I feel thy wild heart pounding,
    O lovely water-sprite."

"Truly, my heart is pounding,
    Pounding, alas, too wild!
I love thee past telling or sounding,
    Too dear, too mortal child."

15

Wenn ich an deinem Hause

I pass your little window
    Each morning that is fair,
And I am thrilled, my darling,
    Whenever I see you there.

Your deep brown eyes disturb me,
    They question and condole,
"Who art thou, and what ails thee,
    Oh, pale and wandering soul?"

I am a German poet,
    In German lands I shine;
And where great names are mentioned
    They're bound to mention mine.

As for my sickness, darling,
    It's rather a common sign . . .
And where great griefs are mentioned
    They're bound to mention mine.

16

Das Meer erglänzte weit hinaus

The vastness of the ocean shone
  In the sunset's final gleaming.
We sat in the fisher's hut alone;
  We sat there, silent and dreaming.

The mist crept up, the waters hove,
  The gulls kept coming and going;
And from her eyes that welled with love
  The quiet tears were flowing.

I saw them fall upon her hand,
  And then, as quickly sinking
Upon my knees, from that white hand
  I drank the tears, unthinking.

And from that hour my life has turned,
  And sorrow leaves me never.
That wretched woman's tears have burned
  And poisoned me forever.

17

Da droben auf jenem Berge

High up on yonder mountain
  A castle stands, and three
Fair maidens live within it;
  They love me generously.

Saturday, Yetta kissed me;
  Sunday, Julia was free;
On Monday, Kunigunda
  With love near smothered me.

But Tuesday, my three fair charmers
  Gave an imposing fête;
The neighborhood's lords and ladies
  Came riding in wagons of state.

But me they had skipped or forgotten,
  And that was a poor thing to do.
Those gossips, the old aunts and cousins,
  They noticed, and laughed at it, too.

18

Die Lilje meiner Liebe

My sweetheart has a lily
  That dreams by a brook all day,
It turns from me, and stilly
  Its beauty seems to say:

"Go, faithless man, your rapture
  Has left me cold. Depart!
I saw you bend and capture
  The rose with your faithless heart."

19

Am fernen Horizonte

Wrapped in the distant sunset,
  Like phantoms in a mist,
I see the town and its towers,
  All rose and amethyst.

A damp sea-breeze is rising;
  The sea grows rough and dark.
With slow and sad precision
  The boatman rows my bark.

The sun looks up a moment,
Piercing the clouds above,
And shows me, all too clearly,
The place I lost my love.

20

Sei mir gegrüsst, du grosse

Greetings to you, great city
Of power and mystery,
That once, within your bosom,
Shielded my love for me.

Tell me, O gates and towers,
Where is my loved one, where?
Into your care I gave her;
You should have kept her there.

I do not blame the towers,
They could not stir where they stood,
When she, with her trunks and boxes,
Stole off as fast as she could.

The gates, those fools, *they* let her
Pass through them—and were still.
Well, fools are always willing
When foolish women will.[1]

[1] The original:

> *Die Thore jedoch die liessen*
> *Mein Liebchen entwischen gar still;*
> *Ein Thor ist immer willig,*
> *Wenn eine Thörin will.*

Heine puns here untranslatably on the word "*Thor*," which is either a "gate" or a "fool," "*Thörin*" being the feminine.

21

So wandl' ich wieder den alten Weg

To old paths and familiar streets
  My footsteps have reverted;
And lo, there stands the beloved's house,
  Desolate and deserted.

How close and narrow the streets have grown;
  The pavement itself is unstable!
The houses topple and seem to fall . . .
  I'm off as fast as I'm able!

22

Ich trat in jene Hallen

I stood as in a spell
  Where she swore faith undying;
And where her tears once fell
  Serpents were hissing and lying.

23

Still ist die Nacht, es ruhen die Gassen

The night is still; the streets are quiet;
  My sweetheart dwelt in this house of yore.
Long since she left the city's riot;
  The house still stands as it stood before.

Here, too, there stands a man who gazes
  On heaven and wrings his hands in despair.
Lo, when his face the moonlight glazes—
  It is myself that is standing there.

Oh, pale, worn shadow, oh, phantom double,
Why ape my bitter, love-sick tears,
That drove me here to an endless trouble,
Many a night in the vanished years.

24

Wie kannst du ruhig schlafen

How can you sleep so soundly,
    Knowing I'm living. See,
When the old rage comes on me,
    What is a yoke to me!

There is a song that tells how
    A lover dead and brave
Came to his lass at midnight,
    And brought her to his grave.

Believe me, child of beauty,
    Bright as the fiercest star,
I live—and am ten times stronger
    Than all the dead men are!

25

Die Jungfrau schläft in der Kammer

A maiden lies in her chamber
    Lit by a trembling moon;
Outside there rises and echoes
    A waltz's giddy tune.

"I wonder who breaks my slumber;
    I'll go to the window and see—"
And lo, a skeleton stands there;
    He fiddles and sings with glee:

"A dance you swore to give me,
  And you have broken your vow;
Tonight there's a ball in the churchyard;
  Come out and dance with me now!"

The maid, as though moved by magic,
  Obeys, and she leaves the house;
The skeleton, fiddling and singing,
  Goes on with its wild carouse.

It fiddles and leaps and dances
  And rattles its bones to the tune;
Its skull keeps nodding and nodding
  Crazily under the moon.

26

Ich stand in dunkeln Träumen

I stood bewildered, seeing
  Her picture there—and lo,
That fair, beloved likeness
  Began to live and glow.

About her lips there trembled
  A laughter, strange and dear;
And, through the tears of sorrow,
  Her gleaming eyes shone clear.

Wet were my cheeks; the tear-drops
  Were falling fast and free . . .
And oh, I cannot believe it,
  That you are lost to me!

27

Ich unglücksel'ger Atlas! eine Welt

I, unfortunate Atlas! A whole world,
A monstrous world of sorrows I must carry.
I bear a weight unbearable; a burden
That breaks the heart within me.

Oh, foolish heart, you have what you desired!
You would be happy, infinitely happy,
Or infinitely wretched, foolish heart.
And now—now you are wretched.

28

Die Jahre kommen und gehen

The years keep coming and going,
　Men will arise and depart;
Only one thing is immortal:
　The love that is in my heart.

Oh, once, only once, might I see thee,
　Ere I break these fetters in shards,
And kneel to thee, dying, and murmur:
　"Madam, my best regards."

29

Mir träumte: traurig schaute der Mond

I dreamed: The moon shone sadly down,
　Sadly the stars were grieving;
They led me to the distant town
　Where my beloved was living.

They led me safely to her abode;
  I kissed the stones of the stairway,
Pressing the very steps she trod
  Where her skirts had trailed their fair way.

The night was long; the night was cold;
  Cold were the stones on the landing;
The moon revealed her, aureoled,
  Still at the window standing.

30

Was will die einsame Thräne

Why does this lonely tear-drop
  Disturb my eyes again?
It lingers, a last reminder
  Of days too distant for pain.

Once it had shining sisters;
  But, with the old delights
And passing griefs, they left me,
  Lost in the windy nights.

Lost, like the mist, those blue orbs,
  Stars with a smiling dart,
That shot the joys and sorrows
  Laughing into my heart.

Even my love has perished,
  A breath that I have drawn . . .
Oh, lone, belated tear-drop,
  'Tis time you too were gone.

31

Der bleiche, herbstliche Halbmond

The pale, autumnal half-moon
Breaks through the cloudy skies;
Quietly by the churchyard
The lonely parsonage lies.

The mother reads in her Bible;
The son just stares and stares;
The elder daughter dozes;
The younger one declares:

"Oh, Lord, how stupid the days are,
Endlessly dull and drear!
Only when there's a funeral
Is there anything doing here."

"You're wrong," says the mother still reading,
"They've only buried four;
That is, since they laid your father
There, by the churchyard door."

"Well," yawns the elder daughter,
"I'll starve no longer with you.
I'll go to the Count tomorrow;
He's rich, and he loves me, too."

The son then bursts out laughing,
"At the 'Star' there are hunters three;
They're making gold and gladly
They'll teach the secret to me."

The mother flings her Bible
At his head, half-crazed with grief,
"That's what you'll be, God help you,
A common gutter-thief!"

Lo, there's a tap at the window;
They turn to a beckoning hand.
There, in his moldy cassock,
They see the dead father stand.

32

Das ist ein schlechtes Wetter

Well, this is awful weather,
Storming with rain and snow.
I sit at the window staring
Into the darkness below.

A little glimmering brightness
Goes down the uncertain street:
A lantern, and a mother
With tired and stumbling feet.

I think it's eggs and flour
That the old lady has bought
To bake a cake for her daughter,
The lazy good-for-naught.

Yawning at home on the sofa
She lies in front of the blaze—
The golden hair is falling
Around her golden face.

33

Man glaubt, dass ich mich gräme

They think that I am tortured
  Beneath a bitter yoke;
And I have come to believe it
  As well as other folk.

Child with the large eyes, I've said it
  Too often, but still it's true
I love you beyond all telling,
  And love tears my heart in two.

But in my own room only
  I've said this thing—for see,
When I am in your presence
  No word escapes from me.

For there were evil angels
  That sealed my lips somehow;
And through these evil angels
  I am so wretched now.

34

Deine weissen Liljenfinger

Oh, your slim, white lily-fingers,
Only once more might I kiss them;
And, as to my heart I press them,
Lose myself in quiet weeping.

Your clear, violet-eyes pursue me;
Dance before me, day and night.
And I wonder how to answer,
How to solve those sweet, blue riddles.

35

"Hat sie sich denn nie geäussert"

"Has she never even shown you
   That your hot avowals moved her?
Did her dark eyes tell you nothing,
   When you swore how much you loved her?

"Could you never find an entrance
   To her soul through sighs and glances?
And they say you're not a donkey,
   But a Hero of Romances!"

36

Sie liebten sich beide, doch keiner

They loved one another, though neither
   Would speak to the other thereof;
They looked at each other like strangers
   The while they were dying of love.

They parted; and only in visions
   They met, and the dream soon fled.
And at last these two were buried—
   They scarcely knew they were dead.

37

Und als ich euch meine Schmerzen geklagt

When I told of my sorrows that wounded and tore
   You answered with yawns and nothing more.
But now, since I've added a lyrical phrase
   And put them in verse, you are lavish with praise!

38

Ich rief den Teufel und er kam

I called the devil and he came;
And then I saw, with a wondering gaze,
He was not hideous, he was not lame,
But a genial man with charming ways.
A man in the very flush of his prime;
Experienced, suave, and in touch with his time.
As a diplomat, his talent is great,
And he speaks wisely of Church and the State.
True, he is pale; but it's little wonder,
For Sanskrit and Hegel he's staggering under.
His favorite poet is still Fouqué;
As critic he finds that the work is a bother,
So Hecaté now, his beloved grandmother,
Has taken the task and enjoys it, they say.
My legal studies called forth his laudation;
He too, in his youth, found them quaint recreation.
He said that my friendship could never be
Too dear for him, and bowed to me,
And asked had we not met some place—
Perhaps the ambassador's? And with that sentence
I looked more closely at his face,
And recognized an old acquaintance.

39

Mensch, verspotte nicht den Teufel

Mortal, mock not at the devil,
   Life is short and soon will fail,
And the fire everlasting
   Is no idle fairy-tale.

Mortal, pay your debts, delay not.
  Years are long; and while they last
You will borrow in the future
  Just as much as in the past.

40

Mein Kind, wir waren Kinder

My child, we once were children,
  Two children, blithe and gay,
We used to crawl up to the hen-house
  And hide ourselves under the hay.

We cackled and crowed whenever
  People passed down the road—
"Kikerikee!" they thought it
  Was really the cocks that crowed.

The boxes in our courtyard
  We draped with what we could find,
And lived in them together,
  A home of the coziest kind.

Our neighbor's cat came often
  To visit us in our bower;
We met her with bows and curtsies
  And compliments by the hour.

Politely we asked how her health was,
  In the course of a friendly chat.
(Since then we've said the same thing
  To many a grave, old cat.)

And often like old folk we gossiped,
  Aping their serious ways;

Complaining how things were better
In the vanished "dear old days."

How Love and Faith and Honor
Were lost without regret;
How coffee was so expensive,
And money so hard to get! . . .

Gone are the plays of childhood,
And all things seem a wraith—
Time and the world and money,
And Love and Honor and Faith.

41

Das Herz ist mir bedrückt, und sehnlich

My heart is crushed with grief, for sadly
I think of old times, clean of strife,
When all the world went far from badly,
And people lived a normal life.

But now the world seems madly driven;
Scrambling to pull and push ahead!
Dead is the good Lord up in Heaven,
And down below the devil's dead.

All things, with this eternal shoving,
Become a cheap and sodden brawl;
And if it were not for a little loving
There'd be no rest for us at all.

42

Wie der Mond sich leuchtend dränget

As the moon through heavy cloud-drifts
Bursts with his effulgent rays,

So a shining memory rises
  From the old and darkened days:

On the deck we sat, and drifted
  Down the Rhine as on a throne;
And the banks, bright green with summer,
  In the radiant twilight shone.

And there was a gracious lady;
  At her feet I sat and dreamed.
On that pale, dear face the ruddy,
  Burnished gold of sunset gleamed.

Lutes were ringing, boys were singing;
  Happiness on every side!
And the vault of heaven grew bluer,
  And the very soul grew wide.

And there passed, as in a legend,
  Cliff and castle, wood and field . . .
And I saw them through her beauty;
  In her eyes they lay revealed.

43

Im Traum sah ich die Geliebte

I saw in a dream the belovéd,
  A woman careworn and gray;
That radiant, blossoming body
  Withered and fallen away.

One child in her arms she carried,
  And one by her hand was led;
And struggle and sorrow were written
  In her look, her clothes, her tread.

She stumbled toward the market,
    And there she looked at me,
And there I waited, saying
    Calmly and mournfully:

"Oh, come with me to my dwelling,
    For thou art sick and pale;
And meat and drink I'll work for
    To make thee whole and hale.

"And I will tend and cherish
    Thy children undefiled;
But thee, before all others,
    Thou poor, unfortunate child.

"And I will never speak of
    My love so torn and deep.
And when at last thou diest,
    Upon thy grave I'll weep."

44

Teurer Freund! Was soll es nützen

"Why, my friend, this same old fretting,
    In the same, monotonous fashion?
Will you be forever setting
    On the addled eggs of passion?"

"Ah! It's no small task to tackle!
    First the chicks come, thin and sickly;
Then, when they begin to cackle,
    In a book you clap them, quickly."

45

Werdet nur nicht ungeduldig

Listen; do not grow impatient,
  Though I keep the old note ringing,
And you hear the old heart-sickness,
  Even in my latest singing.

Only wait—these dying echoes
  Soon will cease; and with new power,
Lo, a new, poetic Springtime
  In a heart that's healed will flower.

46

Nun ist es Zeit, dass ich mit Verstand

Now it is time that I should start
  And leave all folly behind me.
As comic actor I've played my part
  In a comedy that was assigned me.

The settings were painted brilliant and bold
  In the latest romantic fashion;
My knightly mantle was splendid with gold;
  I thrilled with the noblest passion.

And now at last I must say good-by
  To speeches once distracting.
But I am wretched, and I sigh
  As though I still were acting.

O God! unknown I spoke in jest
  The things I felt most deeply;
I've acted, with death in my very breast,
  The dying hero, cheaply.

47

Den König Wiswamitra

The good king Wiswamitra
Has little quiet now;
He'll fight, he'll fret, he'll famish
To get Wasishta's cow.

Oh, good king Wiswamitra,
Oh, what an ox art thou;
Such penance and such passion—
And all for that one cow!

48

Herz, mein Herz, sei nicht beklommen

Heart, my heart, let naught o'ercome you;
Bear your destiny and pain.
Spring will bring you back again
What the Winter's taken from you.

And how much is left! The small things
And the whole of earth is fair!
Heart, you never need despair;
You can love, not one, but all things!

49

Du bist wie eine Blume

Child, you are like a flower,
So sweet and pure and fair;
I look at you, and sadness
Touches me with a prayer.

I must lay my hands on your forehead
And pray God to be sure
To keep you forever and always
So sweet and fair—and pure.

50

Kind! es wäre dein Verderben

Child, I know 'twould be your ruin,
  And my thoughts keep guard and turn there,
That your heart may not be kindled
  With the love that used to burn there.

But my too successful triumph
  Somehow does not quite delight me.
And I keep on thinking, hoping
  You might love me yet—despite me.

51

Wenn ich auf dem Lager liege

When I lie down for comfort
  Upon the pillows of night,
There rises and floats before me
  A phantom clothed in light.

As soon as smiling slumber
  With soft hands locks my eyes,
Into my dream the vision
  Creeps with a sweet surprise.

But even with the morning
  The dream persists and stays;
The sunlight cannot melt it—
  I carry it all my days.

52

Mädchen mit dem roten Mündchen

Girl, whose mouth is red and laughing;
  Girl, whose eyes are soft and bright,
All my being moves about you,
  Thinking of you day and night.

Long, how long, this winter evening;
  And I yearn the whole night through
To be sitting, talking lightly,
  In the little room with you.

To my lips I would be pressing,
  Love, your slender, tender hand;
And my tears would tremble, blessing
  That beloved and blesséd hand.

53

Mag da draussen Schnee sich türmen

Snows and storms may whirl in torrents;
And I watch, without abhorrence,
Hail at all my windows storming;
For they never seem alarming
While my heart can hold this grace:
Spring—and one dear, Spring-like face.

54

Andre beten zur Madonna

Mary's praise is never done;
  Others pray to Paul and Peter;
  But my only prayer is sweeter,
For I worship thee, my sun.

Give me kisses, sweetly won,
  Give my songs their shining cadence,
  Loveliest sun among the maidens,
Loveliest maid beneath the sun!

55

Verriet mein blasses Angesicht

Did not my pallid face betray
  The passion that I bore you?
And did you think my haughty lips
  Would, beggar-like, implore you?

These haughty lips were only made
  For kisses, jests, and lying—
They'd form a mocking, scornful word
  Even though I were dying.

56

"Teurer Freund, du bist verliebt"

"Ah, my friend, you are in love
  And new torments chain you tighter;
For your brain is growing duller
  As your foolish heart grows lighter.

"Yes, my friend, you are in love,
  Though the truth is unconfessed;
Why, I see your heart's blood glowing—
  Blushing, even through your vest!"

57

Ich wollte bei dir weilen

I sought your side, the only
  Peace that I ever knew;

You left me, worn and lonely.
  You had so much to do.

I said I gave you wholly
  Body and soul; and how
You laughed, laughed long and drolly,
  And made a twinkling bow.

With all these things you tried me;
  You even dared do this:
You roused me, then denied me
  A single, parting kiss.

Think not because of my snarling
  I'll shoot myself at your door!
All this, my precious darling,
  Has happened to me before.

58

Saphire sind die Augen dein

Sapphires are those eyes of yours,
  None lovelier or braver;
Thrice happy is the lucky man
  On whom they shine with favor.

Your heart is a warm diamond,
  A light that never dwindles.
Thrice happy is the lucky man
  For whom that fire kindles.

Twin rubies are those lips of yours,
  A rich and radiant measure.
Thrice happy is the lucky man
  Who can possess this treasure.

Oh, could I know that lucky man,
And find that happy lover,
Nicely alone in some deep wood,
His luck would soon be over.

59

Habe mich mit Liebesreden

I have lied to win you, precious;
    Now my breast against yours burns.
And I lie in my own meshes,
    And the jest to earnest turns.

And if ever you should leave me,
    With a jest, as is your right,
Earnestly, while fiends receive me,
    I will shoot myself that night.

60

Zu fragmentarisch ist Welt und Leben

Life in this world is a muddled existence—
Our German professor will give me assistance.
He knows how to whip the whole thing into order;
He'll make a neat System and keep it in line.
With scraps from his nightcap and dressing-gown's border
He'd fill all the gaps in Creation's design.

61

Ich hab' mir lang den Kopf zerbrochen

My head and brain are almost broken
    With dreams and thinking, night and day;
But now your eyes have solved the problem,
    They sweep my hesitance away.

And I will come to you quite boldly,
  And meet your eyes' sweet, silent call.
And once again I am a lover—
  Something I cannot grasp at all.

62

Sie haben heut' Abend Gesellschaft

They're having a party this evening
  And the house is gay with light.
Above, at a brilliant window,
  A shadow trembles in sight.

You see me not; in darkness
  I move alone, apart;
How little can you see, then,
  Into my darkened heart.

My darkened heart still loves you,
  Loves you and tortures me,
And breaks and lies here bleeding—
  But you will never see.

63

Ich wollt' meine Schmerzen ergössen

Oh, could I capture my sadness
  And pour it all into one word;
The glad-hearted breezes would lift it
  And carry it off, like a bird.

They'd bear it to you, oh, belovéd,
  That word of passionate care;
And every hour you'd hear it,
  'Twould follow you everywhere.

Yes, when you have scarce closed your eyelids,
   And slumber over them streams,
That word will arise and pursue you—
   Even into your dreams.

64

Du hast Diamanten und Perlen

You've pearls and you've diamonds, my dearest,
   You've all that most mortals revere;
And, oh, your blue eyes are the fairest—
   What else could you ask for, my dear?

Upon those blue eyes, my dearest,
   I've written for many a year
A host of immortal poems—
   What else could you ask for, my dear?

And with those blue eyes, my dearest,
   You wrought a bright torture here,
And lightly you led me to ruin—
   What else could you ask for, my dear?

65

Wer zum erstenmale liebt

He who, for the first time, loves,
   Even vainly, is a God.
But the man who loves again,
   And still vainly, is a fool.

Such a fool am I; the second
   Time I love, still unrequited.
Sun and moon and stars are laughing;
   And I laugh with them—and perish.

66

Zu der Lauheit und der Flauheit

In your tepid soul and vapid,
   There's no strength to stand the shocks
Of my wild love, with its rapid
   Force that breaks a path through rocks.

You, you want Love's broad, safe high-roads,
   And a husband's arm through life;
Scorning all the glades and by-roads—
   Just a prim and pregnant wife.

67

O, mein gnädiges Fräulein, erlaubt

Oh, loveliest of ladies, may
   This pale son of the Muses,
Upon thy swan-like bosom lay
   His head with Love's own bruises.

"Oh, sir! To say such things to me
Out loud—in front of company!"

68

Gaben mir Rat und gute Lehren

Of words and advice they were the donors;
They even promised me lavish honors.
My future was rosy, my fame would be great;
They'd be my patrons—I need only wait.

But still, with all their patronization,
I would have died of slow starvation,

Except for a man who chanced to be made
Of splendid stuff and who came to my aid.

Excellent fellow! I look on and let him
Work for my dinner; I'll never forget him!
Ah, it's a pity that I never can
Kiss him—for I am that worthy man.

69

Diesen liebenswürd'gen Jüngling

This most amiable youngster
  Can't be spoken of too highly;
Oft with wine, liqueurs, and oysters
  He regales me, almost shyly.

Charming are his coat and trousers,
  And his ties are most appealing;
And he comes here every morning
  Just to ask how I am feeling.

Of my wide renown he gushes,
  Of my grace, my wit and humor;
And he swears to serve and help me,
  Grieving that he cannot do more.

And at many an evening party
  'Mid the ladies' panegyrics,
With inspired voice and features
  He recites my deathless lyrics.

Oh, to find so rare a fellow
  Makes me see the whole world gaily;
In these sorry times, above all,
  When his betters vanish daily.

70

Mir träumt: ich bin der liebe Gott

I dreamt I was the dear Lord God
  And sat in Heaven gaily,
The angels thronged about my feet
  And praised my verses daily.

And cakes I ate and sweetmeats, too,
  My costly taste displaying.
I washed them down with rare old wines,
  Without a thought of paying.

But the inaction bored me so,
  I longed once more to revel;
I thought, were I not God Himself,
  I'd rather be the devil.

"Ho, long-legged Gabriel," I called,
  "Put on thy boots, I prithee;
Seek out my good old friend Eugene
  And fetch him quickly with thee.

"Seek him not at the college halls,
  Seek him where wine inspires;
Seek him not at St. Hedwig's church—
  Seek him at Ma'm'selle Meyer's."

The angel spread his plumes and flew
  Swift as a wingéd stallion,
And found and carried up to me
  My friend, the old rapscallion.

"Yes, lad, I am the Lord Himself,
  I rule each great and dumb thing;
I always told you some fine day
  I would amount to something.

"And I work wonders every hour,
  Things that would quite enthuse you;
Today, for instance, I will change
  All Berlin, to amuse you.

"The cobble-stones in every street
  Shall split; and in their moister,
New-opened centers shall be found,
  Juicy and fresh—an oyster.

"A rain of gentle lemon-juice
  Shall fall on them, bestowing
A grace; and lo, through all the streets,
  Rhine wine shall keep on flowing.

"See how the folk of Berlin run;
  Their joy's too great to utter;
The heads of all the City Courts
  Are drinking from the gutter.

"And look how glad the poets are,
  How hungrily they rally!
The ensigns and lieutenants, too,
  Lap up each street and alley.

"The soldiers are the cleverest,
  Their shrewdness they display there.
They know that miracles like this
  Don't happen every day there."

71

Von schönen Lippen fortgedrängt, getrieben

Torn from bright lips I loved; departing sadly
From those warm eyes that held me in their heaven.
I would have stayed another day, and gladly,
But then the coach came up, and I was driven.

Child, that is life! A constant cry and wailing;
A constant parting, though your arms enfold me.
Keep me. But see, no heart can be unfailing;
Even your eyes were powerless to hold me.

72

Wir fuhren allein im dunkeln

Alone in the darkened post-chaise
We sat and rode through the night;
Closely together we nestled,
With laughter the hours were light.

But, oh, my love, next morning—
And how we stared to find,
Sitting between us, Cupid,
The boy that seemed so blind! [1]

[1] The original:

> *Doch als es Morgens tagte,*
> *Mein Kind, wie staunten wir!*
> *Denn zwischen uns sass Amor,*
> *Der blinde Passagier.*

It is possible that in *"der blinde Passagier"* Heine was half punning on a bit of German slang—a "blind passenger" being one who, like a stowaway, gets in anywhere without paying.

73

Wie dunkle Träume stehen

Like a dark dream the houses
  Stretch in a ghastly row;
Wrapped in my heavy mantle
  I pass them, silent and slow.

The tower of the cathedral
  Rings with the midnight hour;
And now my sweetheart is waiting
  With all her charms in flower.

The moon's my friend and companion,
  He lights the ways that are dim;
And as I come to her dwelling
  Gladly I call to him:

"I thank you, good old comrade,
  Through you no path was furled;
And now, since I must leave you,
  Go light the rest of the world.

"And if you find a lover
  Heaving a lonely sigh,
Console him as you consoled me,
  My friend, in the days gone by."

74

Das weiss Gott wo sich die tolle

God knows where I'll find that silly
  Madcap of a girl again;
I have searched this endless city,
  Wet and cursing in the rain.

Inns I've ransacked, tap-rooms, taverns—
    Everywhere that she was not;
I have asked each surly waiter,
    And a shrug was all I got.

Then I see her at a window.
    And she giggles—beckons— Well!
Who could guess she'd ever stop at
    Such an elegant hotel!

75

Hast du die Lippen mir wund geküsst

With kisses my lips were wounded by you,
    So kiss them well again;
And if by evening you are not through,
    You need not hurry then.

For you have still the whole, long night,
    Darling, to comfort me!
And what long kisses and what delight
    In such a night may be.

76

Und bist du erst mein ehlich Weib

And when you're once my wedded wife
    You'll be the gayest one, dear;
For then you'll live the happiest life,
    With nought but pleasure and fun, dear.

And if you should scold I will not curse,
    'Twill be a matter of course, dear;
But, ah, should you disdain my verse,
    I'll get me a divorce, dear.

77

Als sie mich umschlang mit zärtlichem Pressen

When I am wrapped in her tender embraces
  My soul seeks the skies like a thing that is driven!
I let it ascend; and meanwhile no place is
  As sweet as her lips, where I drink draughts of heaven.

78

In den Küssen, welche Lüge

Oh, what lies there are in kisses!
  And their guile so well prepared!
Sweet the snaring is; but this is
  Sweeter still, to be ensnared.

Though your protests overwhelm me,
  Still I know what you'll allow.
Yet I'll swear by all you tell me;
  I'll believe all you avow.

79

An deine schneeweisse Schulter

Upon your snow-white shoulder
  My weary head's at rest,
And I can hear the longing
  That stirs within your breast.

The blue Hussars come bugling,
  Come riding past your door;
And tomorrow, my love, you'll leave me
  And I shall see you no more.

But though you will leave me tomorrow,
    Today you are wholly mine;
Today you shall bless me doubly,
    Closer your arms shall twine.

80

Es blasen die blauen Husaren

The blue Hussars go bugling
    Out of the town and away;
I come to you now, my sweetheart,
    Bringing a rose bouquet.

That was a mad, wild uproar;
    Crowding in every part!
But there was a place for many,
    Even in your small heart.

81

Habe auch in jungen Jahren

In my youth when love was yearning,
I was often sad, and burning
    Like a cord of wood.
Now the price of fuel's higher,
And the cost has quenched the fire,
    Ma foi! and that is good.

Think of this, my pretty darlings,
Cease your silly tears and quarrelings,
    Stupid griefs and harms.
You have life, that precious bubble;
So forget love's ancient trouble,
    Ma foi! within my arms.

82

Bist du wirklich mir so feindlich

Have you really grown to hate me?
  Is the dreaded change completed?
Then the world shall hear my grievance,
  Hear how badly I've been treated.

Oh, ungrateful lips, how could you
  Utter such a shameful story
Of the man whose kisses thrilled you
  In those days of perished glory.

83

Ach, die Augen sind es wieder

Ah, these eyes again which always
  Made my welcome seem completer;
And these are the lips which always
  Made my harsh life somehow sweeter.

And the voice is just as always,
  When its lightest whisper gladdened.
Only *I* am not as always;
  I am home, but changed and saddened.

Now I feel white arms about me
  Close and passionately twining—
Yet I lie upon this bosom
  Unresponsive and repining.

84

Himmlisch war's, wenn ich bezwang

'Tis a heavenly pleasure indeed,
    Curbing passion's wild excess;
And when I do not succeed
    'Tis a pleasure none the less.

85

Blamier mich nicht, mein schönes Kind

Don't shame me, darling; keep your place;
In public turn your pretty face.
But when we're home, and just us two,
Why, then I'll make it up to you.

86

Ja, Freund, hier unter den Linden

Yes, friend, here *Unter den Linden* [1]
    Your heart will be made gay
By women who have sinned in
    The very nicest way.

They blossom brightly, and know it;
    Their silks light up the street.
"Warm flowers," said a poet,
    "On little wandering feet."

Ah, those lovely hats and plumes!
    Ah, those lovely shawls that vex!
Lovely cheeks with their red blooms!
    And the lovelier, swan-like necks.

[1] *Unter den Linden:* The promenade where the fashionable ladies always
could be seen.

87

Selten habt ihr mich verstanden

Hard to understand your gabble;
  And my thoughts you fail to reach.
Only when in filth we dabble
  Do we find a common speech.

88

Doch die Kastraten klagten

And still the eunuchs grumbled,
  Whene'er my voice arose;
They grumbled as they mumbled
  My songs were far too gross.

And, oh, how sweetly thrilling
  Their little voices were;
Their light and limpid trilling
  Made such a pretty stir.

They sang of love, the leaping
  Flood that engulfs the heart . . .
The ladies all were weeping
  At such a feast of art!

89

Auf den Wällen Salamancas

On the walls of Salamanca
  Where the very winds are fonder,
Slowly, with my lovely Donna,
  In the summer dusk we wander.

And my arm is bent about her
  Slender body, and it lingers
As I feel her haughty bosom
  Heave beneath my happy fingers.

But a vague and threatening whisper
  From the linden makes me gloomy;
And the millwheel's evil murmur
  Sends a dark foreboding through me.

"Ah, Señora, something tells me
  Nevermore we two shall wander
On the walls of Salamanca,
  Where the very winds are fonder."

90

Kaum sahen wir uns, und an Augen und Stimme

As soon as we met we were rapt in each other,
  Your eyes and your voice showed you would not resist;
And had it not been for that dragon, your mother,
  There, in that instant, I think we'd have kissed.

Tomorrow, alas, I must leave the quaint city
  And go the old way, as if bound by a spell.
And you will look down from your window in pity;
  And I—I will wave back a friendly farewell.

91

Über die Berge steigt schon die Sonne

Over the mountains the sun throws his fire;
  The bells of the lambs in the distance are low.
My love and my lamb, my own sun of desire,
  Once more I would see you before I must go.

I gaze at her window, impatient and muffled—
"My child, fare thee well; I am parting from thee!"
In vain! Nothing moves, not a curtain is ruffled;
For still she lies sleeping and dreaming . . . of me?

92

Zu Halle auf dem Markt

In Halle's market-place
There stand two mighty lions.
Observe their hollow boldness; see
How quickly men have tamed them.

In Halle's market-place
There stands a mighty giant.
He has a sword, but wields it not;
Some fear has petrified him.

In Halle's market-place
There stands a great cathedral,
Where peasantry and bourgeoisie
Have plenty of room to pray in.

93

Schöne, wirtschaftliche Dame

Lovely and efficient lady,
House and farm are well endowed;
And your cellar's well appointed,
And your fields are all well plowed.

In your clean and shining garden
Weeds can never raise their heads;
And the straw, when threshing's over,
Will be used to stuff the beds.

But your heart and lips, fair lady,
Fallow lie, as hard as stone;
And the bed is but half useful
Where you lie, and sleep alone.

94

Dämmernd liegt der Sommerabend

Softly now the summer twilight
Lies upon the woods and meadows;
And a golden moon looks downward
With a comforting and shy light.

By the brook and in its islands
Crickets chirp; the water murmurs;
And the wanderer hears a plashing
And a breathing in the silence.

There, alone, unclad, unfrightened,
See, a water-nymph is bathing.
How those white limbs in the water
And the moon are doubly whitened!

95

Nacht liegt auf den fremden Wegen

Night lies on the strange, dark roadways;
Weary limbs and heart distress me . . .
Ah, sweet moon, through you my load weighs
Lighter, as your soft beams bless me.

Radiant moon, your gentle wonder
Sends night's ancient terrors reeling;
All my fears are torn asunder,
And the happy tears come healing.

96

Der Tod, das ist die kühle Nacht

Death, it is but the long, cool night,
And Life's a dull and sultry day.
It darkens; I grow drowsy;
I am weary of the light.

Over my bed a strange tree gleams;
There a young nightingale is loud.
He sings of love, love only . . .
I hear it, even in dreams.

97

"Sag, wo ist dein schönes Liebchen"

"Where now is your precious darling,
That you sang about so sweetly,
When the magic, flaming torrent
Fired and filled your heart completely?"

Ah, that fire is extinguished,
And my heart no longer flashes;
And this book's an urn containing
All my love—and all its ashes.

DUSK OF THE GODS

Der Mai ist da mit seinen goldnen Lichtern

Young May is here with all her golden glamor,
And silken zephyrs, and warm, spicy odors.
She lures me, laughing, with her snowy blossoms,
And greets me with the thousand eyes of violets.

She spreads a wide green carpet, rich with flowers,
Woven throughout with sun and morning dew;
And thus she calls to all her well-loved mortals.
The pale-faced, shut-in people hear her first;
The men put on their fancy trousers
And Sunday coats with gold and glassy buttons;
The women all wear white—for innocence;
Youths start to train and twirl the vernal mustache;
Young girls begin a heaving of the bosom;
The city poets stuff into their pockets
Pencil, and pad, and opera-glass! And gladly
The gaily-colored crowds make for the gates,
Camping outside upon the verdant hillsides,
Amazed to see the trees so busily growing;
Playing with sweet and brightly-colored flowers,
Hearing the songs of birds, clear-toned and joyful,
And shouting exultations up to heaven.

May called upon me, too. She knocked three times
Upon my door and cried, "I am the May!
Thou pallid dreamer, come—and I will kiss thee!"
I held my door closed tight, and called to her:
Your lures are all in vain, false visitor.
I have seen through you, May; I have seen through
The world's vast plan—and I have looked too long,
And much too deep; for all my joy has vanished,
And deathless troubles rankle in my heart.
I see right through the hard and stony cover
Of all men's houses and of all men's hearts,
And see in both lies and deceit and torture.
I read men's thoughts by looking at their faces,
Most of them evil. In the blush of maidens
I see the trembling wish beneath the shame;
Upon Youth's proud and visionary head

I see the cap-and-bells of stupid folly;
And twisted phantom-pictures, crazy shadows
Are all I see—until I scarcely know
If earth's a madhouse or a hospital.

I see right through the earth to its foundations,
As though 'twere crystal, and I see the horrors
That May, with all her green and gladdening cover,
Hides all in vain. I see the dead:
They lie below there in their narrow coffins,
Their still hands folded and their blind eyes open.
White are their robes and whiter still their faces.
And through black lips the yellow worms are crawling.
I see the son sitting beside his mistress,
Taking their pleasure on his father's grave;
The nightingales sing mocking songs around them;
The gentle meadow-flowers grin and chuckle.
Deep in his grave the father stirs and shivers—
And Mother Earth is torn with painful spasms.

Oh, Earth, poor Earth, I know your pains and sorrows;
I see the fire raging in your bosom,
I see you bleeding from a thousand veins,
I see your countless wounds torn wide and gaping,
Pouring out streams of flame and smoke and blood.
I see those stark, defiant sons of giants,
Your primal brood, climb from the gloomy chasms
Swinging red torches in their horny hands.
They fix their iron ladders to the skies
And rush to storm the citadel of Heaven.
Black dwarfs swarm hotly after them; and, crackling,
The golden stars crumble to dust and ashes.
Dark, impious hands tear down the golden curtain
From God's own shrine; and with a frightful shrieking

The holy angels fall upon their faces.
Upon his throne a pale and frightened God
Plucks off his diadem and tears his hair . . .
And still the savage horde draws nearer, nearer.
The giants hurl their rain of blazing torches
Into the vaults of Heaven; the dwarfs belabor
The backs of angels with their flaming scourges.
In fear the stricken spirits cringe and cower,
And by the hair they are pulled down and vanquished.

And there, I see my own dear angel stand
With her blonde locks, her sweet, inspiring features,
And with eternal love about her lips,
And with great blessings in her great, blue eyes.
When lo, a frightful, black, and evil goblin
Tears from the ground my pale and trembling angel.
Grinning, he gloats upon her noble beauty,
And clasps her close with tightening embraces . . .

A shriek of horror cleaves the universe;
Its pillars topple; Earth and Heaven crumple.
And Night resumes its dark and ancient rule.

DONNA CLARA

In dem abendlichen Garten

In the evening-colored garden
Wanders the Alcalde's daughter;
Trumpets' and the drums' rejoicings
Rise and echo from the castle.

"Oh, I weary of the dances,
And the cloying, fatuous phrases

Of the knights, who, bowing deeply,
To the sun itself compare me.

"Everything seems dull and tiresome
Since by moonlight I beheld him,
Him, my hero, whose sweet lute-strings
Draw me nightly to my window.

"How he stood; so slim and fiery,
And his eyes were burning boldly
From his pale and classic features—
Looking like St. George, the valiant."

Thus mused lovely Donna Clara,
Gazing at the ground beneath her;
As she looked up—lo, the handsome
Unknown knight stood there before her.

Clasping hands with trembling passion,
Now they wander in the moonlight;
Now the flattering breeze is friendly;
Great, enchanted roses greet them.

Great, enchanted roses greet them,
Redder than love's flaming heralds . . .
"Ah, but tell me, my belovéd,
Why these deep and sudden blushes."

"Gnats were stinging me, my dearest,
And I hate these gnats in summer;
Hate them, love, as though they might be
Nasty Jews with long, hooked noses."

"Jews and gnats—let us forget them,"
Says the knight, with soft persuasion . . .
From the almond tree a thousand
Flower-flakes of white are falling.

Flower-flakes of white are falling,
And their perfume spills about them.—
"Ah, but tell me, my belovéd,
Is your heart mine, and mine only?"

"Yes, I love but you, my dearest,
And I swear it by the Saviour,
Whom the Jews, God's curse upon them,
Did betray and foully murder."

"Jews and Saviour—let's forget them,"
Says the knight, with soft persuasion . . .
Far off in the dreamy distance
Lilies gleam, with light surrounded.

Lilies gleam, with light surrounded,
Gazing at the stars above them.—
"Ah, but tell me, my belovéd,
Have you not perhaps sworn falsely?"

"Nothing's false in me, my dearest;
Just as in my breast there courses
Not a drop of blood that's Moorish,
Nor a taint of Jewish foulness."

"Jews and Moors—let us forget them,"
Says the knight, with soft persuasion,
And, into a grove of myrtle,
Guides the fair Alcalde's daughter.

With Love's soft and supple meshes
He has secretly entrapped her.
Short their words, but long their kisses;
And their hearts are running over.

Like a melting, poignant bride-song,
Sings the nightingale, uplifted;
Like a thousand torchlight dancers
Leap the fireflies from the bushes.

In the grove the stillness deepens.
Nought is heard except the murmurs
Of the wise and nodding myrtle
And the breathing of the flowers.

But the shock of drums and trumpets
Breaks out wildly from the castle,
And it wakes the lovely Clara
From the arms of her belovéd.

"Hark! they call to me, my dearest;
But before we part, pray tell me
What, my love, your own dear name is
That you've hidden so long from me."

And the knight, with gentle laughter,
Presses kisses on her fingers,
On her lips and on her forehead;
And at last he turns and answers:

"I, Señora, your belovéd,
Am the son of the respected,
Erudite and noble Rabbi
Israel of Saragossa."

THE PILGRIMAGE TO KEVLAAR

1

Am Fenster stand die Mutter

The mother stood at the window;
    The son lay on the bed.
"Will you not rise up, William,
    And see the throng?" she said.

"I am so sick, my mother,
    I cannot hear or see;
The thought of my dead Gretchen
    Is all that lives in me."

"Rise up, and then to Kevlaar
    With book and cross we'll go;
God's Mother, She will heal you
    And rid your heart of woe."

The churchly banners flutter,
    Louder the chanting grows;
From Köln, beside Rhine River,
    The long procession goes.

The mother joins the pilgrims,
    She leads her son in the line,
And they, too, swell the chorus:
    "Queen Mary, praise be Thine!"

2

Die Mutter-Gottes zu Kevlaar

The Mother of God in Kevlaar
    Puts on her finest cloak—

Today they will keep her busy,
The crowds of wretched folk.

For all the sick in Kevlaar
Bring her, as offerings meet,
Limbs made of cunning waxwork,
Wax arms and waxen feet.

And whoso brings a wax arm
His arm is healed of its wound,
And whoso brings a wax foot
His foot grows strong and sound.

Oh, many have come to Kevlaar
On crutches who danced away;
And many whose fingers were palsied
Can take up the fiddle and play.

The mother bought a wax light,
And molded therefrom a heart;
"Take this to Mother Mary,
And She will ease the smart."

And sighing he took the wax heart,
And sighing he knelt and prayed;
The tears in his eyes were trembling,
And tremblingly he said:

"Oh, Holiest of the Holy,
Virgin, divinely fair,
Empress of all the Heavens
To Thee I bring my care.

"At Köln with my aging mother
I live within the town,

Town of a hundred churches
And chapels of renown.

"And near us lived my Gretchen
Who now lies underground—
Mary, I bring Thee a wax heart,
Heal Thou my heart's great wound.

"Cure Thou my long heart-sickness,
And daily, rain or shine,
Fervently I will worship.
Queen Mary, praise be Thine!"

3

Der kranke Sohn und die Mutter

The heartsick son and his mother
Were sleeping in the gloom,
And the Mother of God came softly,
And entered the little room.

She bent down over the lover,
And one white hand was drawn
Over his heart so gently . . .
And, smiling, She was gone.

In a dream the mother saw this,
And would have seen still more,
But the dogs' loud baying awoke her;
She stumbled to the floor.

And there, stretched out and quiet,
He lay—and he was dead.

And on his cheeks the daybreak
  Shone with a sudden red.

She folded her hands and sat there,
  She did not rail or whine;
She murmured over and over,
  "Queen Mary, praise be Thine!"

FROM "THE HARZ JOURNEY"
(1824)

PROLOG

Schwarze Röcke, seidne Strümpfe

Black dress-coats and silken stockings,
  Cuffs of snowy white—beshrew them!
Soft embraces, oily speeches.
  Ah, if but a heart beat through them!

If a storm could stir your shirt-fronts,
  Ruffle them in any fashion!
Oh, you kill me with your maudlin
  Bursts of imitation passion.

I will go and climb the mountains,
  Where the simple huts are standing,
Where the winds blow fresh and freely,
  And a chest may try expanding.

I will go and climb the mountains,
  Where the mighty pine-trees tower,
Where the birds and brooks are singing,
  And the heavens grow in power.

Fare ye well, ye polished Salôns,
  Polished folk and polished chaffing—
I will climb the rugged mountains,
  And look down upon you, laughing.

MOUNTAIN IDYL

1

Auf dem Berge steht die Hütte

On the mountain stands a cabin,
　Wherein lives a mountaineer;
All the evergreens are rustling
　And the moon turns golden here.

In the cabin there's an armchair
　Curiously carved and high.
He who sits in it is lucky;
　And that lucky man am I.

On the footstool there's a maiden,
　In my lap her arms repose;
Eyes like two blue stars that sparkle,
　And her mouth's a crimson rose.

And those dear blue eyes grow larger
　While the wonder in them grows;
And she lays a lily finger
　Shyly on the crimson rose.

No, the mother does not see us,
　For she spins and spins away;
And the father plays the zither,
　Singing some forgotten lay.

And the maiden whispers softly,
　Softly, almost breathlessly;
While a host of weighty secrets
　Gravely she confides to me.

"But since Auntie died," she tells me,
  "We can never hope to go
To the picnic-grounds at Goslar;
  That's the loveliest place I know.

"On the mountains here, it's lonely;
  Colder far than down below;
And in Winter we are almost
  Lost and buried in the snow.

"Though I'm quite a girl, I tremble
  Like a child that's seized with fright,
At the evil mountain spirits
  And the things they do by night."

Suddenly she stops, as though her
  Own words chill and terrorize;
And she raises both hands quickly,
  Quickly covering her eyes.

In the trees the rustling's louder,
  Faster still the wheel is stirred,
And above the tinkling zither
  Something of the song is heard:

"Do not fear, my child, my darling,
  Fear no spirit's evil might!
Overhead, my child, my darling,
  Angels guard thee day and night!"

2

Tannenbaum, mit grünen Fingern

Now the fir-tree's long, green fingers
  Tap against the window-pane,

And the moon, that quiet listener,
　Sheds a flood of golden rain.

Father, mother, sleeping soundly,
　Snore for hours without a break;
But we two, with lively chatter,
　Keep each other wide awake.

"That you spend much time in praying
　I've my doubts; for always there
Is a sneer about your features
　That was never caused by prayer.

"Oh, that sneer, so cold and evil,
　Frightens me and terrifies—
But my terror seems to vanish
　When I see your gentle eyes.

"And I doubt that you believe in
　The inspired faith of most.
Don't you worship God the Father,
　And the Son and Holy Ghost?"

"Ah, my child, while still an infant,
　While at mother's knee I stood,
I believed in God the Father,
　He whose rule is great and good.

"He who made the earth we dwell on,
　And the people here below;
He who made sun, moon, and planets,
　Teaching them the way to go.

"Then, my child, as I grew older,
　My belief had but begun,

And I mastered many new things,
 And I worshiped God—and Son;

"The Belovèd Son, who, loving,
 Gave us love to bless and guide;
And for his reward, as usual,
 Was condemned and crucified.

"Now that I've matured and learned much,
 Read and roamed from coast to coast,
Now my heart, with deep conviction,
 Bows before the Holy Ghost.

"He has worked the greatest wonders,
 And he works them still; he broke,
Once for all, the tyrant's power,
 And he burst the bondman's yoke.

"All the ancient scars have vanished,
 Justice takes its rightful place;
Now all men are free and equal
 In a pure and noble race.

"Mists and every evil fancy
 That had filled each night and day,
Cares that crowded out our gladness—
 These have all been swept away!

"And a thousand armored champions
 He has sanctified and sent
To fulfill his sacred mission,
 Fired with their high intent.

"Lo, their splendid swords are shining
 And their tossing flags are bright!—

What, my child, you long to look on
  Such a proud and holy knight?

"Well, my child, come here and kiss me;
  Look at me and you can boast
You have known just such a doughty
  Champion of the Holy Ghost."

3

Still versteckt der Mond sich draussen

Still the bashful moon is hiding
  Close behind the evergreen;
And the lamp upon the table
  Flickers and is scarcely seen.

But those two blue stars are shining
  O'er the heaven of her cheeks;
And the crimson rose is glowing,
  And the lovely child still speaks.

"Tiny goblins, imp-like faeries,
  Clean our little cupboard bare;
It is full of food at evening,
  But at daylight—nothing's there!

"And the thieving Little People
  Skim our cream, our very best;
Then they leave the pans uncovered
  And the cat licks up the rest.

"And that cat's a witch, I know it;
  For she slinks off every night
To the old and ruined castle
  On the haunted mountain-height.

"Once a mighty castle stood there,
  Full of armor and romance;
Shining knights and lovely ladies
  Laughed in many a torchlight dance.

"Then an old enchantress cursed it,
  Cursed each stone and winding stair.
Now there's nothing left but ruins;
  And the owls are nesting there.

"But my dear old aunt once told me
  If one speaks the Word of Might
At the proper, magic moment,
  And the hour and place be right,

"Then the castle shall be lifted
  From the ruined stones—and then
All the vanished knights and ladies
  Will arise and dance again.

"And who speaks that word of magic,
  Knights and ladies, wall and tower,
All are his; while drums and trumpets
  Hail his new and happy power." . . .

Thus the faery legends blossom
  From her mouth, that rose-in-bloom,
While her eyes are pouring starlight
  In the still and darkened room.

Round my hands she winds her golden
  Tresses, binding me at will;
Gives my fingers pretty nicknames;
  Kisses, laughs—and then grows still.

And the hushed room edges closer,
  Watching with a friendly light . . .
Table, chest—it seems I must have
  Seen them all before tonight.

Amiably the old clock gossips,
  And the zither, scarcely heard,
Plays itself with airy fingers;
  And, as in a dream, I'm stirred.

This must be the proper hour;
  Yes, the time and place are right.
And I think I feel it gliding
  From my lips—that Word of Might.

Do you see, my child, how quickly
  Midnight trembles now and breaks!
Brooks and pine-trees murmur louder,
  And the ancient mountain wakes.

Clang of zither, elfin voices
  Rise from glens and faery bowers;
And a wild, fantastic Springtime
  Brings a forest full of flowers.

Flowers, trembling and audacious,
  Flowers, strangely broad and tall,
Fling their eager scents and colors
  As though passion swayed them all.

Roses, red as flame, and burning
  From the brilliant tumult, rise;
Lilies, like great crystal columns,
  Tower straight into the skies.

And the stars, with fiery longing,
  Great as suns, look down and blaze,
Till the lilies' hearts are flooded
  With those eager, showering rays.

But ourselves, my child, are altered
  More than all of these—and see!
Gleaming torches, silks and jewels
  Shimmer 'round us radiantly.

You, you have become a princess,
  And this hut's a castle tall;
Knights and ladies dance rejoicing;
  And there's magic over all.

Ah, but *I* have won the castle,
  Knights and ladies, wall and tower;
Even you—and drums and trumpets
  Hail my new and happy power!

THE HERD-BOY

König ist der Hirtenknabe

He's a king, this happy herd-boy,
  And his throne's the grassy down;
And the sun above his forehead
  Is his great and golden crown.

At his feet the sheep are lying,
  Flattering courtiers, soft and sly;
And his cavaliers are cattle,
  Pompously parading by.

And the kids are his court-players;
  Flutes of birds that hold carouse

Make a splendid chamber-music
With the gentle bells of cows.

And they ring and sing so sweetly,
And the soothing murmurs creep
From the waterfall and forest,
That the young king falls asleep.

Like a minister, his watch-dog,
Governs with an open ear;
And his loud, suspicious barking
Makes the very echoes fear.

Sleepily the young king mutters:
"Ah, to rule is hard and mean;
How I wish that I were home now
With my cozy little queen!

"On her dear and queenly bosom
Soft my regal head would lie;
And I'd find my ancient kingdom
Shining in each love-lit eye."

ON THE BROCKEN

Heller wird es schon im Osten

Comes a spark, the sun's first glimmer;
And the eastern sky's in motion.
Far and faint the mountain summits
Float upon a misty ocean.

Had I seven-league boots, I'd hasten
With the wind, as fast as telling;

Running on the tops of mountains
Till I reach my dear one's dwelling.

I would draw the curtains softly
From her bed, where she lies dreaming;
Softly I would kiss her forehead
And her lips twin rubies gleaming.

And still softer I would whisper
In her frail and lily ear, "Love,
Dream we've never lost each other;
Dream we're lovers still, my dear love."

THE ILSE [1]

Ich bin die Prinzessin Ilse

I am the Princess Ilse
And I dwell at Ilsenstein.
Come with me to my castle,
Thou shalt be blest—and mine.

[1] Here Heine has personified the famous stream and given to it one of those *loreleys* that fill German tradition and verse. As an introduction to this poem he has written, in *"Die Harzreise,"* an exquisite description of the river itself:

"It is indescribable, the merriment, the grace and the *naïveté* with which the Ilse leaps down upon and glides over the fantastically piled rocks that she finds in her path, like a sprightly girl. Yes, the saying is true, the Ilse is a Princess, who, laughing and blossoming, runs down the mountains. How her white garment of foam glitters in the sunlight! How the silver band about her bosom flutters in the wind! How the diamonds sparkle and flash! The high beech-tree stands near her, like a grave father, secretly smiling at his forward and favorite child; the white birches move about like delighted aunts, who are nevertheless a bit anxious over such daring leaps; and the proud oak looks on like a troubled uncle, who might have to pay for this lovely weather. The flowers on the bank murmur softly 'O, take us along, take us along, dear sister.' But the wild girl, not to be held by anything, runs on . . . And suddenly she seizes the dreaming poet; and over me there streams a flower-like rain of resounding gleams and gleaming sounds, and all my senses lose themselves in a rush of Beauty—and I hear only a sweet and fluty voice singing: *'I am the Princess Ilse . . .'* "

There I shall bathe thy forehead
  With waters clear and glad,
Until thy pain shall vanish,
  Thou sick and sorrowing lad.

With my white arms about thee
  Upon my breast thou'lt be;
And thou shalt lie there dreaming
  Of faery legendry.

And I shall kiss and hold thee
  As I would kiss and hold
My lover, dear King Heinrich,
  Who now lies dead and cold.

The dead stay dead forever,
  Only the living live;
My laughing heart is leaping,
  I've youth and joy to give.

Then come down to my castle,
  Come to my crystal halls;
The knights and maidens are dancing,
  Happy are all my thralls.

There's rustling of silk and clatter
  Of spurs, and the bright air hums;
The nimble dwarfs are playing
  On fiddles and horns and drums.

But always my arms shall enfold thee
  And I shall keep thee enthralled;
As I stopped the ears of King Heinrich
  When the brazen trumpets called.

THE NORTH SEA
(1825-1826)

CORONATION

Ihr Lieder! Ihr meine guten Lieder!

Ye songs! Ye valiant songs of mine
Up, up, and arm yourselves!
Let all the trumpets echo,
And lift this blossoming girl
Upon my shield.
For now my restless heart
Longs for her rule, proclaims her Queen.

Hail to thee, hail—oh, youthful Queen!

From the fierce sun at noon
I'll tear the red and gleaming gold,
And it shall be a diadem
For thy belovéd head.
From the great, waving, blue silk tent of heaven,
Where all the diamonds of the night are flashing,
I'll cut a mighty piece;
And hang it, like a royal mantle,
About thy royal shoulders.
I'll give thee a kingly dower
Of starched and polished sonnets,
Haughty tercets, proud and courtly stanzas.
For Pages I shall give thee my wit;
For Court-fool, my wild imagination;
For Herald, with laughing tears in his escutcheon,

My Humor shall serve thee . . .
But I, myself, dear Queen,
I humbly kneel before thee,
And present to thee, from the velvet cushion,
With deepest homage,
The little reason
That mercifully has been left me
By thy predecessor in the realm.

TWILIGHT

Am blassen Meeresstrande

On the pale strip of seashore
I sat alone, lost among fugitive thoughts.
The sun was sinking lower and threw
Glowing, red beams upon the water.
And the white, widening line of waves,
Pulled by the urging tide,
Rolled in and rumbled nearer and nearer—
A curious mingling of wailing and whistling,
Of laughing and murmuring, sighing and shouting;
And, under it all, the strange croon of the ocean.
It was as though I heard forgotten stories,
Ancient and lovely legends,
That once I had heard as a child
From our neighbor's children,
When we, in the summer evening,
On the stone-steps before the door,
Huddled together and listened
With eager hearts,
And sharp, inquisitive eyes . . .
While the growing girls
Sat at the opposite windows;

Their heads showing above the fragrant flower-pots,
Faces like roses;
Laughing and moon-illumined.

NIGHT ON THE STRAND

Sternlos und kalt ist die Nacht

The night is starless and cold,
The ocean yawns.
And, flat on his belly, the monstrous North-wind
Sprawls upon the sea.
Wheezing and groaning,
He babbles his hoarse confidences,
Like a crotchety grumbler who has grown good-humored;
Babbles to the listening waters.
Wild tales he tells them,
Tales of giants, tales of furious slaughter,
And old-world stories out of Norway.
And, between times, he laughs and bellows
Incantations from the Eddas,
And oaths and runes
So potent and so darkly magical
That the white sea-children
Leap up turbulently,
In waves of exultation.

Meanwhile, on the flat shore,
Over the surf-dampened sands,
A stranger walks
With a heart that is wilder than winds or waters.
Wherever he tramps
Sparks fly and sea-shells crunch and crumble.
He wraps himself in his gray, gloomy mantle

And strides on quickly through the windy night—
Led safely by the little taper
That beckons and shimmers with promise
From the lonely fisherman's cottage.

Father and brother are out at sea,
And alone,
All alone in the cottage, she sits,
The fisher's lovely daughter.
She sits at the hearth
And listens to the kettle
Singing its droning, drowsy song.
And she shakes fuel and heaps sticks on the fire
And blows on it,
So that the flickering red light
Lights up, with a lovely magic,
That blossoming face,
Those soft white shoulders
That stand out strangely from the coarse, gray shirt;
Shines on those small and careful hands
That are binding the little petticoat
Tighter about her waist.

Suddenly the door springs open
And the nocturnal stranger enters.
Confident with love, his eyes are fixed
On the white, slender girl,
Who trembles before him,
Like a frail and frightened lily.
And he drops his mantle on the ground
And smiles and says:

"Behold, my child, I keep my word;
I come—and with me come

The ancient times, when all the gods
Came down from heaven to the daughters of men,
And embraced them
And begat with them
Scepter-bearing races of kings,
And heroes, shakers of the world . . .
But, child, do not stand astonished any longer,
Amazed at my divinity;
But get me, I beg of you, some tea with rum,
For it's cold outside.
And on such raw nights
We shiver—even we, who are immortal;
And, being gods, we catch ungodly sneezings,
With colds and coughings that are almost deathless."

POSEIDON

Die Sonnenlichter spielten

The sun's broad beams were playing
Over the wide and rolling sea.
Far off, and anchored, I saw the ship
That was to take me home;
But the right wind was lacking
And I was still sitting on a white sand-dune
Upon the beach.
And I read the song of Odysseus,
That old and ever-youthful song,
From whose leaves, with the breath of the ocean rushing through
     them,
Rises joyfully,
The breath of the gods,
And the radiant Springtime of man,
And the blue, smiling heaven of Hellas.

My noble heart was loyal, and accompanied
The son of Laertes through terror and travail;
Sat down with him, suffered and wept with him
At friendly hearths
Where queens regaled him, spinning purple cloths.
It helped him with his lies, and aided his escape
From giants' caverns and the arms of sirens.
It followed him down the Cimmerian night,
Through storm and shipwreck—
It stood with him through struggles past all telling.

And then I sighed, "Oh, harsh Poseidon,
Thy anger is fearful;
And I, myself, am afraid
Of my own home-coming."

Scarcely had I spoken,
When the sea was churned into foam,
And out of the whitening waters rose
The head of the sea-god,
Sea-weed crowned,
And mockingly he called:

"Have no fear, little poet!
I haven't the least intention of harming
Your poor little boat,
Nor scaring your precious little soul
With a lusty, long-to-be-remembered rocking.
For you, bardlet, have never vexed me.
You have never, that I know of, shaken the smallest turret
Of Priam's holy city.
Nor have you singed a single hair
From the eyelash of my son, Polyphemus.
And, surely, never have you been befriended or counseled
By Pallas Athene, the goddess of Wisdom!"

Thus cried Poseidon
And dived back in the sea.
And at the coarse old sailor's joke
I heard Amphitrite, the fat fish-wife,
And the stupid daughters of Nereus,
Laughing under the waters.

DECLARATION

Herangedämmert kam der Abend

The evening came, dusk-enshrouded,
The tide tossed in wildly;
And I sat on the beach, watching
The white dance of the breakers.
My bosom heaved like the sea,
And yearning seized me—a keen home-sickness
For you, and your fair image
That rises over all things,
And calls me forever,
Over all and forever,
In the howling of the winds, in the roaring of the sea
And in the sighing clamor of my own heart.

With a light reed I wrote upon the sand
"Agnes, I love you!"
But heartless waves crept up and poured themselves
Over that sweet confession,
And blotted it out.

Frail reed, shifting and treacherous sand,
Unstable waters, I'll trust you no more!
The heaven grows darker, my heart grows wilder;
And with strong hands, from Norway's mighty forests

I'll tear the highest pine;
And dip it deep
In Aetna's glowing crater.
And with such a pen,
Fiery and gigantic,
I'll write upon the darkening dome of heaven
"Agnes, I love you!"

Thus every night that flaming line shall burn
And blaze down from the furthest skies;
And all the vast generations of men
Shall read and thrill with the rapturous words:
"Agnes, I love you!"

THE SEA HAS ITS PEARLS
(FROM "NIGHTS IN THE CABIN")

Das Meer hat seine Perlen

The sea has its pearls,
The heaven its stars,—
But my heart, my heart,
My heart has its love.

Great is the sea and the heaven,
But my heart is greater still;
And fairer than pearls or stars
Glistens and sparkles my love.

Oh, young and lovely maiden,
Come to my fathomless heart;
My soul, and the sea, and the heavens
Are wasting away with love.

THE EYES OF HEAVEN
(FROM "NIGHTS IN THE CABIN")

1

Eingewiegt von Meereswellen

Soothed and rocked by rhythmic billows,
Lulled by soft and dreamy fancies,
In my narrow berth I ponder,
Lying in the little cabin.

And I see, beyond the port-hole,
Two great stars serenely shining—
The great, steadfast, and belovéd
Eyes of all eyes, deepest, dearest.

The great, steadfast, and belovéd
Eyes keep watch; they glow and guard me
As they burn their golden beacons
On the highest peaks of heaven.

Toward the highest peaks of heaven
I look up for hours and hours,
Till a veil of floating silver
Mists the eyes serene and steadfast.

2

Es träumte mir von einer weiten Heide

I dreamed about a wide and lonely prairie,
Covered to silence with fine, silver snow;
And, underneath the silence, I was buried,
And slept at last, a cold and lonely sleep.

But high above, the starry eyes of heaven
Looked down upon me in my darkened grave.
Those knowing eyes! They sparkled with clear triumph,
Serenely silent, and with futile love.

STORM

Es wütet der Sturm

The storm rages now
And whips the waves,
And the waters, boiling and furious,
Tower into a moving waste
Of white and flowing mountains.
And the ship climbs them
Sharply, painfully;
And suddenly plunges down,
Into a black and yawning chasm of flood.

O Sea!
Mother of Venus, born of your quickening foam,
Grandmother of Love! Help me!
Already, light of wing, and smelling for corpses,
The white and ghostly sea-mew hovers
And whets its bill on the mast-head,
And lusts to feed on my heart
Which rings with the praise of thy daughter;
The heart that thy grandson, the little scamp,
Has taken for plaything.

Fruitless my prayers and entreaties.
My cry dies in the rushing storm,
In the alarum of the wind.
It roars and rattles and whistles and wails—

A madhouse of sounds!
And between times I can hear,
Far off but distinctly,
Magical harp-tones,
Passionate singing,
Soul-melting and soul-tearing—
And I know the voice . . .

Far on the rocky coast of Scotland
Where an old, gray castle
Juts into the boiling sea;
There, at a high-arched window,
A woman stands, lovely and sick at heart,
Delicate-featured and marble-pale.
And she plays on the harp and sings;
And the storm tosses her long hair,
And carries her dark song
Over the wide and darkening sea.

CALM AT SEA

Meeresstille! Ihre Strahlen

Calm at sea! The sun is throwing
Great long beams upon the water,
And the ship plows through the furrows,
Through a sea of tossing jewels.

And the bosun on his belly
Softly snores beside the tiller;
While a shrinking, tar-smeared ship's boy
Patches sail beside the foremast.

Underneath the dirt, his cheeks are
Reddening slowly; fear or sorrow

Makes his broad mouth twitch and tremble
And his large, deep eyes are troubled.

For the Captain stands before him,
Storms and swears and scolds him: "Rascal!
Rascal! You've been at the barrel.
Rascal! You have stolen a herring!"

Calm at sea! . . . Above the rollers
Lo, a little fish leaps gaily;
Warms his little head with sunlight,
Flaps his little tail with ardor.

But a sea-gull, from high spaces,
Shoots down on the giddy spratling;
And, her prey held in her talons,
Back into the blue she circles.

PEACE

Hoch am Himmel stand die Sonne

The sun stood high in the heavens
Swathed in white clouds;
The sea was still.
I lay in the helm of the vessel,
Dreamily musing . . . When, half awake
And half asleep, I saw the Christ,
The Saviour of the world.
In a white, waving garment
He walked, tall as a giant,
Over land and sea.
His head rose into the heavens,
His hands were stretched in blessing

Over land and sea;
And, like a heart in his breast,
He carried the sun,
The great, red, burning sun.
And that flaming heart, that fiery splendor,
Poured all its hallowed sunbeams,
And all its tender, compassionate light,
Wide-spread and warming,
Over land and sea.

Clear and happy bells were ringing,
Drawing on the gliding vessel;
Drew, like swans with ropes of roses,
Lightly to a fair, green harbor
Where men lived in a lofty, towering
Sky-scraping city.

Wonder of peace! How quiet the town!
The cries and the clamor were hushed;
The clatter of trade was over.
And, through the clean-swept, echoing streets,
Men in white raiment wandered
Carrying palm-branches.
And where two met in that city,
They gazed at each other with understanding,
And, thrilling with love and a sweet abnegation,
Kissed each other on the brow.
And both looked up
At the glowing heart of the Saviour
That joyfully sacrificed its red blood
In streams of ruddy light.
And they, thrice-blest, would cry,
"Praise be to Jesus Christ!"

*

If such a conception would have been granted you,
What would you have given,
Dearly belovèd brother!
You who are so weak in the head and the loins
And so strong in the faith!
You who worship the Trinity so religiously
And kiss the cross and the pup and the paw
Of your noble protectress daily.
You who talked yourself into the council
And a place on the bench
And, at last, to a part in the governing
Of that virtuous city,
Where dust and faith arise,
And the long-suffering Spree, with its holy waters,
Washes the souls and dilutes the tea of the faithful—
Had you but conceived this vision,
Dearly belovèd,
You would have taken it to market
And offered it in high places.
Your white, simpering features
Would melt with devotion;
And the high and mighty lady,
Enraptured and trembling with bliss,
Would sink, praying, on her knees beside you.
And her eyes, beaming with happiness,
Would promise you an increase of salary
Of a hundred sterling Prussian dollars.
And you would fold your hands and stammer,
"Praise be to Jesus Christ!"

SECOND CYCLE

SEA GREETING

Thalatta! Thalatta!

Thalatta! Thalatta!
Hail to thee, O Sea, ageless and eternal!
Hail to thee, from a jubilant heart—
Ten thousand times hail!
Hail, as you were hailed by
Ten thousand Grecian hearts;
Calamity-conquering, homeward-hungering,
Immortal Grecian hearts.

The billows rolled higher,
Heaving and howling;
The sun poured eagerly downward
A rain of rosy lights;
The startled sea-gulls
Flew off with loud cries;
And there were sounds of horses stamping,
And the clashing of shields,
And echoes ringing, like a battle-shout:
"Thalatta! Thalatta!"

Hail to thee, Sea, ageless and eternal!
The whisper of your waters is as the speech of my own land;
The shimmer and surge of your billowy wastes
Is as the dreams of my childhood;
And old memory reveals in new colors

All of those lovely, wonderful playthings,
All of those glittering Christmas presents,
All of those rosy branches of coral,
Goldfish and pearls and shining sea-shells,—
All that you cherish and guard
Down in your clear and crystal depths.

Oh, how I have suffered in strange places!
My heart lay in my breast
Like a fading flower
In the tin box of a botanist.
It seems as though I had sat through the whole Winter,
A sick man in a dismal room,—
And now I leave it!
And suddenly there streams upon me
The emerald Spring, the sun-awakened;
And white branches rustle
And the young flowers look at me
With bright and odorous eyes,
And there's perfume and humming and laughter in all that
    breathes,
And in the blue heavens the very birds are singing:
"Thalatta! Thalatta!"

Oh, dauntless, home-returning heart,
How often, oh, how often,
The barbarian girls of the North have assailed you!
How often have they shot burning arrows
With their great, conquering eyes;
How often have they threatened to cleave the breast
With curved, two-edged words;
How often their chiseled, hieroglyphic letters
Have beaten on my poor, bewildered brain.
I raised my shield against them vainly.

The arrows whistled, the blows came crashing,
And the barbarian girls of the North
Drove me to the sea—
And now, with a great breath, I greet it,
The long-loved, rescuing sea,
"*Thalatta! Thalatta!*"

SUNSET

Die schöne Sonne

The splendid sun
Has slipped quietly into the sea;
The waving waters are already clouded
With the shadows of night;
Only the afterglow
Stretches a web of gold and rosy lights over them.
The restless tide
Urges the billows toward the shore,
And the white waves leap and gambol
Like a flock of woolly lambkins
At evening, when a singing herd-boy
Drives them home.

"How splendid is the Sun!"
Thus, after a long silence, spoke my friend
Who had been walking with me on the beach.
And, half in fun and half in earnest,
He assured me that the sun was a lovely woman
Who had married the old sea-god for convenience.
All day long she wanders happily
Through the high heavens, robed in red and purple,
Blazing with diamonds;
Beloved and worshiped

By every creature in the world;
And all creation is made happy
With the light and warmth of her glance.
But at evening she is forced ruthlessly
To turn back again
To the damp house and the sterile embraces
Of her senile spouse.

"Believe me," my friend continued,
And laughed and sighed and laughed again,
"They live in a sweet wedlock there below!
Either they sleep or else they quarrel
Till the sea above them towers and storms,
And the sailors hear, in the roar of the billows,
How the old one scolds at his wife:
'Whore of the heavens!
Glittering harlot!
All day long you glow for others,
And at night, for me, you are tired and frosty!'

After such curtain-lectures
It's no wonder that the proud sun
Breaks into tears and bewails her lot,
And weeps so long and bitterly, that the sea-god
Springs from his bed in sheer desperation
And swims swiftly up to the surface of the sea
To recover his wind and his wits.

So it was I saw him, a few nights ago,
Looming up, breast-high, above the waves.
He wore a yellow flannel jacket,
And a lily-white nightcap,
And a lined and withered face."

THE GODS OF GREECE

Vollblühender Mond! In deinem Licht

Great blossoming moon! Your yellow light
Turns all of the sea to liquid gold;
Into the distance the long beach stretches
As clear as day with the glamor of evening.
And through the starless, pale-blue heavens,
Massive, white clouds are moving;
Like colossal statues of the gods,
Of glistening marble.

No! Those white images never are clouds!
They are the very gods of old Hellas,
Who ruled the ancient world so gladly,
Who now, dead and supplanted,
Drift, like great ghosts, in a spectral procession
Through the hushed heavens at midnight.

Awed and enraptured I wondered, and looked on
This air-molded Pantheon,
These solemn, majestic, and fearfully-moving
Towering figures . . .
That one is Kronion, king of the heaven,
Snow-white are the locks on his head,
Those time-renowned locks that could shake all Olympus;
He holds in his hands dead, powerless bolts,
And his lined face is feeble with care,
Yet firm with a touch of the ancient pride.
Those times were better and nobler, O Zeus,
When you took a lordly delight in
The nymphs, and the youths, and the sweet, smoking altar.
But even the gods cannot rule on forever;

The young ones will drive out their elders,
As you yourself drove out your hoary father,
Supplanting your uncles, the Titans,
Jupiter Parricida!
And I see you too, haughty Juno!
In spite of all your jealous fears,
The scepter is wielded today by another,
And you are no longer the Queen of heaven.
And your large eyes are watery and dull,
And your white arms have lost their power,
And never can your vengeance trouble
The mild, God-bearing Virgin
And the miracle-working Son of God.
You too I see there, Pallas Athene!
Could not your shield and wisdom ward
Disaster from the deities?
And you are there, you too, Aphrodite,
Once the golden girl, now the silvered one!
Truly, the girdle of love scarce adorns you,
Yet I am still strangely awed by your beauty;
And if you would give yourself and bless me
As you have blessed other great heroes, I'd perish of fear—
A corpse-like goddess you seem to me,
Venus Libitina!
No longer the terrible Ares
Looks at you with the eyes of love.
And how the youthful Phoebus Apollo
Is saddened! His lyre is mute
That joyfully sweetened the feasts of the gods.
Hephaestus is even sadder,
And truly the limping one never again
Shall take Hebe's place,
Or busily serve the great assembly

With heavenly nectar.—Time has extinguished
The inextinguishable laughter of the gods.

Ye gods of Greece, I have never loved you!
For hateful to me are all the Greeks,
And even the Romans are odious.
Yet holy compassion and tremulous pity
Flow through my heart
When I see you there above me,
Forgotten divinities,
Dead and night-wandering shadows;
Weak as the mist, torn by the wind.—
And when I think how vapid and spineless
The new gods are who have conquered you,
These new, sad gods, who now are the rulers,
Who take joy at our pain in their sheep's cloak of meekness—
Oh, then I am seized with a rancorous hate
And I would break down their newly-built temples
And fight for *you*, ye ancient rulers,
For you and your sweet, ambrosial right;
And before your highest altars,
Built up again, and smoking with sacrifice,
I humbly would kneel and invoke you,
Raising my arms in a prayer.—

For, even though, ye ancient deities,
When you joined in the furious combats of mortals,
You always fought on the side of the victor;
Now you will see that man is greater than you.
For I stand here in the combat of gods
And fight on for you, the vanquished.

.   .   .   .

Thus I spoke, and high above me
I saw those cloudy figures blushing,

Gazing on me as though dying;
Transfigured by sorrow—and then they vanished.
The moon was suddenly hidden
Under the clouds that rolled on darkly.
The sea came up with a rush.
And into the heavens, calm and victorious,
Walked the eternal stars.

QUESTIONS

Am Meer, am wüsten, nächtlichen Meer

By the sea, by the dreary, night-colored sea,
A young man stands;
His heart full of anguish, his head full of doubts,
And with pale lips he questions the billows:

"Oh, solve me the riddle of Life,
The torturing, deathless riddle
Which has cracked so many heads,
Heads in hieroglyphic bonnets,
Heads in black birettas and turbans,
Heads in weighty wigs, and a thousand other
Poor, perspiring heads of people—
Tell me, what is Man? And what's his meaning?
Where does he come from? Where is he going?
Who dwells up there among the golden stars?"

The billows are whispering their eternal whispers.
The wind blows on; the clouds go sailing;
The stars keep twinkling, indifferent and cold;
And a fool waits for his answer.

THE PHOENIX

Es kommt ein Vogel geflogen aus Westen

A bird comes flying out of the West.
It flies eastward
Toward its Orient garden-home,
Where strange spices blossom and breathe,
And palm-trees rustle and fountains are cooling.
And the glad bird sings as he flies:
"She loves him! She loves him!
She carries his picture in her small heart,
And carries it sweetly, shyly hidden,
And scarcely knows it, herself!
But in her dreams he stands before her;
She pleads and cries and kisses his hands,
And calls him by name,
And, calling, she wakes and lies half-frightened,
And rubs her eyes with a trembling wonder—
She loves him! She loves him!"

I leaned on the mast on the upper deck;
And stood and listened to the bird's song.
The white-curling billows leaped up and sprang
Like dusky green horses with silvery manes.
With shimmering sails, the Heligolanders,
Those daring nomads of the sea,
Went by, like lines of soaring swans.
Over me, in the eternal blue,
White clouds were floating,
And the eternal sun,
The Rose of the heavens, the fire-blossoming,
Laughed at its splendor mirrored in the sea—
And sky and sea and my own wild heart

Rang with the echo:
"She loves him! She loves him!"

SEA-SICKNESS

Die grauen Nachmittagswolken

The gray clouds of late afternoon
Sag and hang heavily over the sea
Which heaves darkly against them;
And the ship drives on between them.

Sea-sick, I sit by the mainmast,
And give myself up to a host of reflections;
Reflections that are ash-gray and very old,
That were already made by Father Lot
After he had been enjoying good things too freely,
And found himself in a bad way.
With this I think of other old stories:
How the cross-bearing pilgrims, in the days of their stormy sea-
    journeys,
Would be soothed by kissing the picture
Of the blessèd Virgin.
How sea-sick knights, in similar distress,
Would press the precious glove of their adored
Against their lips—and straightway would be cured . . .
But here I sit, and keep on chewing
An old dried herring, that salty consoler
When one's sick as a cat or down as a dog.

All this time the ship is battling
With the wild, tossing tide.
Like a rearing war-horse, she poises herself
On her trembling stern, till the rudder cracks.

Then down she plunges, headlong
Into the howling watery chasm once more.
Then again, like one reckless and weak with love,
She seems about to rest herself
On the black bosom of a giant wave,
That, with a huge roaring, comes toward her.
And suddenly, a furious sea-cataract,
Seething and foaming, rushes upon us,
And souses me with foam.

This tumbling and tossing and rocking
Is beyond bearing!
In vain my eyes strain to seek
The German coast. Alas! only water—
Nothing but water; endless, treacherous water.

As the winter-wanderer longs at evening
For a warm and comforting cup of tea,
So my heart longs for thee,
My German fatherland!
Though forever thy sweet soil is encumbered
With madness, hussars, poor verses,
And thin and vapid pamphlets!
Though forever thy donkeys
Feed upon roses, instead of on thistles!
Though forever thy high-born monkeys
Prink and preen themselves in idle splendor,
And think themselves better than all other
Dull, heavy-footed, stupid and common cattle!
Though thy feeble old snail-councilors
Think they will live forever
Since they move forward so slowly;
Daily clearing their throats to argue
"Does not the Cheese belong to the Cheese-mites?"

Or consuming long hours discussing
"Methods of Improving Egyptian Sheep"
So that the shepherd may shear them like others,
Without a difference—
Though forever folly and wrong and injustice
May cover thee, oh, Germany,
Still am I yearning for thee now:
For thou, at least, art good, dry, solid land.

EPILOG

Wie auf dem Felde die Weizenhalmen

Like the ears of wheat in a wheat-field growing,
So a thousand thoughts spring and tremble
In the minds of men.
But the tender fancies of love
Are like the happy colors that leap among them;
Red and blue flowers.

Red and blue flowers!
The sullen reaper destroys you as worthless;
Block-headed fools will scornfully thresh you; [1]
Even the penniless wayfarer
Who is charmed and cheered by your faces,
Shakes his poor head,
And calls you pretty weeds!
But the young girl from the village,
Twining her garland,
Honors and gathers you.
And with you she brightens her lovely tresses.

[1] *Hölzerne Flegel zerdreschen euch höhnend,*
In this line Heine again makes use of a satiric and subtle play on words;
"hölzerne" is "wooden," and *"Flegel"* can mean either a "flail" or a "clown."

And thus adorned, she hurries to the dancing,
Where fiddles and flutes are sweetly sounding;
Or runs to the sheltering beech-tree,
Where the voice of her lover sounds even sweeter
Than fiddles and flutes.

NEW POEMS

NEW SPRING
(1828-1831)

PROLOG

In Gemälde-Galerieen

Galleries show him painted brightly
 As the warrior of romance;
Marching forth to combat knightly,
 Flourishing a sword and lance.

But insistent *amoretti*
 Steal his armor, mock his powers,
And, though peevish and upset, he
 Lets them wreathe his neck with flowers.

So I yield, as love and prattle
 Steal my strength, command my rhymes;
Marking time while others battle
 In the grim war of our times.

SONGS

1

Unterm weissen Baume sitzend

Sitting underneath white branches
 You can hear the gathering breezes;
You can see clouds high above you
 Wrap themselves in fog that freezes.

Woods are barren, fields are naked,
 And the chilling blasts continue
Till the wintry heart is frozen—
 Ice without and ice within you.

Suddenly white flakes are falling,
  Falling, as though some forgetful
Tree discharged a heavy snowdrift
  While you sat there, cold and fretful.

But, behold! it is no snowdrift
  Falling from the trees to freeze you;
'Tis an avalanche of petals
  Loosed by Spring to please and tease you.

Winter's gone and May's the magic.
  Heart, be glad you were mistaken!
Snow-flakes, somehow, turn to blossoms,
  And the heart exults to waken.

2

In dem Walde spriesst und grünt es

Now the wood blooms like a maiden
  Running to a lover's meeting;
And the sun laughs down upon it:
  "Welcome, Spring! A fervent greeting!"

Nightingale, I hear your flute-call
  As it starts the woodland ringing.
What a poignant, long-drawn cadence:
  "Love"—'Tis all you know of singing!

3

Die schönen Augen der Frühlingsnacht

The stars of Spring with their gentle glow
  Bring comfort after pain:
And love that belittled and laid you low
  Is quick to exalt you again.

Upon a lime-tree, late and long
A lonely nightingale sings;
And, as the soul drinks in the song,
The spirit lifts its wings.

4

Gekommen ist der Maie

Here's May, with all its lifting
Of leaves and voices high;
And rosy clouds are drifting
Across an azure sky.

A nightingale is singing
In every bower and croft;
And little lambs are springing
Where fields are clover-soft.

But I am not singing or springing;
I lie on a grassy plot,
Hearing a distant ringing,
And dreaming of God knows what.

5

Leise zieht durch mein Gemüt

Lightly swinging bells are ringing
With a soft insistence;
Tinkle, tiny tunes of Spring,
Tinkle through the distance.

Fill the air and run to where
All the flowers grow sweeter.
If you see a rosebud there
Tell her that I greet her!

6

Der Schmetterling ist in die Rose verliebt

The butterfly is in love with the rose
  And flutters about her all day,
While he, in turn, is pursued by a bright
  Sunbeam that follows his way.

But wait—with whom is the rose in love?
  For whom does she tremble and pale?
Is it the silent evening star?
  The passionate nightingale?

I do not know whom the red rose loves;
  But I love you all, for I
Sing nightingale, sunbeam, and evening star,
  The rose and the butterfly!

7

Es erklingen alle Bäume

All the trees are full of music;
  Nests are singing, high and small.
In this green, orchestral concert,
  Who's conductor of it all?

Can it be that old, gray plover
  Who keeps nodding to the beat?
Or that pedant, who, up yonder,
  Marks his *"Cuckoo"* strong and sweet?

Or is it the stork, who gravely
  Keeps on tapping with his bill,
Just as though he were directing,
  While the others soar and trill.

No; my own heart holds the leader;
   Well he knows the stress thereof!
And I feel the time he's beating,
   And I think his name is love.

8

Im Anfang war die Nachtigall

"In the beginning was the word,
   Sung by the nightingale, '*Sweet! Sweet!*'
While grass and apple-blossoms stirred,
   And violets found their dancing feet.

"He bit his breast until the blood
   Ran freely, and from that bright stream
A tall and lovely rose-tree stood;
   And there he sings his passionate dream.

"All of us birds now live in peace;
   His blood redeemed all things that fly.
Yet if the rosy song should cease
   The wood, and all it holds, would die."

So, to his brood, the sparrow speaks,
   As though he had them all in church;
The mother-bird is proud, and squeaks
   Upon her high and lawful perch.

She's a good housewife, every day
   She only lives to build and breed;
While he, to pass the time away,
   Lectures his children in the creed.

9

Es hat die warme Frühlingsnacht

The warm Spring night, the humid air,
　Draw flowers from the stubborn plain;
And if my heart does not take care
　'Twill find itself in love again.

But which new flower will ensnare
　My heart with unexpected doom?
The nightingale bids me beware
　Of one young lily just in bloom.

10

Es drängt die Not, es läuten die Glocken

I must go forth, the bells are pealing;
　And, oh, I've lost my head completely.
A pair of eyes, in league with Springtime,
　Have been conspiring far too sweetly.

A pair of brilliant eyes and Springtime
　Storm at my heart and have incensed me—
Even the nightingales and roses
　I think are in a plot against me.

11

Ach, ich sehne mich nach Thränen

Ah, I long for tears returning
　Love and all its tender pain;
And I fear that very yearning
　Soon will be fulfilled again.

Love, that unction never failing,
 Love, that torture self-revealed,
Steals once more into an ailing
 Bosom that is barely healed.

12

Die blauen Frühlingsaugen

The deep, blue eyes of Springtime
 Peer from the grass beneath;
They are the tender violets
 That I will twine in a wreath.

I pick them and I ponder—
 And all my hopes and aims,
All of my hidden fancies
 The nightingale proclaims!

Yes, all that I think, he echoes
 In a loud and lyric mood;
And now my deepest secret
 Is known to all the wood.

13

Wenn du mir vorüberwandelst

When you pass me on your way
 And your light dress touches me,
My heart leaps, and I would follow
 Wheresoever you may be.

Then you turn, and your great eyes
 Half invite me to pursue.

And my fool heart halts and trembles;
And I dare not follow you.

14

Die schlanke Wasserlilie

The slender water-lily
   Stares at the heavens above,
And sees the moon who gazes
   With the luminous eyes of love.

Blushing, she bends and lowers
   Her head in a shamed retreat—
And there is the poor, pale lover,
   Languishing at her feet!

15

Wenn du gute Augen hast

If your eyes are very keen
   And you search my latest poem,
You will see a fair youth hiding
   There, and (what is more) you know him.

If your ears are very sharp,
   You will hear—part voice and part strings—
Singing, sighing, laughing, crying
   Songs to trouble your poor heart-strings.

For they come, with look and word,
   Like their author, to perplex you:
A fantastic, love-sick dreamer,
   Whose queer dreams can only vex you.

16

Was treibt dich umher in der Frühlingsnacht

What drives you out in this night of Spring
To set the flowers murmuring?
    The violets are affrighted;
The roses, flushed with shame, are red;
The lilies, paler than the dead,
    Bend low as though they were blighted.

O lovely moon, what second sight
Inspires the flowers, for they are right—
    My crime is not forgiven.
How could I know the flowers had heard
The frantic prayers and the absurd
    Vows I had made to heaven!

17

Mit deinen blauen Augen

Your eyes' blue depths are lifted,
    With love and friendship stirred.
They smile; and, lost in dreaming,
    I cannot speak a word.

Your eyes and their deep heavens
    Possess me and will not depart—
A sea of blue thoughts rushing
    And pouring over my heart.

18

Wieder ist das Herz bezwungen

Once again my heart is shaken
    Free of all that's grim and gloomy;

Once again the sweet awaking,
  And May's breath comes coursing through me.

Once again I pace the side-walks,
  Peering under every bonnet,
Seeking Her, that dear dilemma,
  As though life depended on it.

Once again I haunt the rustic
  Bridge above the little river.
Ah, perhaps, She'll have to cross it;
  And my arms yearn to receive her.

Waterfalls bring foreign gossip,
  Like all garrulous musicians;
And my heart, that clever linguist,
  Understands the repetitions.

Once again I lose myself in
  Dreams, dark paths, and ways new-wooded.
And the birds in all the branches
  Mock love's fool, the self-deluded.

19

Die Rose duftet—doch ob sie empfindet

The rose is fragrant—but can she be feeling
  All she breathes forth? Can the nightingale
Feel half his own rapture, half the appealing
  Poignance that wakes to his lyrical hail?

I do not know. The truth may grieve us;
  And why should we be quick to see
That such deceptions may deceive us;
  If these are lies—well, let them be.

20

Weil ich dich liebe muss ich fliehend

Because I love your shining features
  I must avoid them, for behold
How ill they match this sullen creature's
  Unhappy visage.—Do not scold.

Because I love you, I must wait full
  Day after day with fear and cold.
No wonder when you find me hateful
  I must avoid you.—Do not scold.

21

Ich wandle unter Blumen

I wander where budding bowers
  Infect me with romance;
My soul expands with the flowers,
  Dizzy, as though in a trance.

Hold me! or drunken with utter
  Joy at the spell you invoke,
Here at your feet I totter—
  And the garden is full of folk!

22

Wie des Mondes Abbild zittert

As the moon's pale image trembles
  In the sea's wild billows, even
While the moon herself in silence
  Calmly walks across the heaven,

So you wander, my belovéd
Calm and silent; while there waken
Tears and tremblings, as your image
Shakes because my heart is shaken.

23

Es haben unsre Herzen

Our hearts have made a holy
Alliance, firm and fast;
They understand each other,
And beat as one at last!

But ah, the poor young rosebud
That lent your bosom grace,
Our helpless, little confederate
Was crushed in our embrace.

24

Sag mir wer einst die Uhren erfund

Come, tell me whose super-intelligent power
Invented the second, the minute, the hour.
It must have been someone afraid of delight
Who sat in his house through a long winter night
And counted the strokes of the mice pick-picking,
And the measured beat of the death-watch ticking.

And who do you think first invented the kiss?
A lover who laughed when he tasted his bliss.
He kissed with conviction that brooked no delay;
He kissed all through April, he kissed all through May;
He kissed till the thrushes were shamed into singing,
And the great, laughing sun set the whole world springing.

25

Küsse, die man stiehlt im Dunkeln

Kisses that one steals in darkness,
  And, in darkness, are returned,
Those are blesséd kisses, kindling
  Hearts afresh where love has burned.

Sad with thoughts and premonitions,
  Then the spirit loves to view
All the past it can remember,
  Wandering in the future, too.

But to think too much is harmful,
  Most of all, when lovers kiss.—
Weep, my soul, instead of thinking;
  Weeping's easier than this.

26

Es war ein alter König

There was an aged monarch,
  His heart and head were gray with strife;
This poor old monarch wedded
  A young and lovely wife.

There was a pretty page-boy,
  His hair was light, his heart was clean;
He carried the long and silken
  Train of the fair young queen.

You know the old, old story
  So sweet to hear, so sad to tell:
Both of them had to perish;
  They loved each other too well.

27

In meiner Erinnrung erblühen

In memory many pictures
　Arise and reassemble—
What gives your voice the magic
　That makes me burn and tremble?

Oh, do not say you love me!
　All that may bloom most brightly,
Love and the fires of April,
　You put to shame so lightly.

Oh, do not say you love me!
　But kiss in quiet closes,
And laugh when, in the morning,
　I show you withered roses.

28

Durch den Wald im Mondenscheine

Through the woods last night at moonrise
　Rode the elves on airy highways.
I could hear light bugles calling,
　And small bells rang through the byways.

Tiny silver stallions sported
　Golden horns. Was it a vision?
Like wild swans, they floated past me
　With miraculous precision.

And the queen smiled back upon me,
　Answering the look I gave her.
Was she blessing love's renewal?
　Or was death to be her favor?

29

Morgens send' ich dir die Veilchen

Every day I send you violets
  Which I found in woods at dawn;
And at evening I bring roses
  Which I plucked when day was gone.

Do you know what these two flowers
  Say, if you can read them right?
Through the day you shall be faithful
  And shall love me through the night.

30

Der Brief, den du geschrieben

Your letter does not move me
  Although the words are strong;
You say you will not love me—
  But ah, the letter's long . . .

Twelve pages, neat and double.
  A little essay! Why,
One never takes such trouble
  To write a mere good-by.

31

Sorge nie, dass ich verrate

Do not fear that I'll betray my
  Love for you. The world ignores
What I say about your beauty
  When I gush in metaphors.

Underneath a glade of flowers
  In a hushed and hidden field,
Lies our warm and glowing secret,
  Burning still—but still concealed.

Though the rose may flame too boldly,
  Never fear—they will not see!
For the world believes that fire
  Only burns in poetry.

32

Sterne mit den goldnen Füsschen

Stars with golden feet are walking
  Through the skies with footsteps light,
Lest they wake the earth below them,
  Sleeping in the lap of night.

All the silent forests listen;
  Every leaf's a small, green ear;
And the dreaming mountain stretches
  Shadowy arms that reach me here.

Hush, who called there? My heart trembles
  As the dying echoes fail.
Was it my beloved, or was it
  Just a lonely nightingale?

33

Schon wieder bin ich fortgerissen

Once more we two are torn asunder,
  Once more the summons comes to part;
And may you never stop to wonder
  How much the torture twists my heart.

The carriage groans; the old bridge rumbles;
  Even the brook has lost its cheer.
Good fortune goes, my poor heart grumbles,
  As I depart from all that's dear.

The very constellations scatter,
  Hunted, it seems, from Heaven's plains.
Farewell, belovéd. But no matter
  Where I am driven, my heart remains.

34

Die holden Wünsche blühen

The sweet desires blossom
  And fade, and revive, and spend
Their beauty and wither, and blossom—
  And so on, without end.

I know this, and it saddens
  My life and all its zest.
My heart's so wise and clever
  It bleeds away in my breast.

35

Spätherbstnebel, kalte Träume

Autumn mists, cold dreams are filling
  Height and valley, while the thinned
Trees, poor ghosts, give their unwilling
  Leaves to bait the brutal wind.

One tree there, and one tree only,
  Holds its leaves untouched by dread;
There, among the gaunt and lonely
  Crowd, it lifts a dauntless head.

The scene's my heart: the same grim capture
Kills the dearest dreams we knew.
Yet where all is stripped and sapped, your
Face appears. The tree is you.

A MISCELLANY
(1832-1839)

SERAPHINE

1

Wandl' ich in dem Wald des Abends

Through the dusky wood I wander,
  Through the dream-invoking glade,
While your spirit is beside me
  Like the shadow of a shade.

Is not that your white veil drifting;
  This your softly shining face?
Or is merely moonlight sifting
  Through dark fir-trees for a space.

And this sound of weeping, is it
  My own sorrow that I hear?
Can it, somehow, be my loved one
  Who has really shed a tear!

2

An dem stillen Meeresstrande

Night has come with silent footsteps,
  On the beaches by the ocean;
And the waves, with curious whispers,
  Ask the moon, "Have you a notion

"Who that man is? Is he foolish,
  Or with love is he demented?
For he seems so sad and cheerful,
  So cast down yet so contented."

And the moon, with shining laughter,
  Answers them, "If you must know it,
He is both in love *and* foolish;
  And, besides that, he's a poet!"

3

Das ist eine weisse Möwe

That is a silver sea-gull
  Floating against the sky
Above the darkening waters.
  The moon is cold and high.

The shark and the ray observe her
  With calculating eye;
The sea-gull swoops and circles;
  The moon is cold and high.

Oh, dear and desperate spirit,
  I hear your pitiful cry.
The waters are much too near you.
  The moon is cold and high.

4

Im Mondenglanze ruht das Meer

The moon's white spell has calmed the sea;
  It lies here, gently gleaming.
A gradual fear steals over me;
  A legend sets me dreaming.

A legend, old as time, that tells
  Of sunken towns and peoples,
And how, beneath deep water, bells
  Still sound from sunken steeples.

Alas! Those bells will never save,
  Nor prayers restore one building;
For what is given to the grave
  Lies still. The grave's unyielding.

5

Dass du mich liebst, das wusst' ich

I was aware you loved me,
  I knew it long, my dear;
Yet, when at last you said it,
  My heart was torn with fear.

I climbed high up the mountain,
  And sang a joyful air;
I walked the seashore weeping
  To see the sunset there.

My heart's the sun; it blazes
  High in the heavens above,
And sinks, immense and glowing,
  In a burning sea of love.

6

Wie neubegierig die Möwe

How this too anxious sea-gull
  Follows us even here,
Because your lips come closer
  And closer to my ear.

Need I confess I'm filled with
  More wonder than the bird's;
Anxious if I'm to be thrilled with
  Your kisses or your words.

If I were only certain
   What shakes my pulse like this!
Tauntingly intermingled
   Are promise and the kiss.

7

Auf diesen Felsen bauen wir

Upon these rocks we shall erect
   A church, superb and splendid,
Built on the third New Testament . . .
   The sufferings are ended.

Ended at last the difference
   Between us, false and shoddy;
Ended the stupid rage of flesh,
   The torments of the body.

Listen how God in that dark sea
   Speaks with a thousand voices,
How, in the thousand-lighted skies,
   His loveliness rejoices.

God's beauty moves through light and dark,
   Through bright and secret places;
His spirit lives in all that is—
   Even in our embraces.

8

Graue Nacht liegt auf dem Meere

Gray night lies upon the waters;
   Stars appear with shy persistence;

Underneath the surf are gradual
  Voices drawn from some great distance.

Now the north-wind smites a music
  From the waves, as though compelling
Chords from some gigantic organ,
  Chords majestic and upswelling.

Partly pagan, partly sacred—
  Thus the song reflects his spirit,
While the music mounts to heaven,
  And the stars rejoice to hear it.

Now the stars grow large and larger,
  Reaching unrecorded phases
Till, as great as suns, they light up
  Heaven's dark and endless mazes.

Blending with the ocean's music
  They create the maddest measure:
Solar nightingales that circle
  In a sky of gold and azure.

Earth and heaven out-sing each other;
  Infinity grows still more roomy;
And, to such gigantic promptings,
  New desire goes storming through me.

9

Schattenküsse, Schattenliebe

Shadow-love and shadow-kisses,
  Shadow-life—you think it strange?

Fool! Did you imagine this is
Fixed and constant, free from change?

Everything we love and cherish
   Like a dream, goes hurrying past;
While the hearts forget and perish,
   And the eyes are closed at last.

10

Das Fräulein stand am Meere

Upon the shore, a maiden
   Sighs with a troubled frown;
She seems so sorrow-laden
   To see the sun go down.

Don't let the old thing grieve you,
   Look up and smile, my dear;
For, though in front he may leave you,
   He'll rise again in the rear.

11

Mit schwarzen Segeln segelt mein Schiff

With great, black sails my ship sails on,
   On through a storming sea;
You know how deathly sick I am,
   And how you have tortured me.

But you are faithless as the wind
   That rushes fast and free . . .
With great, black sails my ship sails on,
   On through a storming sea.

12

Wie schändlich du gehandelt

I've told no man how shameful
  You were, and how malicious;
But I have sailed away to the sea
  And told it to the fishes.

Upon the land I've left your
  Good name, so none may doubt you.
But through the length and depth of the sea,
  Everyone knows about you!

13

Es ziehen die brausenden Wellen

The waves draw in and stumble
  Upon the strand;
They crumble as they tumble
  Over the sand.

With strength and an increasing
  Power they roar;
Their energy's unceasing—
  And what's it for?

14

Es ragt ins Meer der Runenstein

The runic stone juts into the sea;
  I sit beside it, dreaming.
The sea-gulls cry, the waves run free,
  The wind is whistling and screaming.

Many have been beloved by me,
Many I thought were unfailing.
Where are they now? The waves run free;
The wind is whistling and wailing.

15

Das Meer erstrahlt im Sonnenschein

The sea is sparkling in the sun,
Golden and glad to be.
My brothers, when I come to die,
Bury me in the sea.

For I have always loved it; yes,
And it was kind to me;
It cooled my heart, how often!
We were good friends, were we.

ANGELIQUE

1

Nun der Gott mir günstig nicket

Now that God has given me gladness
Must I mope in dumb displeasure?
I, who sang so much when sadness
Was the theme that set the measure?

I, who turned the old desires
To a new poetic fashion,
Till a hundred versifiers
Learned to simulate my passion?

Come, you birds so hushed and shaken
In my soul, what can deter you?

Fill your throats! Arise! Awaken!
Let men know joy still can stir you!

2

Wie rasch du auch vorüberschrittest

Although you hurried coldly past me,
Your eyes looked backward and askance;
Your lips were curiously parted,
Though stormy pride was in your glance.

Would I had never tried to hold you,
Nor seek your white and flowing train.
Would I had never found your footsteps,
Or seeking them, had sought in vain.

Now, all your pride and wildness vanished,
You are as tame as one could be;
Gentle, and sweet beyond endurance—
And, worse, you are in love with me!

3

Nimmer glaub' ich, junge Schöne

Never think I heed, my beauty,
What your virtuous lips may say;
Such dark eyes make mock of virtue,
Such dark eyes drive fear away.

Let us leave all poor pretenses;
Give me those half-willing hands.
Lips are witless, hearts have wisdom—
And your wise heart understands.

4

Wie entwickeln sich doch schnelle

How from such a chance beginning
   And in what a casual fashion,
There has grown so close a union,
   Such a great and tender passion.

Every day this charming creature
   Holds me faster in her power,
And the feeling that I love her
   Grows upon me hour by hour.

And her soul has beauty? Frankly,
   That's a matter of opinion;
But I'm sure of all the other
   Charms she shows to me, her minion.

Those white lips and that white forehead!
   Nose that wrinkles on occasion,
When her lips curve into laughter—
   And how swift is their persuasion!

5

Ach, wie schön bist du, wenn traulich

Ah, how sweet you are, confiding
   All your thoughts to me, your lover,
When, with noble words and phrases,
   Your impulsive mind runs over.

When you tell me that your thoughts are
   Large and of a lofty fashion;
How your heart's pride, not too stubborn,
   Is at war with your compassion.

How you'd never give yourself for
  Millions—no, you could not bear it!
Ere you sold yourself for money
  You would rather die, you swear it!

And I look at you and listen,
  And I listen till you've finished,
Like a thoughtful, silent statue
  Whose belief is undiminished.

6

Ich halte ihr die Augen zu

I close her eyes, and keep them tight
  Whene'er we come to kiss;
Her laughter, curious and bright,
  Asks me the cause of this.

From early morn till late at night
  She questions why it is
I close her eyes and keep them tight
  Whene'er we come to kiss.

I do not even know—not quite,
  What my own reason is—
I close her eyes, and keep them tight
  Whene'er we come to kiss.

7

Wenn ich, beseligt von schönen Küssen

When in your arms and in our kisses
  I find love's sweet and happiest season,
My Germany you must never mention—
  I cannot bear it: there is a reason.

Oh, silence your chatter on anything German;
   You must not plague me or ask me to share it.
Be still when you think of my home or my kindred—
   There is a reason: I cannot bear it.

The oaks are green, and the German women
   Have smiling eyes that know no treason;
They speak of Love and Faith and Honor!
   I cannot bear it: there is a reason.

8

Fürchte nichts, geliebte Seele

Do not fear, my love; no danger
   Ever will approach us here;
Fear no thief or any stranger—
   See, I lock the door, my dear.

Do not fear the wind that's quarreling,
   For these walls are strong and stout;
To prevent a fire, my darling,—
   See, I blow the candle out.

Let my arms fold close and thickly
   Here about your neck and all—
One can catch a cold so quickly
   In the absence of a shawl.

9

Während ich nach andrer Leute

While I seek forbidden pastures,
   While, to put it briefly, I

Underneath some stranger's window
  All night long parade and sigh,

Then, perhaps, some other lover
  Paces just as anxiously
Underneath the very window
  Where my sweetheart lives with me.

That is human. God in heaven,
  Who can tell what may befall
In this labyrinth of living!
  So it goes. God keep us all.

10

Ja, freilich, du bist mein Ideal

Yes, surely, you are my ideal;
  Your beauty makes me dizzy.
Have I not proved the fact with zeal?
  But just today I'm busy.

Tomorrow between two and three,
  Impatient little sinner,
Immoderate flame will quicken me—
  And after, there'll be dinner.

Perhaps, if there is still a seat,
  I'll take you, on the level,
To opera as a special treat;
  They're playing *Robert the Devil.*

It is a very grand affair
  Of spells and love unlawful;
The music is by Meyerbeer,
  The text by Scribe—godawful!

11

Schaff mich nicht ab, wenn auch den Durst

Don't send me off, now that your thirst
    Is quenched, and all seems stale to you;
Keep me a short three months or more,
    Then I'll be sated, too.

If now you will not be my love
    Then try to be my friend;
Friendship is something that may come
    When love comes to an end.

12

Dieser Liebe toller Fasching

This mad carnival of loving,
This wild orgy of the flesh,
Ends at last and we two, sobered,
Look at one another, yawning.

Emptied the inflaming cup
That was filled with sensuous potions,
Foaming, almost running over—
Emptied is the flaming cup.

All the violins are silent
That impelled our feet to dancing,
To the giddy dance of passion—
Silent are the violins.

All the lanterns now are darkened
That once poured their streaming brilliance
On the masquerades and mummers—
Darkened now are all the lanterns.

And tomorrow is Ash Wednesday,
And I put a cross of ashes
On your lovely brow, and tell you:
"Woman, you are dust. Remember!"

DIANE

1

Diese schönen Gliedermassen

Such magnificent expanse,
    Such long lines of bone and muscle
Should provoke inspired chants;
    They are, may I say, colossal.

Should I overcome them by
    Unforeseen romantic ruses,
I'd be sorry for it; I
    Would emerge a mass of bruises.

Goddess with a heavenly length,
    Bosom, throat and neck enslave me;
Ere I love you, give me strength,
    But should *you* embrace, God save me.

2

Am Golfe von Biscaya

Beside the Bay of Biscay,
    She saw the light of day,
And in her cradle strangled
    Two kittens, so they say.

On naked feet she ran
    Across the Pyrenees,

And then at Perpignan
   She did her best to please.

Now she is quite the lady
   In the Faubourg Saint-Denis,
She's cost the small Sir William
   A fortune. *C'est la vie!*

3

Manchmal wenn ich bei Euch bin

Sometimes when I am with you,
   Often-loved and lofty Doña,
Memory brings back the view
   Of the great square in Bologna.

There's a massive fountain of
   Marble called "The Giant's Fountain,"
With a Neptune perched above,
   Like a mole-hill on a mountain.

HORTENSE

1

Ehmals glaubt' ich, alle Küsse

Once I thought that all the kisses
   Women give us soon or late
Were the justly reckoned blisses
   Preordained by grudging fate.

Then I kissed by measure, praying
   Each time long and seriously,
Just as though I were obeying
   Some divine economy.

Now I know that kissing's rarely
  Quite as serious as this;
I approach the matter fairly,
  And I kiss, and kiss, and kiss.

2

Wir standen an der Strasseneck

We stood upon the corner, where,
  For upwards of an hour,
We spoke with soulful tenderness
  Of love's transcending power.

Our fervors grew; a hundred times
  Impassioned oaths we made there.
We stood upon the corner—and,
  Alas, my love, we stayed there!

The goddess Opportunity,
  A maid, alert and sprightly,
Came by, observed us standing there,
  And passed on, laughing lightly.

3

In meinen Tagesträumen

In all my dreams by daylight
  And nights that follow after,
My spirit throbs and rings with
  Your long and lovely laughter.

Remember Montmorency?
  The ass you dared not straddle?
And how, into the thistles,
  You fell from that high saddle?

The donkey stood there browsing
Upon the thorns thereafter—
Always will I remember
Your long and lovely laughter.

4

Steht ein Baum im schönen Garten

She Speaks:

Deep within a lovely garden
   There's an apple on a tree;
And, about the boughs, a serpent
   Coils itself and looks at me.
I can't take my eyes from off it,
   While I hear its gentle hiss,
While its eyes burn with a promise
   And a prophecy of bliss.

The Other Speaks:

'Tis the fruit of life you see there,
   Taste it, do not let it fall;
Lest you throw away a lifetime
   Without knowing life at all.
Come, my darling, my sweet pigeon,
   Try it, taste it, do not fear;
Follow my advice and thank me.
   Trust your wise old aunt, my dear.

5

Nicht lange täuschte mich das Glück

No longer does your beauty seem
   My lying hope, my hunger;

Your face is like a foolish dream
That came, but comes no longer.

Daybreak was clean; it brought the sun;
The dubious mist departed.
And we, quite casually, were done
With what was scarcely started.

CLARISSA

1

Meinen schönsten Liebesantrag

Spurn my suit, and, when I ask it,
Keep your kiss. Delay; deny.
If I say, "Is love a basket?"
Roll your childish eyes and cry.

Prayers are not my style, so listen;
I may never pray again:
"God, please dry those tears that glisten,
And put something in her brain!"

2

Hol' der Teufel deine Mutter

May the devil fetch your father,
May the devil take your mother,
Who so cruelly at theater
Kept us hidden from each other.

There they sat; he large in velvet,
She intolerably begauded;

Then the hapless lovers perished.
And, my God! how they applauded!

3

Geh nicht durch die böse Strasse

Do not go into the furious
    Street alert with curious eyes;
Shield yourself from the injurious
    Glances that no men disguise.

Everything that's good befriends you
    Till I, burning in suspense,
Watch while even laughter lends you
    Lovely arts of innocence.

Yet, in some repeated dream, I
    Know, though you seem born to bless,
You, so good, will come to be my
    Bosomful of bitterness.

4

Es kommt der Lenz mit dem Hochzeitgeschenk

Spring comes laughing with honeymoon zest,
    With music and celebrations.
Bride and bridegroom put on their best
    To receive his congratulations.

Jasmine and roses fill the room,
    And, since he does nothing sparsely,
There's celery for the bride and groom,
    And ever-fertile parsley.

5

Schütz' euch Gott vor Überhitzung

Here's advice and wedding wishes:
    God save you from perspiration,
From anemia that's pernicious,
    Goiter, gout, and constipation.

Watch your diet; don't grow shoddy;
    Free yourself of hives and hernia.
Keep, in short, a healthy body—
    And the rest need not concern ye.

6

Jetzt kanst du mit vollem Recht

Now, my innocent, you can
    Think (and you'll be right) about me:
"He's a really wicked man
    Thus to jeer in verse and flout me—

"Me, who never hinted once
    Of the many things that ailed him;
Who upheld him, like a dunce,
    Though most everyone assailed him—

"Me, who, as a matter of fact,
    Stood quite ready to adore him,
Had he known the way to act,
    Had he known the best thing for him!"

7

Es kommt zu spät, was du mir lächelst

Too late your sighs and smiles of promise,
　Your little hints of love, too late.
Emotion's dead. The pulse is quiet
　That beat at such an anxious rate.

Too late the thought of mutual passion;
　Too late the talk of being brave.
Your ardent look is no more rousing
　Than sunlight falling on a grave.

This would I know: When life is over
　Where can the tired spirit go?
Where is the fire that we extinguished?
　Where is the wind that ceased to blow?

YOLANDA AND MARIE

1

Diese Damen, sie verstehen

Both of them know how to honor
　Poets; they do not discuss
Art. Instead, they give me luncheon,
　Me and my great genius.

Ah! The soup was most auspicious,
　And the wine increased the mood;
The roast chicken was delicious,
　And the larded hare was good.

And the Muse? We dined upon her,
　Full to tears, and loath to part;

And I thanked them for the honor
That they showed me and my art.

2

In welche soll ich mich verlieben

Which of them shall I fall in love with?
Both of them make my senses swirl.
The mother's still a lovely woman;
The daughter's an enchanting girl.

In those young arms and virgin beauties
My trembling heart is almost caught!
But thrilling too are genial glances
That understand each casual thought.

My heart resembles our gray brother,
Who stands, a jackass self-confessed,
Between two bundles of his fodder,
Uncertain which may taste the best.

3

Vor der Brust die trikoloren

Flowers on your breast—I heed 'em!
For the tricolor explains:
"This proud heart exults in freedom,
And it cannot live in chains."

Queen Marie, though I adore you,
Listen well, though you are crowned:
Many that have reigned before you
Have been shamefully dethroned!

4

Die Flaschen sind leer, das Frühstück war gut

The bottles are empty, the breakfast was good,
  The ladies are gay as at night;
They pull off their corsets (I knew that they would);
  I think they are just a bit tight.[1]

The shoulders—how white! The young breasts—how neat!
  I stand, like the dumbest of lovers.
They throw themselves down on the bed's snowy sheet,
  And, giggling, dive under the covers.

They draw the bed-curtains; I watch them prepare
  To shed the last wisp of their clothing;
And there, like the fool of the world, I stare
  At the foot of the bed, and do nothing.

5

Jugend, die mir täglich schwindet

Youth is leaving me; but daily
  By new courage it's replaced;
And my bold arm circles gaily
  Many a young and slender waist.

Some were shocked and others pouted;
  Some grew wroth—but none denied.
Flattery has always routed
  Lovely shame and stubborn pride.

Yet the best is gone. Too late, I'd
  Give my soul for it, in truth.

[1] Which, as Heine indicates in another untranslatable pun, applies either to the corsets, or their wearers, or both.

Can it be the blundering, great-eyed,
Sweet stupidity of youth?

EMMA

1

Er steht so starr wie ein Baumstamm

He stands as stark as a tree-trunk
    In wind and frost and heat;
His arms reach up to the heavens,
    Into the ground, his feet.

Thus suffers and stands Bagaritha,
    But Brahma will end his woe;
Down from the heights of heaven
    He lets the Ganges flow.

But I, beloved, must suffer
    Worse torments and in vain.
Your eyes, that are my heaven,
    Shed not a drop of rain.

2

Vierundzwanzig Stunden soll ich

I must wait for four-and-twenty
    Hours on the happy chance
That there was a more than senti-
    Mental favor in her glance.

Words are fatuous and futile;
    Speech itself is far too rough;

Passion makes the utterance brutal . . .
And the butterfly is off.

But a loving glance can carry
    The warm bosom's eloquence,
Like a promised heaven, starry
    With divine benevolence.

3

Emma, sage mir die Wahrheit

Emma, tell me, tell me truly:
    Was it love that made me foolish?
    Or is love itself the simple
Consequence of all my folly?

Oh, I'm troubled, darling Emma,
    Troubled by my foolish passion,
    Troubled by my passionate folly—
Most of all, by this dilemma.

4

Bin ich bei dir, Zank und Not

When I'm with you, jar and strife!
    All my words are wasted breath!
But away from you, this life
    Is not living, it is death.

All night long I lie and brood:
    Is it death or hell I've had?
Certain, in this wretched mood,
    That I am not ill but mad.

5

Schon mit ihren schlimmsten Schatten

Now with shadows dark and eerie
  Evil night is creeping on;
Now our souls are dull and weary,
  Weary-eyed we sit and yawn.

You grow old and I grow older,
  And our Spring has lost its grace.
You grow cold and I grow colder
  As the Winter comes apace.

Ah, the end is sad; the tearless
  Sighs when love begins to pall.
So, when life grows cold and cheerless
  Let death come and end it all.

FRIEDERIKE

Verlass Berlin, mit seinem dicken Sande

Leave Berlin, with its ever-thickening sand,
Its tea too thin for anyone to drink,
Its clever folk who think they understand
What Hegel told them that they ought to think.
Come, let's to India, to some sunny brink
Where sandal-blossoms perfume all the land,
Where white-robed bands of pilgrims meet, and sink
In prayer upon the Ganges' holy strand.

To that inspiring haven, let's away,
Where lotus-flowers overtop the height

Of towering Indra, and the palm-trees sway;
There faith still lives, and there in happy flight,
I'll kneel, like any pilgrim, and I'll pray:
"Loveliness, be my dream and my delight."

KATHARINE

1

Ein schöner Stern geht auf in meiner Nacht

A lovely star has risen in my night,
A star of smiling comfort and delight,
   A golden promise to the eye—
      O, do not lie!

As the young moon draws up the swelling sea,
My soul is drawn to you, and wild and free
   It bursts into a passionate cry—
      "O, do not lie!"

2

"Wollen Sie ihr nicht vorgestellt sein?"

"And don't you really want to meet her?"
   Inquired the duchess; unperturbed
I said, "Denial is the sweeter
   When one can keep emotion curbed."

The lovely creature is so winning
   I start and tremble, for it seems
With her new life might be beginning
   New pleasures, and new painful dreams.

Fear cautions me, "Remain a stranger,"
   Yet longing urges, "Do not wait."

Her eyes spell secrecy and danger,
   Yet they are my dark stars of fate.

Her brow is clear and always brightening.
   But even now I think I see
The storm-clouds gather and the lightning
   Burn its imperative way through me.

Her mouth is pure. But rose-lips bring me
   No comfort when the rose hides this:
The serpent that will some day sting me
   With the sweet poison in its kiss.

Longing compels me near and nearer;
   Fate drives me on; for this I came . . .
She turns. She speaks. Now I can hear her,
   And every word is like a flame.

"Monsieur," she says amidst the clamor,
   "Who was the singer we just heard?"
And there I stand, and there I stammer,
   "Madam, I did not hear a word."

3

Wie Merlin, der eitle Weise

Like old Merlin, the enchanter,
   I'm enslaved by my own thought;
   I, who came to snare, am caught.
I possess her, yet I want her.

Bound, and at her feet, I languish,
   Gazing always in her eyes;
   Hour after hour flies,
Half in ecstasy, half anguish.

While the wasted hours upbraid me,
  Days and weeks and months go by.
  All I've said's forgotten. Why,
Even her own words evade me.

Sometimes, in a dream, I fancy
  Her mouth lies on mine. And then
  Unknown depths are stirred again
With her flaming necromancy.

4

Den Tag, den hab' ich so himmlisch verbracht

I spent the day in a heavenly way;
  Evening still found me elated.
We wined and dined; Kitty was kind;
  And love remained unsated.

The red lips warmed and pleaded and stormed;
  Hot and wild were her hands;
The brown eyes yearned, the bosom burned
  With ever-increasing demands.

She held me fast, and only at last
  I slipped the amorous tether;
In the living snare of her own bright hair
  I tied her hands together.

5

Du liegst mir so gern im Arme

You lie in my arms so gladly,
  The cries of the world seem far.
I am your own dear heaven,
  You are my dearest star.

Below us the foolish people
  Quibble and quarrel and fight;
They shriek and bellow and argue.
  And all of them are right.

With jingling bells on their fool's caps,
  They rise from their stupid beds;
Swinging their clubs in anger,
  They crack each other's heads.

But we, we two are lucky
  That they are all so far—
You bury within its heaven
  Your head, my dearest star!

6

Unsre Seelen bleiben freilich

Our platonic souls are surely
  In a state of rare perfection,
Firm as faith, upheld securely
  By some spiritual connection.

And, though spirits slip their tether
  It would not be such a bother,
For our souls have wings of ether
  And they soon would find each other.

Spirits likewise are immortal,
  And Eternity's untiring;
Anyone with time and patience
  Can achieve the heart's desiring.

Yet our bodies are but bodies;
  Arms they have which we must cherish;

Quite devoid of wings of ether
    They have mortal legs, and perish.

Think of this, and so take pity;
    Do not lift one restless feather
Till the Spring, my clever Kitty,
    When we'll fly away together.

7

Ich liebe solche weisse Glieder

I love this white and slender body,
    These limbs that answer love's caresses,
Passionate eyes, and forehead covered
    With a wave of thick, black tresses.

You are the very one I've searched for
    In many lands, in every weather.
You are my sort; you understand me;
    As equals we can talk together.

In me you've found the man you care for.
    And, for a while, you'll richly pay me
With kindness, kisses, and endearments—
    And then, as usual, you'll betray me.

8

Kitty stirbt! und ihre Wangen

Kitty's dying; pale her cheeks,
    But her forehead's hot with fever.
Pitiful it is that I
    Now, before her death, must leave her.

Kitty's dying; soon she'll lie
   In the grave next to her mother's.
And she knows! But even now
   All she does is care for others.

And she asks me to remember
   When the winter winds are flying
To put on the warm, wool stockings
   Knit for me as she lies dying.

9

Jüngstens träumte mir: spazieren

Once I dreamed that I went walking
Up and down the streets of Heaven,
She with me; for, lacking Kitty,
Heaven itself were Purgatory.

There I saw the chosen spirits,
The most pious and the saintly,
Those who, when they lived as mortals,
Starved the flesh to serve the spirit.

Churchmen—patriarchs, apostles,
Self-denying monks and hermits,
Hideous graybeards, youthful zealots—
And the young ones were the ugliest.

Pale, attenuated faces,
Grim ascetics, strictly tonsured
(Various Jews were there among them)
Passed us, frowning circumspectly,

Seeing nothing, eyes averted,
Although you, my ever lovely,

Pressed my arm and hung upon me,
Hung upon me, laughing, teasing.

One alone looked straight upon you,
And it was the only handsome
Man in the entire assembly;
And his face was wonder-working.

Lips were molded by compassion,
Eyes were carved with understanding,
As once on the Magdalene
Now he looked, looked long upon you.

Oh! I know how well he meant it—
No one is so pure and holy—
But (I might as well admit it)
Jealous anger burned within me.

And I must confess, in Heaven
Heaven itself grew hateful to me,
Irritated—God forgive me!—
By our Saviour, Jesus Christ.

10

Gesanglos war ich und beklommen

Songless I was, immersed in mourning,
  Now song, at last, the gloom disperses;
Like tears that come with never a warning
  So, without warning, come the verses.

Once more melodic strains are starting
  To sing of great love, greater anguish,
Of hearts that have to break at parting,
  And hearts that only live to languish.

Sometimes I feel mysterious fleetings
  And German oaks about me glimmer;
They hint of home and early meetings—
  But they are dreams, and they grow dimmer.

Sometimes it seems I hear them singing,
  Remembered German nightingales!
In jets of song the notes are springing—
  But they are dreams; the music fails.

Where are the roses, those bright vagrants,
  In German fields? They rise and haunt me
Though they are withered, ghostly fragrance.
  In dreams they bloom, in dreams they taunt me.

KITTY

1

Augen, die ich längst vergessen

Eyes that I had long forgotten
  Snare me with their old romances;
And once more I am held captive
  By a maiden's tender glances.

Now her kisses bear me backward
  To the time we lived so sweetly,
When the days were spent in folly
  And the nights in love completely.

2

Mir redet ein die Eitelkeit

Your love for me (so says my pride)
  Is of a godlike fashion;

But deeper wisdom tells me that
It's only your compassion.

You give me more than is my due
When others underrate me;
And you are doubly sweet and kind
Because they wound and hate me.

You are so fond, you are so fair,
Your goodness overpowers!
Your speech is music, and your words
More perfumed than the flowers.

You are a friendly star to me,
Shining with gentle gladness;
You make this earthly night less black,
And sweeten all my sadness.

3

Es glänzt so schön die sinkende Sonne

The sun is fair when it sinks in splendor,
Yet fairer still are your eyes that shine;
Your beaming eyes and this splendid sunset
Illumine and trouble this heart of mine.

For the sunset means an end and a parting;
Night for the heart, and an endless woe.
And soon, between your eyes and my heart, love,
The wide and darkening sea shall flow.

4

Er ist so herzbeweglich

Her letter leaves me breathless—
She says (at least she writes me)

Her love, that so delights me,
Is timeless, speechless, deathless.

She's bored and dull and sickly
  And never will recover
  Unless . . . "You must come over
To England, yes—and quickly!"

5

Es läuft dahin die Barke

Swift as a deer, my bark
  Cuts through the waters, leaping
  Over the Thames, and sweeping
Us on to Regent's Park.

There lives my darling Kitty,
  Whose love is never shoddy;
  Who has the whitest body
In West End or the City.

She smiles, expecting me there,
  And fills the water-kettle,
  And wheels the tiny settle
Forward—and we have tea there!

6

Das Glück, das gestern mich geküsst

The joy that kissed me yesterday
  Has disappeared already;
Long years ago I found it so:
  True love is never steady.

Oft curiosity has drawn
   Some lovely ladies toward me;
But when they looked deep in my heart
   They left, and then abhorred me.

Some have grown pale before they went,
   And some with laughter cleft me;
But only Kitty really cared—
   She wept before she left me.

CELIMENE (MATHILDE)

Glaube nicht, dass ich aus Dummheit

Do not think that it is weakness
   Pardons you and your deceiving;
Do not think I am the good Lord,
   Whose whole business is forgiving.

With your whims I've been as patient
   As a statue gathering mildew;
Others faced with what I've suffered
   Long before this would have killed you.

Heavy cross! And still I bear it,
   Knowing well what every groan meant;
Loving you, my purgatory,
   You, my sin and my atonement.

Yes, you are my dark enchantress,
   But, although your arms are Circe's,
In their shameful depths they bring me
   God's own grace and all His mercies.

JENNY

Ich bin nun fünfunddreissig Jahr' alt

My years now number five-and-thirty
  And you are scarce fifteen, you sigh . . .
Yet, Jenny, when I look upon you,
  The old dream wakes that will not die.

In eighteen-seventeen a maiden
  Became my sweetheart, fond and true;
Strangely like yours her form and features,
  She even wore her hair like you.

That year, before I left for college,
  I said, "My own, it will not be
Long till I come back home. Be faithful!"
  "You are my world," she answered me.

Three years I toiled; three years I studied;
  And then—it was the first of May—
In Göttingen the tidings reached me:
  My love had married and gone away.

It was the first of May! With laughter
  The Spring came dancing through the world.
Birds sang, and in the quickening sunshine
  Worms stretched themselves and buds uncurled.

And only I grew pale and sickly,
  Dead to all beauties and delights;
And only God knows how I suffered
  And lived throughout those wretched nights.

But still I lived. And now my health is
   Strong as an oak that seeks the sky.
Yet, Jenny, when I look upon you,
   The old dream wakes that will not die.

ABROAD

1

Es treibt dich fort von Ort zu Ort

Now you must race from place to place
   With never a reason why;
The wind confides a word of grace.
   But what can you reply!

The love you left cries out its lack,
   Unable to pursue:
"My errant love, come back! come back!
   Dear heart, I wait for you!"

But onward, onward; never rest,
   No matter what the pain.
The very thing you loved the best
   You must not see again.

2

O, des liebenswürd'gen Dichters

"Oh, this dear, delightful poet
   Whose great poems charm and cheer us!
How we'd love to make him happy
   If we only had him near us!"

While these dear, delightful ladies
   Promise me a sweet existence,

I am in a foreign country,
　Pining safely at a distance.

What's the good to know, up North, it's
　Fairer in the South than this is . . .
And a hungry heart can't feed on
　Promissory, verbal kisses.

3

Du bist ja heut so grambefangen

Today you are so plunged in sorrow,
　I've never seen you more depressed.
Your tears have almost made a furrow;
　The sobs still shake within your breast.

Are all your cheerless thoughts still turning
　To where your home once used to stand?
Confess, how often you've been yearning
　For your belovéd Fatherland.

Do you still think of her who sweetly,
　With little scoldings, bound you fast?
And how you raged, and how completely
　You both made peace and kissed at last.

Do you still think of friends who sought you,
　And cherished you through good and ill,
When storms of inner turmoil caught you,
　Although your trembling lips were still?

And are you thinking of your mother
　And sister, dear as no one else?
Ah, now, I think that memories smother
　Your pride, and all your hardness melts.

And are you thinking of that fated
Old garden where you often groped
Among the boughs and dreams, and waited
And trembled anxiously—and hoped. . . .

The hour is late. The night is shining
  With snow that gleams like splintered glass.
And I must cease this aimless pining,
  And dress for company. Alas!

4

Ich hatte einst ein schönes Vaterland

I had, long since, a lovely Fatherland.
  The oaks would gleam
And touch the skies; the violets would nod.
  It was a dream.

You'd kiss me, and in German you would say
  (Oh, joy supreme—
How sweet the sound of it!) *"Ich liebe dich"* . . .
  It was a dream.

TRAGEDY

1

Entflieh mit mir und sei mein Weib

"Oh, fly with me and be my love,
  Rest on my heart, and never rouse;
And in strange lands my heart shall be
  Thy fatherland and father's house.

"But if you stay, then I die here,
And you shall weep and wring your hands;
And even in your father's house
You shall be living in strange lands."

2

Es fiel ein Reif in der Frühlingsnacht
(A genuine folk-song; heard by Heine on the Rhine)

The hoar-frost fell on a night in Spring,
It fell on the young and tender blossoms.
And they have withered and perished.

A boy and a girl were once in love;
They fled from the house into the world—
They told neither father nor mother.

They wandered here and they wandered there—
They had neither luck nor a star for guide . . .
And they have withered and perished.

3

Auf ihrem Grab da steht eine Linde

Upon their grave a tree stands now
With winds and birds in every bough;
And in the green place under it
The miller's boy and his sweetheart sit.

The winds grow tender, soft and clinging,
And softly birds begin their singing.
The prattling sweethearts grow silent and sigh,
And fall to weeping, neither knows why.

SONGS OF CREATION

Im beginn schuf Gott die Sonne

1

God made sun in the beginning;
   Stars came next in his creation;
Thereupon he fashioned cattle
   From his excess perspiration.

Wild beasts followed; haughty lions,
   Grim with claws, were given admittance;
Then, with lions for his models,
   God made cats and little kittens.

After this began to bore Him,
   God shaped men, and deer, and donkeys;
Then, with man set up before Him,
   He made interesting monkeys.

Satan looked, and cried, "Already
   God's gone stale. It is to laugh.
What's creation? Imitation!
   First the cow—and then the calf."

2

Then God turned upon the devil:
   "Satan, look your fill and laugh.
True, I crowd the world with copies:
   Sun and planet, cow and calf.

"After men I model monkeys;
   Cats are lions, not so great.

Imitative? True. But tell me,
  Satan, what do *you* create?"

3

"And why, you ask, I made it all?
  Satan, are you undiscerning?
  Within my spirit's depth, a burning
Consciousness began to call.

"Was it sickness or a lure?
  Headlong passions forced and filled me.
  Creation came; it almost killed me;
But creation was my cure."

BALLADS

(1839-1842)

BALLADS

A WOMAN

Sie hatten sich beide so herzlich lieb

They loved each other beyond belief—
She was a strumpet, he was a thief;
Whenever she thought of his tricks, thereafter
She'd throw herself on the bed with laughter.

The day was spent with a reckless zest;
All night she lay upon his breast.
So when they took him, a moment after,
She watched at the window, with laughter.

He sent word, pleading, "Oh, come to me,
I need you, need you bitterly,
Yes, here and in the hereafter."
Her little head shook with laughter.

At six in the morning they swung him high;
At seven the turf on his grave was dry;
At eight, however, she quaffed her
Red wine, and sang with laughter!

SPRING FESTIVAL

Das ist des Frühlings traurige Lust!

It is the Springtime's wild unrest.
  Blossoming maidens everywhere
  Storm through the woods with streaming hair;
Echoing, as they beat their breast,
      "Adonis—Adonis!"

As dusk grows thick, the torches flare
 And frantic voices fill the night.
 With wails, mad laughter, sudden fright,
They seek him, shouting everywhere:
  "Adonis—Adonis!"

And he, that boy of beauty, lies
 Upon the ground, so strangely dead;
 His blood stains all the flowers red,
And every wind, lamenting, cries:
  "Adonis—Adonis!"

CHILDE HAROLD

Eine starke schwarze Barke

A black-shrouded, night-beclouded
 Funeral bark comes gliding by.
The attendants speak no sentence
 Through the tight-lipped scrutiny.

Their regard is the dead bard, his
 Brow is marble, stone his face;
His blue-blazing eyes are gazing
 Into heaven's hollow space.

Soul-assailing comes a wailing
 As from some deep-water bride;
And the troubled waters bubble
 On a doubly threatening tide.

THE ADJURATION

Der junge Franziskaner sitzt

The young Franciscan sits alone
Within his cloister-cell;
He reads a book of magic called
"The Mastery of Hell."

And as the midnight hour strikes,
He raves and calls upon
The powers of the Underworld,
And cries, distraught and wan:

"For this one night, you spirits, raise
From all the hosts that died
The fairest woman—give her life,
And place her at my side."

He breathes the aweful, secret word,
And, answering his commands,
In white and drooping cerements
The perished Beauty stands.

Her face is sad. With frightened sighs
Her poor, cold breasts are stirred.
She sits beside the startled monk.
They stare—without a word.

EVIL STAR

Der Stern erstrahlte so munter

The star that sparkled happy and high
Has fallen suddenly out of the sky.
What's love, you ask, that's so richly sung?
A star, my child, in a heap of dung.

Like a dying dog, befouled with slime,
It lies there forgotten, covered in grime.
The rutting sow will salute it with grunts;
The cock will crow over a star for once.

Oh, when I fall let me fall to where
A flower of some sort tries the air;
Whatever's denied me, may I have
A decent death, a sweet-smelling grave.

ANNO 1829

Dass ich bequem verbluten kann

Give me a nobler, wider sphere
    Where I, at least, can bleed to death.
Oh, do not let me stifle here
    Among these hucksters. Give me breath!

They eat and drink with greedy pride
    Dull and complacent as the mole;
Their generosity is wide—
    As wide as, say, the poor-box hole.

Cigar in mouth they stroll along;
    Their hands are fat with many a gem;
Their stomachs are both huge and strong.
    But who could ever stomach *them!*

They deal in spices, but the air
    Is filled, alas, with something else;
Their souls pollute the atmosphere,
    And foul it with their fishy smells.

If they but had some human vice,
    Some lust too terrible to see—
But not these virtues, not this nice
    Flabby and smug morality.

Ye clouds above, take me away
    To Africa or furthest North;
Even to Pomerania. Pray
    Carry me with you, bear me forth.

Take me away . . . They pass me by.
    The clouds are wise; they do not heed.
For when they see this town they fly,
    And anxiously increase their speed.

ANNO 1839

O Deutschland, meine ferne Liebe

O Germany, for which I weary,
    Thinking of you, I have to weep;
This merry France grows somehow dreary,
    This light folk puts my mind to sleep.

Reason alone, dry and unfeeling,
    Is crowned in every Paris street—
O bells of home! O happy pealing!
    O faith so foolish, and so sweet!

These courtly manners! I distrust 'em!
    The mincing bow, the formal kiss!
The German peasant's rudest custom
    Means more to me than all of this.

These grinning ladies' endless clatter:
A mill-wheel grinding in each head!
Give me the girls, who, without chatter,
Smile and go quietly to bed.

Here, round and round in frantic motion,
All things are whirled, a headlong race.
There everything's nailed down with caution,
And stays in its appointed place.

Somewhere at home the muted blowing
Of a night-watchman's horn prevails;
There his nocturnal song is growing
And mingling with the nightingale's.

That was the poet's native clime, with
Sheltering oaks on Schilda's heath.
'Twas there I wove the happy rhyme with
Moonbeam-light and violet breath.

EARLY

Auf dem Faubourg Saint-Marceau

Through the Faubourg Saint-Marceau
Fog crept everywhere this morning;
A queer fog the end of autumn,
Like a white night, strange and solid.

As I walked through this white world,
Softly, slowly, coming toward me
I observed a woman's figure
Molded (so it seemed) of moonlight.

Yes, the moon itself had carved
Those smooth limbs, that form ethereal;
Not in all of France was ever
Such a slender apparition.

Was it Luna, who, perhaps,
Spent the night—and early morning—
With some boulevard Endymion,
Coyly in the Latin Quarter?

Then, on my way home, I thought:
Why did she avoid my glances?
Did the goddess think I might be
The sun-guiding, golden Phoebus?

THE NIXIES

Am einsamen Strande plätschert die Flut

The shore was lipped by the tide; the moon,
    Whiter than ever, had risen.
The young knight lay on a shining dune,
    Held in a dream's bright prison.

The amorous nixies in filmiest dress
    Rose from the sea-floor, creeping
Closer and closer, presuming to bless
    The youth who was seemingly sleeping.

The first nixie lay an inquisitive hand
    On the feathers that hung from his bonnet;
The second fingered the fine-woven band
    Of chain and the belt upon it.

Then sighed the third and her eyes were blurred
As she drew the blade from its sheathing,
And, leaning her lovely weight on the sword,
She hung o'er the youth, scarcely breathing.

The fourth came dancing, and swayed above
The knight like a spray in a bower:
"Oh, if I only could be your love,
Mortality's finest flower!"

The fifth one fondled the mortal's wrist,
Gently she laid her hand on.
The sixth held off, but at last she kissed
His lips and cheeks with abandon.

The young knight was wise. He kept his eyes
Closed, there was naught he was missing.
Under the moon he heard their sighs . . .
And the nixies kept on kissing.

THE UNKNOWN

Meiner goldgelockten Schönen

My adored and golden-haired one,
Every day I'm sure to meet her,
When beneath the chestnut branches
In the Tuileries she wanders.

Every day she comes and walks there
With two old and awful ladies.
Are they aunts? Or are they dragons?
Or dragoons in skirts and flounces?

No one even seems to know her.
I have asked friends and relations;

But I ask in vain. I question,
While I almost die of longing.

Yes, I'm frightened by the grimness
Of her two mustached companions;
And I'm even more upset by
This, my heart's unusual beating.

I have scarcely breathed a whisper
Or a sigh whene'er I passed her;
I have never dared a burning
Glance to tell her of my longing.

But today I have discovered
What her name is. It is Laura;
Like the sweet, Provençal maiden
Worshiped by the famous poet.

She is Laura! I'm as great now
As was Petrarch when he chanted
And extolled his lovely lady
In those canzonets and sonnets.

She is Laura! Yes, like Petrarch,
I can hold platonic riots
On this name, and clasp its beauty—
He himself did nothing more.

ALI BEY

Ali Bei, der Held des Glaubens

Ali Bey, the Faith's defender,
Lies surrounded by his maidens;
Paradise on earth, a foretaste
Of the Paradise in heaven.

Odalisques as fair as houris,
Graceful as gazelles, attend him;
While one softly strokes his forehead,
Others curl his beard with perfume.

To a lute another dances,
Sings and sways and clings with kisses
To his heart, where all the blessèd
Flames of happiness are kindled.

From beyond there comes a sudden
Clash of trumpets, scabbards rattle;
Kiss of steel and call of rifles—
"Lord! The Franks are seen approaching!"

And the warrior mounts his war-steed.
Yet, throughout the crash of battle
Still he acts as though surrounded
By the fairest of his maidens.

When the Frankish heads are severed
By the dozen, he regards them
Smiling, like a tender lover
When he kisses his belovèd.

FORTUNE

Frau Fortuna, ganz umsonst

Frowning Fortune, you had best
Smilingly surrender, lest
I compel you, lest I force you,
Seize your weapons and unhorse you.

Have you favors to bestow?
Grant them, or your overthrow

Will be sudden and unheeding—
Ah, but how my wounds are bleeding!

I had scarcely felt the fray,
Yet my red blood runs away.
I can boast, brave as a drunkard;
But the conqueror is conquered.

PSYCHE

In der Hand die kleine Lampe

With a small lamp in her fingers
    And a great glow in her breast,
Psyche creeps into the chamber
    Where the sleeper is at rest.

She grows frightened and she blushes
    As she sees his beauty bare—
While the god of love awakens,
    And his pinions beat the air.

Eighteen hundred years of penance!
    She, poor soul, still fasts with awe;
Almost dead, because she came where
    Love lay naked—and she saw!

DAME METTE

(FROM THE DANISH)

Herr Peter und Bender sassen beim Wein

As Peter and Bender sat at their wine
    Sir Bender spoke up, "I fear you
Are wasting your voice. Though the world rejoice,
    Dame Mette will never hear you."

Sir Peter replied, "I'll wager my horse
  Against your dogs, I'll sing her
Into my bed." He smiled and said,
  "This very night I'll bring her."

And as the hour of midnight came
  Sir Peter began his singing.
His voice was good, over water and wood
  The notes went roundly ringing.

The gossiping pines were suddenly still;
  The stream, that babbler and lisper,
Grew silent soon; the inquisitive moon
  And the stars forgot to whisper.

It woke Dame Mette out of her sleep.
  "Who sings this song of wooing?"
She threw on a dress, nor stopped to guess
  What mischief might be brewing.

Over the water and through the wood
  With a purpose blind and tragic
She hurried along; Sir Peter's song
  Drew her with its dark magic.

And when she returned at early morn
  Sir Bender arose and met her.
"Where spent you this night? If I see aright
  You are wet and your clothes are wetter."

"Oh, I have been to the nixies' pool
  To hear their prophesying.
Dancing so free, they spattered me,
  And there's been no time for drying."

"The sand at the nixies' pool is fine,
  And soft is the path that's leading
From here to there; but bloody and bare
  Are your feet, and your cheeks are bleeding."

"Last night I was in the elfinwood
  To watch the fairy dances.
A thorn or two— What is it to you?
  I went and took my chances."

"The elves do dance, but only in May,
  And on a carpet of flowers;
But this is fall. The cold winds call
  And leaves come down in showers."

"I was—I was with Sir Peter last night;
  He sang, and his song was magic.
Through water and wood, careless of blood
  I went, though the end is tragic.

"His song is powerful as death;
  The notes still echo through me,
Who now must learn what makes them burn
  And why they turn to doom me."

They've hung the old church-door with black;
  Thickly the crowds are massing;
The organ rolls, the one bell tolls;
  Dame Mette's soul is passing.

Sir Bender weeps beside the bier;
  His cries make a doleful jargon:
"Oh, woe betide, I've lost my bride
  And my good hounds in the bargain."

AWAY!

Der Tag ist in die Nacht verliebt

The day is enamored of night,
And spring is entranced by winter,
Life is in love with death,
And you—are in love with me!

You love me—look, and even now
Gray shadows seem to fold you;
All of your blossoming fades
And your white soul lies bleeding.

Oh, shrink from me, and only love
The butterflies light-hearted,
That sport among the golden beams.
Oh, shrink from me—and all things bitter.

A MEETING

Wohl unter der Linde erklingt die Musik

Under the linden the music is gay,
    The couples are gossiping loudly;
And two are dancing whom nobody knows,
    They carry themselves so proudly.

Now here, now there, they glide and sway
    In wave-like measures beguiling.
They bow to each other, and as they nod,
    She whispers, gently smiling:

"A water-pink is hanging from
    Your cap, my fair young dancer;

It only grows in the depths of the sea—
  You are no mortal man, sir.

"You are a merman, and to lure
  These village maids your wish is.
I knew you at once by your watery eyes
  And your teeth as sharp as the fishes'."

Now here, now there, they glide and sway
  In wave-like measures beguiling.
They bow to each other, and as they nod,
  He answers, gently smiling:

"My lovely lady, tell me why
  Your hand's so cold and shiny?
And why is the border of your gown
  So damp and draggled and briny?

"I knew you at once by your watery eyes,
  And your bow so mocking and tricksy—
You're not a daughter of earth, my dear;
  You are my cousin, the nixie."

The fiddles are silent, the dancing is done;
  They part with a ripple of laughter.
They know each other too well and will try
  To avoid such a meeting hereafter.

KING HAROLD HARFAGER

Der König Harald Harfager

The good King Harold Harfager
  Lies in the depths below;
His water-witch beside him,
  He sees time come and go.

Held in the lovely mermaid's arms
  He neither lives nor dies;
Resigned to his delicious doom
  Two hundred years he lies.

The King's head lies in the mermaid's lap;
  His dark eyes strain above;
Yearning to meet her burning eyes,
  He cannot look enough.

His golden hair is silver-gray,
  His yellow face forlorn;
On ghostly cheeks the bones stand out,
  The skin is withered and torn.

Yet sometimes from his dream of love
  King Harold suddenly wakes;
He hears the billows roaring above
  While his crystal palace shakes.

Sometimes it seems to him the wind
  Throbs with the Norsemen's call;
Swiftly he lifts his battle arm,
  Then sadly lets it fall.

Sometimes he thinks he hears the chant
  Of sailors crude and strong,
Praising King Harold Harfager
  In some heroic song.

Then groans the King, and wails and weeps,
  His bosom pierced with pain.
The water-witch leans over his mouth
  And kisses him quiet again.

THE FAITHLESS LOUISA

Die ungetreue Luise

The fair and faithless Louisa
    Returned and, lightly flitting,
She came to where the lamps burned low
    And Ulrich still was sitting.

She cozened and she kissed him;
    She smiled, and tried to soften
His grief and said, "How you have changed—
    You used to laugh so often!"

She cozened and she kissed him
    Where he lay, sad and sunken . . .
"My God, your hands are cold as ice,
    And all the flesh is shrunken!"

She cozened and she kissed him;
    Tears wet her lovely lashes . . .
"My God, your hair that was so black
    Is now as gray as ashes!"

And the poor Ulrich sat there,
    Silent and old and broken;
He kissed his faithless sweetheart,
    And not a word was spoken.

POEMS FOR THE TIMES
(1839-1846)

DOCTRINE

Schlage die Trommel und fürchte dich nicht

Beat on the drum and blow the fife
    And kiss the *vivandière*, my boy.
Fear nothing—that's the whole of life,
    Its deepest truth, its soundest joy.

Beat reveillé, and with a blast
    Arouse all men to valiant strife.
Waken the world; and then, at last,
    March on . . . That is the whole of life.

This is philosophy; this is truth;
    This is the burning source of joy!
I've borne this wisdom from my youth,
    For I, too, was a drummer-boy.

A WARNING

Solche Bücher lässt du drucken!

You will print such books as these?
    Then you're lost, my friend, that's certain.
    If you wish for gold and honor,
Write more humbly—bend your knees.

Aye, you must have lost your senses,
    Thus to speak before the people,
    Thus to dare to talk of preachers
And of potentates and princes.

Friend, you're doomed, so it appears:
   For the princes have long arms,
   And the preachers have long tongues,
—And the masses have long ears!

ADAM THE FIRST

Du schicktest mit dem Flammenschwert

With flaming swords you sent police
   Down from The Heavenly City,
And drove me out of Eden's walls
   With neither right nor pity.

Now with my wife I journey forth,
   Through further country ranging;
Yet I have eaten wisdom's fruit—
   A fact beyond your changing.

You cannot change my mind that knows
   How small you are. I wonder
Whether you hope to make yourself
   Great with mere death and thunder.

I will not miss your Paradise
   Miraculously hidden;
Eden is scarcely worth the name
   Where some things are forbidden.

I ask for freedom's fullest rights
   Now freedom's star has risen;
Otherwise heaven becomes a hell
   And Paradise a prison.

THE SECRET

Wir seufzen nicht, das Aug' ist trocken

We do not sigh, the eye is tearless;
　We do not laugh, although we smile.
Not by a look, not by a gesture
　Will we betray our secret guile.

Although our very souls are bleeding,
　The lingering agony must be mocked.
Though it beats loud in our wild pulses,
　We choke it back; our lips are locked.

Go, ask the babe warm in its cradle,
　Go, ask the dead, cold in the grave,
Perhaps these silent ones can tell you
　What we keep secret—secret and brave.

DEGENERATION

Hat die Natur sich auch verschlechtert

Has even Nature altered badly?
　And does she ape what we began?
It seems to me the beasts and flowers
　Deceive as readily as man.

The lily's purity I question;
　She yields to love and seeks to stay
The butterfly that flits above her
　And bears her chastity away.

I even doubt the modest virtue
　Of violets. They have no shame,

But fling their scent like any wanton,
   And thirst in secret after fame.

I half suspect the song-bird's ardor
   Expresses more than he can mean;
He overdoes his trills and raptures,
   And does them only by routine.

The truth has disappeared, I fancy,
   And simple faith has left us, too.
Only the dogs still fawn around us,
   And even they do not seem true.

HENRY

Auf dem Schlosshof zu Canossa

In the courtyard at Canossa
Stands the German Emperor Henry,
Barefoot in his shirt of penance,
And the night is cold and rainy.

From the window two dim figures
Gaze upon him, and the moonlight
Gleams on Gregory, bald-headed,
And the white breast of Matilda.

And the pale-lipped Emperor Henry
Prays his pious paternoster;
But within his kingly heart he
Rends himself and cries in anguish:

"Far in my own German country
High and mighty hills are towering;
And within their depths, the iron
For the battle-ax is growing.

"Far in my own German country
High and mighty oaks are towering;
And in some great trunk, the handle
For the battle-ax is growing.

"Germany, my own belovèd,
You will bear the mighty hero
Who will wield the ax and swiftly
Crush the serpent that torments me!"

TO GEORG HERWEGH

Herwegh, du eiserne Lerche

Herwegh, you lark of iron!
You rise on a swift and jubilant wing
 Toward sunlight and freedom, Liberty's lover!
 Is the long winter really over?
Is Germany really awake to the spring?

Herwegh, you lark of iron,
Because your passionate flight is long,
 You have forgotten earth's condition.
 The Spring you hail with such a vision
Has blossomed only in your song.

THE NEW JEWISH HOSPITAL IN HAMBURG

Ein Hospital für arme, kranke Juden

A hospital for sick and suffering Jews,
For those thrice-cursèd children of affliction,
Burdened forever by the threefold evil:
Poverty, and pain, and Judaism.

And of the three the last is most malignant—
An old disease, a sort of family ailment;
A plague they brought with them from Egypt;
A faith as ancient as it is unhealthy.

Eternal ill! There is no art to cure it.
All that this house can offer to its inmates—
Surgery, lotions, enemas, and steam-baths,
Massage and medicine—are all in vain.

Will Time, perhaps, the one compassionate goddess,
Root out this dark inheritance, which father
Transmits to son? Will some remote descendant
Be cleansed of it, be really whole and happy?

I do not know. I only know that meanwhile,
A loving heart sought to assuage the anguish,
To dull such pain as care and skill may soften.
For such a balsam-dropping heart we should be grateful.

The noble man! Here he has built a refuge
For sufferers, whom the arts of the physician
(Or even Death) may help with the assistance
Of pills and pillows, love and soothing potions.

He gave with generous hands—yet even richer
The tears that fell when he beheld his brothers
Caught in the common illness of his people,
The thousand years' incurable affliction.

TO AN APOSTATE

O des heil'gen Jugendmutes

How the holy zeal of youth
    Dies with all its gay defiance;

Compromise, instead of truth,
  Calls on God for an alliance.

Now the weeks pronounce the loss
  That your soul had never mourned so;
And you creep up to the cross,
  To the very cross you scorned so.

All that's due to Schlegel, Kant,
  Burke, and every logic-spinner—
Yesterday you were a saint,
  And today a shabby sinner.

THE TENDENCY

Deutscher Sänger! sing und preise

German singers! sing and praise
  German freedom, till your song
    Makes the heart leap up to hear it,
    And the deed supports the spirit,
Like the stirring Marseillaise.

Turn from Werther and his wooing—
  For his Lotte let him long! [1]
    Peal the bell and strike the hour.
    Now the people come to power,
Sword in hand, aroused and doing.

Do not sigh, "What does it matter,"
  Like a love-sick flute. Be strong.
    Be a trumpet. Be the thunder.
    Be the charge that tears asunder.
Crash and conquer, blow and shatter!

[1] Here Heine derides Goethe's *Sorrows of Werther*, which, with its sentimental romance of Werther and Charlotte, was wept over by thousands.

Strike, and call for keener actions!
Crush the tyrant! Conquer wrong!
Mix your songs with cries and curses.—
But be sure to keep your verses
Vague and full of dull abstractions.

A PROMISE

Nicht mehr barfuss sollst du traben

Freedom, stumbling through the stews
Barefoot, spat upon, and shocking,
Cheer up! Some day you'll have shoes,
And perhaps (who knows) a stocking.

Freedom, some day you will wear
A warm cap with ear-laps showing;
Then you will not have to care
In the path of all winds blowing.

Men will nod to you, no less;
They may even house and feed you;
They may love you to excess,
But, of course, they will not heed you.

You, however, must, you see,
Listen to your lords *and* heed 'em.
Hold your tongue and bend your knee,
And you'll have a future, Freedom.

A TOPSY-TURVY WORLD

Das ist ja die verkehrte Welt

This is a topsy-turvy world;
Men on their heads are walking.

The woodcocks, by the dozen, shoot
The hunters that are stalking.

The calves are roasting all the cooks;
And men are driven by horses;
On knowledge, light, and liberty
The catholic owl discourses.

The herring is a *sans-culotte;*
The truth Bettina's saying;
And Sophocles upon our stage
A Puss-in-boots is playing.

For German heroes apes have built
A Pantheon enormous!
Massmann at last has combed his hair,
The German prints inform us.

The German bears are atheists,
All former faiths rejecting;
While the French parrots have become
Good Christians, self-respecting.

The *Moniteur* of Uckermark
To madness seems to drive one:
A dead man there has dared to write
An epitaph on a live one.

Let us not swim against the stream;
'Twould be no use whatever.
So let us climb the hill and cry
"May the King live forever!"

GERMANY

Deutschland ist noch kleines Kind

Germany's still a little child.
   The sun's his nurse; she'll feed him
No soothing milk to make him strong,
   But the wild fires of freedom.

On such a diet one grows fast;
   The blood will boil and lurch in
The veins. You neighbors, have a care,
   Before you plague this urchin.

He is a clumsy little giant;
   He'll tear up oaks, and well he
Will use them till your backs are sore,
   And pound you to a jelly.

He is like Siegfried, fearless youth,
   Who did such deeds of wonder;
Who forged his sword, and when he smote
   The anvil flew asunder.

Yes, Siegfried, you shall slay the grim
   Dragon while thanks are given.
Huzzah! How radiantly your nurse
   Will laugh and shine through heaven.

Yours shall be all the hoard, when you
   Have slain the monster horrid.
Huzzah! How bright the king's own crown
   Will blaze upon your forehead!

NIGHT THOUGHTS

Denk ich an Deutschland in der Nacht

Nights when I think of Germany
Sleep is impossible for me;
Tear upon tear so hotly flows
My burning eyes refuse to close.

The years have come, the years have gone;
Twelve years now since an ailing son
Has seen his mother. At the thought
My heart sinks and my nerves grow taut.

My longing mounts to fever-pitch.
That woman—can she be a witch?
As I grow older, love grows deeper
For that old lady, may God keep her.

That frail old lady loves me so
It troubles me. Her letters show
How pitifully the poor hand trembles
And how the mother-heart dissembles.

Germany's an immortal land;
Sound to the core, it's sure to stand.
Its oaks and lindens will survive
And keep the homeward heart alive.

But I could wait; I would not wear
My heart away were she not there.
The fatherland is deathless, aye;
But that poor soul is bound to die.

Since I forsook the German sun
So many friends are dead and gone;
If I should stop to count the roll
I would be stricken to the soul.

Yet count I must, although the count
Reaches a shuddering amount.
The dead press on me, even here,
Until (thank God!) they disappear.

Thank God! upon my windows dance
Dawn and the happy light of France.
My wife comes in with morning gladness,
And smiles away this German sadness.

ONLY WAIT!

Weil ich so ganz vorzüglich blitze

What! Think you that my flashes show me
    Only in lightnings to excel?
Believe me, friends, you do not know me,
    For I can thunder quite as well.

In sorrow you shall learn your error;
    My voice shall grow, and in amaze
Your eyes and ears shall feel the terror,
    The thundering word, the stormy blaze.

Oaks shall be rent; the word shall shatter.
    Yea, on that fiery day, the crown,
Even the palace-walls shall totter,
    And domes and spires come crashing down!

REMEMBERING KRÄHWINKEL'S REIGN OF TERROR

Wir, Bürgermeister und Senat

We, the Senate and the Mayor,
After intensive thought and prayer
For all the various creeds and classes,
Enjoin these lawns upon the masses:

"Beware of aliens, for they sow
Seeds of revolt where'er they go;
Rebellious souls and other vermin
Are scarcely ever (praise God) German.

"Obedience to their ruler's due
From Christian and (much more) from Jew;
And Jew and Christian, every one
Must close their shops when day is done.

"No one shall walk abroad at night
Unless accompanied by a light.
If three shall walk in any street
They shall disperse—before they meet.

"Discard your weapons, bring them all
Hastily to the City Hall;
Retain no sort of ammunition
Unless you long for quick perdition.

"Who holds another point of view,
He shall be shot without ado;
And argument by gesture is
Even more dangerous than this.

"Honor your mayor; it is he
Who guards the State and zealously
Decides what's best for old and young.
So listen well—and hold your tongue."

THE WEAVERS

Im düstern Auge keine Thräne

From darkened eyes no tears are falling;
With gritted teeth we sit here calling:
"Germany, listen, ere we disperse,
We weave your shroud with a triple curse—
    We weave! We are weaving!

"A curse to the false god that we prayed to,
And worshiped in spite of all, and obeyed, too.
We waited, and hoped, and suffered in vain;
He laughed at us, sneering, for all of our pain—
    We weave! We are weaving!

"A curse to the king, and a curse to his coffin,
The rich man's king whom our plight could not soften;
Who took our last penny by taxes and cheats,
And let us be shot like dogs in the streets—
    We weave! We are weaving!

"A curse to the Fatherland, whose face is
Covered with lies and foul disgraces;
Where the bud is crushed before it can seed,
And the worm grows fat on corruption and greed—
    We weave! We are weaving!

"The shuttle flies in the creaking loom;
And night and day we weave your doom.

Old Germany, listen, ere we disperse,
We weave your shroud with a triple curse.
We weave! We are weaving!"

SEVEN SONGS

1

Welch ein zierlich Ebenmass

What a heavenly proportion
Shapes those nobly fashioned members,
And the slender neck is topped with
A small head that's quite enchanting.

Half amusing and half moving
Are those features, where a woman's
Unrestrained voluptuous glances
And a child's clear smile are mingled.

If upon your dazzling shoulders
Here and there, like heavy shadows,
Dust were laid, I would compare you
To no less a form than Venus.

To the sculptured Aphrodite
Rising from her native waters,
Passion-breathing, beauty-spreading,
And, believe me, well-developed.

2

"Augen, sterblich schöne Sterne"

"Eyes, those bright and mortal planets—"
Thus, although it seemed to lack sense,

Went the song I heard one evening
　In the throaty Tuscan accents.

Mending nets, a young girl sang it,
　Who, though she was sewing soundly,
Looked so challenging and charming
　That I kissed her red lips roundly.

Just now, seeing you the first time,
　The whole picture was repeated—
The old song, the sea, the sewing . . .
　Come! The scene must be completed.

3

Es erklingt wie Liebestöne

Through my heart the most beguiling
　Bits of love-songs rise and flit.
And I think the little, smiling
　Eros has a hand in it.

In my heart he's the director,
　Calling forth its dearest themes;
And the music, sweet as nectar,
　Fills and colors all my dreams.

4

Was bedeuten gelbe Rosen

Yellow roses as an offering—
　And they mean? . . . A thorny path;
　Love that is at war with wrath,
And persists, in spite of suffering.

5

Mit dummen Mädchen, hab ich gedacht

With stupid girls, I often thought,
Everything would come to nought;
But if by chance the girl were clever
Things, it seemed, went worse than ever.

The stupid ones made no replies.
The clever ones were far too wise;
Parried the question with "Romancer!"
And left me groping for the answer.

6

Wir müssen zugleich uns betrüben

We laugh and we are troubled
    Whene'er our fingers touch,
That hearts can love so greatly
    And minds can doubt so much.

Do you not feel, my darling,
    My heart beat through the gloom?
She nods her head, and murmurs,
    "It beats—God knows for whom!"

7

Das macht den Menschen glücklich

It makes a man feel happy,
    It drains him to the dregs,
When he has three fair sweethearts
    And just one pair of legs.

I visit the first in the morning;
　I seek the second at night;
The third does not wait, but comes to me
　At noon in a blaze of light.

Farewell, my three fair sweethearts,
　Two legs are all I've got;
I'll go and make love to Nature
　In some more quiet spot.

ROMANCERO

NARRATIVES, LAMENTATIONS,
LAZARUS, HEBREW MELODIES
(1846-1852)

NARRATIVES

NARRATIVES

CHARLES I

Im Wald, in der Köhlerhütte sitzt

In a wood, in a charcoal-burner's hut,
   Far from his lordly city,
A poor king rocks a poor man's child,
   Singing a nursery ditty:

Eya-popeya, what stirs in the straw?
   The sheep in their stalls are bleating—
O child, your face, the mark on your brow,
   Is a thing that my dreams keep repeating.

Eya-popeya, the kitten is dead—
   It's a mark that bears no dissembling.
You'll soon be a man, and you'll swing an ax;
   Already the oaks are trembling.

The charcoal-burner's faith is dead;
   The children no longer are loyal—
Eya-popeya—to God or to king,
   Despising the old blood-royal.

The kitten is dead; the mice are gay—
   We are doomed in lowland and highland—
Eya-popeya—in Heaven the Lord,
   And I, the King, on his island.

My courage is gone; my heart is sick;
   No single hope besteads me—
Eya-popeya—an arm like yours
   Will swing the ax that beheads me.

My death-song is your cradle-song . . .
   I feel the short hair bristling—
Eya-popeya—I hear the blade
   Swiftly and horribly whistling.

Eya-popeya, what stirs in the straw—
   The ax falls—*dead is the kitten—*
My head leaps from the startled trunk;
   'Tis you who will rule in Britain.

Eya-popeya, what stirs in the straw?
   The sheep in their stalls huddle neatly;
The kitten is dead; the mice are gay—
   Sleep, little headsman, sleep sweetly.

MARIE ANTOINETTE

Wie heiter im Tuilerienschloss

Brilliantly in the Tuileries
   The window-panes are aglow,
And in the broadest day one sees
   Old ghosts that come and go.

Flora's Pavilion haunts the air
   With Marie Antoinette;
She holds her morning levee there
   With strict court etiquette.

Court ladies all, they sit or stand
   Each in appointed place;
Jewels upon the throat and hand,
   Bright in brocade and lace.

Each waist is small; each skirt is hooped;
  Lightly the petticoat spreads;
The heels are high; the bows are looped—
  If only they had heads!

Headless they come, headless they go,
  Which is no sinecure,
Especially for her who's so
  Proud of her rich coiffure.

Yes, she of the towering toupée,
  She who was once the wild
Daughter of Emperors, the gay
  Maria Theresa's child,

She, that headstrong and haughty girl,
  Sits headless in a ring
Of maids who cannot boast a curl,
  And cannot help a thing.

The Revolution dealt this blow,
  Pitiful and obscene;
Blame it all on Jean Jacques Rousseau,
  Voltaire, and the guillotine.

Yet strange! As sunlight wanly sheds
  Its light like a pallid star,
They do not feel they have lost their heads,
  Nor know how dead they are.

Each lady bows and fawns and scrapes;
  The curtsies are habitual—
How horrid to watch these headless shapes
  At their unholy ritual.

A Dame of Honor brings a chemise,
　Spun with a silken sheen;
A second Lady sinks to her knees,
　And offers it to the Queen.

Then bow Court Ladies number Three
　And Four, and thereupon,
Kneeling before Her Majesty,
　They draw her stockings on.

The next one holds up filmy things
　That cling about the throat,
Another Maid bows low, and brings
　The royal petticoat.

Fanning her bosom, nobly bred,
　Robe-Mistress stands resigned;
And since, alas, she lacks a head
　She smiles with her behind.

The sun, between the curtains, thrusts
　One sharp inquiring ray.
He sees the queer, affected ghosts,
　And, frightened, slinks away.

THE GOD APOLLO

Das Kloster ist hoch auf Felsen gebaut

1

The convent stands on the highest hill;
　The Rhine goes by and glistens;
Behind barred windows, hidden and still,
　The young nun sits and listens.

A boat is seen, like a tale, like a dream
  Remembered in twilight hours;
Its sails of brilliant taffeta seem
  Wreathed in laurel and flowers.

In the boat, as the evening hazes clear,
  Rises an apparition;
His gold and purple make him appear
  A god in an ancient vision.

Statue-like at his feet there lie
  Nine women, each a goddess;
The clinging tunics show the high
  Breasts underneath the bodice.

The fiery-haired one finds his tongue;
  He sings as he sweeps the lyre.
Into the nun's pure heart the song
  Presses and burns like fire.

She crosses herself again and again;
  She crosses herself like a sinner;
But nothing she does can assuage the pain
  And the longing that throbs within her.

2

"The God of Music, loved am I
  By monarchs and by masses;
In Greece my temple faced the sky,
  High upon Mount Parnassus.

"Upon Parnassus' height in Greece,
  Guarding its holy meadows,

I've often stretched myself at peace
  Beneath the cypress shadows.

"And always, always high and clear,
  Laughter and song were rising.
La-la! La-la! I loved to hear
  The Muses vocalizing.

"Beneath I heard Tra-ra! Tra-ra!
  (The bugle, and a loud one,
Belonged to Artemisia,
  My sister, and a proud one.)

"How it occurred I do not know—
  The sacred river drew me;
And when I sipped Castalia, lo!
  Song always echoed through me.

"I sang, and of its own accord
  My lyre began to quiver;
Like the first glimpse of my adored
  Daphne beside the river.

"I sang, and perfume filled the soul
  With a divine elation;
It was as though an aureole
  Covered the whole creation.

"A thousand years exiled from Greece,
  I left its founts and fanes there;
But still my heart has no release—
  My lyric heart remains there."

3

Muffled in her long black mantle,
Made of serge that's coarse and shoddy,
The young nun starts on her journey
In the habit of a Beguine.

Hotly, anxiously, she wanders
Down the long and narrow highway
Of the Rhine that leads to Holland,
Asking everyone the question:

"Have you seen the god Apollo?
He performs upon the lyre,
Sings, and wears a scarlet mantle,
And he is my heart's dear idol."

No one offers her an answer.
Many turn their backs in silence;
Many stare and smile upon her;
Many merely sigh, "Poor creature!"

Jogging down the German highway
Comes an old tatterdemalion,
Fingering the air and singing
Through his nose a senseless ditty.

On his back he bears a wallet,
On his head a tawdry tricorne;
And he smirks, and leers, and ogles,
As he listens to her asking:

"Have you seen the god Apollo?
He performs upon the lyre,

Sings, and wears a scarlet mantle,
And he is my heart's dear idol."

And the scarecrow stops his singing,
Tugs his beard with queer grimaces,
Strikes a sudden clown-like posture,
And his head wags as he answers:

"You should ask me have I seen him!
Yes, I've seen him more than often
In the streets of Amsterdam,
At the German synagogue.

"There, where he led all the singing,
He was known as Rabbi Faibisch
(In High German that means Phoebus),[1]
But he scarcely is *my* idol!

"Scarlet mantle? Yes, I know it.
It's a really royal scarlet;
Price per ell about eight florins,
And it's not completely paid for.

"And I know his honored father,
Moses Jitscher, circumciser
To the Portuguese Marranos
And (they say) to Christian sovereigns.[2]

[1] In the early centuries many Hellenized Jews adopted the name of Phoebus, which became corrupted into Faibisch, a little-known curiosity which Heine ironically records.

[2] Here Heine again indulges in a pun. The word *Souveraine* means sovereigns in both the monetary and the regal sense. The reference is not merely to circumcision, but to the practice of cutting (or "sweating") goldpieces, especially sovereigns.

"And his mother is a cousin
Of my sister's husband, selling
Sour pickles at the market,
And assortments of odd trousers.

"And their son gives them no pleasure.
True, he plays the lyre not badly,
But he plays taroc and ombre,
And such games of chance far better.

"He's become a non-conformer,
Eaten swine and lost his pulpit;
And he troupes about the country
With a lot of low comedians.

"In the market-place he gives them
Heroes such as Pickle-Herring,
Holofernes, and King David—
As the last he's most successful.

"For he sings King David's raptures
In the Jewish King's own language,
With the very sobs and quavers
Turned according to tradition.

"He enticed nine buxom wenches
From the Amsterdam Casino,
And he's touring with these 'Muses'
Through the country as Apollo.

"One, still heavier than the others,
With her mop of frowsy laurel,
And her squeaking and her grunting
Has been christened 'the great sow.' "

KING DAVID

Lächelnd scheidet der Despot

Tyrants when they come to die
Laugh and look death in the eye,
For they know one thing is sure:
Tyranny will still endure.

There they go, the common folk,
Cattle bowing to the yoke;
Never daring to complain,
Docile to the bit and rein.

To the stalwart Solomon
David, dying, said: "My son,
Apropos of Joab, too,
There is this for you to do:

"This proud general has been
A rankling thorn beneath my skin;
Yet for all my hatred, none
Has done the thing I should have done.

"You, my son, the one I love,
You are good and strong enough;
So, remembering all I've said,
Kill this Joab when I'm dead."

THE ASRA

Täglich ging die wunderschöne

Daily came the lone and lovely
Sultan's daughter, slowly wandering
In the evening to the fountain
Where the plashing waters whitened.

Daily stood the youthful captive
In the evening by the fountain
Where the plashing waters whitened—
Daily growing pale and paler.

Till one dusk the strolling Princess
Stopped, and suddenly addressed him:
"Tell me now thy name, and tell me
Of thy country and thy kindred."

And the slave replied, "My name is
Móhamet; I come from Yemen.
And my people are the Asra,
Who, whene'er they love, must perish."

COUNTESS JUTTA

Pfalzgräfin Jutta fuhr über den Rhein

The Countess Jutta in her frail boat
Under the moonlight seemed to float
Over the Rhine. To her maid she spoke,
"There, did you see where the water broke,
    Seven bodies arise
    With staring eyes?
So mournfully swim the dead.

"Fair knights they were in their fiery youth;
Held on my breast they pledged me truth.
I trusted their oaths, but I knew the way
Of men and their words; so, lest they betray,
    I had them drowned
    Without a sound—
So mournfully swim the dead."

The maid rowed on; the Countess laughed loud;
Grim were the echoes that came from each cloud.
The dead men lifted themselves from the Rhine
And stretched their arms like an oath or a sign,
    And stared at her there
    In a last despair.
So mournfully swim the dead.

NIGHT-JOURNEY[1]

Es wogte das Meer, aus dem dunklen Gewölk

The waters swelled; from the darkening clouds
    The moon rose over the sea;
And as we entered the little boat
    We were three—I know we were three.

There was no sound but the oars that plashed
    In a worn monotony;
With steady progress the foam-capped waves
    Rose and splashed on us three.

She stood in the boat, so slender, so pale,
    So still and silently;
Diana's counterfeit she appeared,
    In marble and ivory.

The moon was hidden; the nightwind played
    A long, cold melody;
When over our heads we heard a scream
    That smote us suddenly.

[1] A nightmare poem which is appropriately blurred in outline, and which achieves its grotesque intensity by mounting suggestions and the insistently repeated rhyme. One of Heine's editors implies that these verses express the theme of the entire *Romancero*—the struggle between beauty and the world—but this "explanation" only adds confusion to obscurity.

It was the voice of the white sea-mew
  That echoed over the sea,
It seemed a warning from some other world
  Or a voice of doom to us three.

Have I a fever? Is it a ghost
  Or a midnight fantasy?
Am I tricked by a dream? Has the dream become
  A horrible mockery?

A horrible mockery!—There, in my dream,
  The Saviour I seemed to be;
'Twas I who carried the heavy cross
  Painfully, patiently.

The poor white beauty is sorely pressed;
  But I will set her free
Of pain and sin, of shame and distress,
  The world's vast misery.

Oh, poor white beauty, do not fear
  The bitter therapy;
Though it must be done with my heart's blood
  I'll summon death for thee.

O gruesome, overpowering dream,
  Sublime insanity!
The black night yawns, the whole sea splits—
  O God! Have pity on me!

Have pity on me, O merciful God!
  O merciful God Shaddei! [2]
Something has plunged—in the sea! Can it be!
  Shaddei! Shaddei! Adonai! [3]

[2] The old Hebrew name for the Almighty.   [3] Hebrew for Lord.

The sun arose. We floated to shore.
   The skies of May were blue.
And as we disembarked, I saw
   We were not three, but two.

PRELUDE

(FROM "VITZLIPUTZLI")

Dieses ist Amerika!

This is America!
This is the new world!
Not the present European
Wasted and withering sphere.

This is the new world,
As it was when Columbus
Drew it first from the ocean.
Radiant with its freshening bath;

Still dripping its watery pearls,
In showers and spurts of color
As the light of the sun kisses them.
How strong and healthy is this world!

This is no graveyard of Romance;
This is no pile of ruins,
Of fossilized wigs and symbols
Or stale and musty Tradition!

Out of healthy ground there blossom
Healthy flowers—not a creature
In that land's *blasé,* or suffers
Rotting of the spinal marrow . . .

A new country! New the fervor,
New the flowers, new the fragrance!
Here the very air is heady
With invigorating perfumes!

EPILOG TO "ATTA TROLL"

(TO VARNHAGEN VON ENSE)

Wo des Himmels, Meister Ludwig

"Where in heaven, Messire Louis,
Did you dig up all this stuff?"
With these words the Cardinal
D'Este cried to Ariosto,

As he read the latter's poem
On the madness of Orlando,
Which was humbly dedicated
To his princely Eminence.

Yes, Varnhagen, my old friend,
Yes, I see your own lips forming
The identical few words
And the same smile, sharp and subtle.

I can even hear you laughing
As you read, although small furrows
Line your high and thoughtful forehead,
And old memories steal on you:

"Are not these the sounds I heard
When my youth dreamed with Chamisso,
With Brentano and Fouqué,
In the blue, romantic moonlight?

"Can that be the holy ringing
Of forgotten forest chapels,
And between the chimes are those the
Cap and bells so pertly jingling?

"Through the nightingales' high choir
Break the bears' peculiar basses,
Rumbling, grumbling—and they change to
Whisperings of sighing spirits.

"Madness in the guise of wisdom!
Wisdom turned upon itself!
The last, dying sob, which quickly
Changes into raucous laughter!" . . .

Yes, my friend, these are the echoes
Of that perished time of dreams,
Save that modern variations
Caper on the ancient ground-bass.

And for all the braggadoccio
You will find despair's dark traces.
To your often-proven kindness
Humbly I commend this poem.

Ah, it is perhaps the final
Wild wood-note of the Romantic!
In these days of din and battle
It will cease and die ignobly.

Other times—and other birds.
Other birds—and other songs.
Listen to them, like the geese, who
Saved the Capitol by cackling!

What a chirping! Those are sparrows;
In their claws are penny-candles;
Yet they fancy they are eagles,
Carrying Jove's thunderbolts.

What a cooing! Doves and pigeons,
Sick of love, now turned to hatred,
And, instead of bearing Venus,
They prefer Mars' bloody chariot!

What a long, world-shaking buzzing!
These must be the giant May-bugs
Of the people's early Spring-time,
Working up a berserk fury!

Other times—and other birds.
Other birds—and other songs.
All, perhaps, would really please me
Had I only other ears!

FAREWELL TO PARIS

(FROM "GERMANY: A WINTER FAIRY-TALE")

Ade, Paris, du teure Stadt

Paris, enchanting town, farewell,
  Today I turn from pleasure
And leave you to distracting joys,
  More than a man can measure.

The German heart within this breast
  Is sick—I can't conceal it—
But in the North at home there lives
  A doctor who can heal it.

He'll care for me and I'll be cured,
　　Thanks to his strict devotions,
But even now I dread to think
　　Of those harsh pills and potions.

You merry folk of France, farewell,
　　Soon I will be returning;
A foolish whim, yet I must yield
　　To this ridiculous yearning.

Imagine! I've a longing for
　　The smell of turf! I burn up
Remembering raw potato-cake,
　　And sauerkraut and turnip.

I long for crude town-councilors
　　And everything they lack. Oh,
I long for timid little blondes,
　　Black bread, and bad tobacco.

And, more than this, I long to see
　　My mother's quaint demeanor;
The dear old soul—'tis thirteen years
　　This autumn since I've seen her.

Farewell, my wife, my lovely wife,
　　My pain you can't perceive, you
Know that I hold you to my heart,
　　And yet, alas, I leave you.

I dread to go. But this deep woe
　　Drives me to desperation:
I must breathe German air again
　　Or die of suffocation.

Not only pain decides; my mind,
  My very limbs determine;
Impatiently my feet demand
  To tread on soil that's German.

At the year's end I will be cured
  Of all that is unpleasant;
I'll come, my pet, and then you'll get
  The loveliest New Year's present.

A VISIT HOME

(FROM "GERMANY: A WINTER FAIRY-TALE")

Von Harburg fuhr ich in einer Stund'

I drove from Harburg—an easy hour—
  As evening came to calm me,
Welcomed by each familiar star;
  The air was kind and balmy.

And when my mother saw me, she
  Clung to me with excitement;
She cried, clasped hands, and stared at me,
  Not sure just what the flight meant.

"My poor child! For these thirteen years
  In France you've had to live; you
Need a good meal, you must be starved.
  Sit down. What can I give you?

"There's fish at home, and there is goose,
  And oranges sweet as honey."
"Good. I'll have fish, and I'll have goose,
  And oranges warm and sunny."

And as I ate, my mother glowed;
  She crowed at my good digestion.
And then, alas, she embarrassed me
  With question after question.

"Do you live well in your home abroad?
  Are all your troubles ended?
Does your wife know how to run the house?
  Are your shirts and socks well mended?"

"The fish is excellent, mother, my own,
  But the bones are a terrible bother;
I'd hate to have one lodge in my throat,
  So let me alone, dear mother."

As soon as I had disposed of the fish,
  The goose was brought to the table.
She asked about that, and she asked about this,
  As quickly as she was able.

"Dear child, do you prefer the French,
  Or Germans, or do you waver?
Is France a pleasanter place than this?
  And which is the land you favor?"

"This German goose is wonderful;
  But, mother, the French have powers
Uncanny, it seems, when it comes to a sauce,
  And their stuffing is better than ours."

After the goose was wholly consumed
  The oranges weren't neglected;
I found them ripe and juicy and sweet,
  Far sweeter than I expected.

And then my mother began again
  With many a curious glance; her
Questions came tumbling; and all in vain
  I sought for the ready-made answer.

"My child, I'm anxious to hear you name
  Your political predilections.
What is your party? What is its aim?
  And what are your own convictions?"

"It was most delicious, mother, my own;
  The oranges really were fine, dear.
I enjoyed the juice to the last sweet drop,
  But I'll leave the bitter rind here."

LAMENTATIONS
AND LAZARUS
(1847-1851)

LAMENTATIONS

PROLOG

Das Glück ist eine leichte Dirne

Good-Fortune is a giddy maid,
    Fickle and restless as a fawn;
She smooths your hair; and then the jade
    Kisses you quickly, and is gone.

But Madam Sorrow scorns all this,
    She shows no eagerness for flitting;
But with a long and fervent kiss
    Sits by your bed—and brings her knitting.

TAKE UP THE LYRE

Wenn man an dir Verrat geübt

When a false word betrays your trust
    And stamps upon your fire,
When what seemed blood is only rust,
    Take up the lyre.

How quickly the heroic mood
    Responds to its own ringing;
The scornful heart, the angry blood,
    Leap upward, singing.

MYTHOLOGY

Ja, Europa ist erlegen

Yes, Europa is forgiven
　And Danaé too. What power
Could subdue a golden shower
Or withstand a bull from heaven?

Semele was not much wiser
　When she lost her precious honor;
　For it never dawned upon her
That a cloud could compromise her.

But our scorn arises quicker
　When we read the tale of Leda—
　Only such a goose would heed a
Silly swan and let it trick her!

TO THE YOUNG

Lass dich nicht kirren, lass dich nicht wirren

Brook no delay; spurn, on your way,
　Apples of gold without regret.
Flashing hordes and clashing swords
　Never have stopped a hero yet.

Boldly begun is almost won.
　An Alexander conquers the world.
No time for debate! For you there wait
　Queens with warm lips when flags are furled.

Never despair! We do and we dare!
　The heir of Darius, we mount the throne.
Defiant of death we draw our last breath
　In drunken triumph in Babylon!

THIS SIDE AND THAT SIDE OF THE RHINE

Sanftes Rasen, wildes Kosen

Tender rages, wild embraces,
Dallying in the rosiest places,
Perfumed promise, pleasant lies,
Lust in a devout disguise,
All the things that love may prize—
Here the French display their graces.

But we Germans, we are great
When it comes to solid hate.
From the deepest depths there runs
German hatred, till the tuns
Of Heidelberg and all its sons
Fill and overflow in spate!

THE SKEPTIC

Du wirst in meinen Armen ruhn!

And you would rest, held in my arms!
   The thought of such a wonder
Sweeps through my blood in magic storms,
   And my heart throbs with thunder.

And you would rest, held in my arms!
   Your head with golden tresses
Would lie upon my shoulder, warm
   With ever-new caresses.

And you would rest, held in my arms!
   This is no day-dream; this is
Earth's taste of all imagined charms
   And heaven's highest blisses!

It is too much! I cannot trust
The too incredible promise,
Till in my joy's wound I have thrust
A finger.—Doubting Thomas!

THE MORNING AFTER

Diese graue Wolkenschar

These gray clouds, so thickly strewn,
    Rose from golden skies and gay;
Yesterday I called the tune,
    And today I have to pay.

Ah, the nectar of last night
    Turns to wormwood. Such is fate!
And the head that was so light
    Cannot even hold its weight.

FOR DOMESTIC PEACE

Viele Weiber, viele Flöhe

Many a woman is like a flea—
    Many a flea, and many a bite—
Though they cause you misery,
    Grin and bear it; that is right.

Otherwise the darlings might
    Plan more devious attacks.
When you grope toward them at night
    They will coolly turn their backs.

PIOUS WARNING

Unsterbliche Seele, nimm dich in Acht

Immortal spirit, beware, despair
  Of evil's quick befriending;
  Soon will your way be wending
Through death, and night, and God knows where.

At the Heavenly Gate there wait for one
  God's army, whose occupation
  Is not to demand your station
Or your name, but what you have done.

Discarding their shoes at the entrance, frees
  The pilgrims, those heavenly trippers.
  Come; enter; draw on your slippers;
Enjoy the music, and take your ease.

FAREWELL

Hatte wie ein Pelikan

Like a pelican I fed you
  With my blood; you ate and drank me.
Now you give me gall and wormwood—
  What a pleasant way to thank me!

It was never meant in malice,
  And your eyes were never fretful;
Nothing creased that placid forehead—
  You were just a bit forgetful.

So good-by; and, though I weep, you
  Will not care or wonder why.
Smile farewell. And may God keep you
  Just a lovely butterfly.

NOW WHERE?

Jetzt wohin? Der dumme Fuss

And now where? My stupid feet
　Want to carry and compel me
Back, a German, in retreat,
　But my wise head seems to tell me

True, the war is over, but
　There are old laws, an immense hoard;
I could certainly be shot
　For the articles they censored.

Therefore, since I cannot go
　Back like an avenging Tartar,
I will save my neck; I know
　I would make a rotten martyr.

Why not fly to England then?
　Gladly, say I, like a comet;
But England's full of Englishmen,
　And the coal-damp makes me vomit.

Sometimes I am bound to see
　Revolution's glorious sequel:
America, the great, the free,
　Land where everyone is equal—

But how could I love a land
　Where the mob is monarch really,
Where there are no King-pins,[1] and
　People chew and spit so freely.

---

[1] *Wo sie ohne König kegeln:* Literally, where they bowl without the king;
a poor pun, and not even Heine's own.

Russia has a heart of gold
  And broad bosom, like a peasant;
But the winters there are cold,
  And the knout is most unpleasant.

Then I lift my eyes, woe's me,
  To the skies, and long to go where
All the stars shine constantly—
  But my own true star is nowhere.

Possibly my star is lost
  In the sky's deep mazes, even
As I have been wrecked and tossed—
  I on earth, and she in heaven.

OLD SONG

Du bist gestorben und weisst es nicht

Dead, you are dead without a doubt;
The lights in your lovely eyes are out;
The roses of your lips will rot;
Yes, you are dead, and know it not.

One summer night, distraught and dread,
I bore you to your final bed.
The nightingales sang a funeral stave;
The stars went with me to your grave.

And as we walked the wood, the trees
Re-echoed with our litanies.
The sable forest bowed its head,
Murmuring prayers to bless the dead.

Then, as we passed the lake, the elves
Danced where the willows crossed themselves;

The dancing stopped. Half curious,
Half pitiful, they looked at us.

And as we reached your grave, with a sigh
The moon itself came down from the sky.
He spoke the Last Words. The loose pebbles ran.
And in the distance the bells began.

SECURITY

Liebe sprach zum Gott der Lieder

Love said to the God of Music,
  "Times are changed. I'd be a dumb thing
If I gave myself without a
  Guarantee or pledge of something."

"Yes," Apollo answered, laughing,
  "Times are changed indeed. You talk like
Some old usurer demanding
  Pledges, cynical and hawk-like.

"Well, I only have my lyre,
  But it's gold, depend upon it.
Tell me, darling, just how many
  Kisses would you lend me on it?"

AUTO-DA-FÉ

Welke Veilchen, stäub'ge Locken

Faded violets, dusty tresses,
  And a band that once was blue;
Things that I had long forgotten,
  Ribbons, crumpled billets-doux—

I have dropped them, smiling sadly,
  In the flames and watch them where
Countless joys and countless sorrows
  Sparkle in the ruins there.

Up the flue go love and lovers,
  Frail and foolish oaths—alas!
And the little Cupid chuckles
  As he sees them burn and pass.

And I sit here by the ruins,
  Dreaming in the lessening light;
While the sparks among the ashes
  Faintly glow . . . Farewell . . .
    Good Night

THE WAY OF THE WORLD

Hat man viel, so wird man bald

He who has, will have much more;
  Each success begets success;
While the man with little, will
  Have (when all is done) still less.

But if there is nothing, then
  Dig your grave for all you're worth.
Only those with something, have
  Right to live on this rich earth.

THE DYING PATRIOT

Flogest aus nach Sonn' und Glück

You sought the sun—and now, alack,
Blind and naked you come back;

Having lost, the Lord knows where,
Both your faith and underwear.

Groping, deathly pale, you come;
But at least you are at home.
Here (take comfort) you may lie
On warm German soil, and die.

Some, too tired and lame to crawl,
Never get back home at all.
Now, poor soul, that you are through,
God (perhaps) will pity you.

RETROSPECT

Ich habe gerochen alle Gerüche

I have smelled every one of the thousand smells
In earth's warm kitchens, have drunk from the wells
Of a thousand pleasures; the great and small
Delights of the world, I have tasted them all.
I've drunk good coffee, have eaten buns;
Have fondled dolls—and the loveliest ones;
Have worn silk vests and the finest hose;
I've even had money in my clothes.
I've ridden a high horse with silver tassels;
I've had fine houses, have lived in castles;
I've thought of myself as a favorite one
Caressed by the golden kiss of the sun;
My brow was crowned with a wreath of laurel,
And I dreamed sweet dreams with never a moral,
Dreams of a soft and endless May,
Where the spirit was free and life's purpose was play;
Never a darkness, disease, nor drouth—
Roast pigeons flew in my open mouth;

Angels distributed golden ducats
And champagne flasks from their inside pockets.
Ah, these were visions, bright soap-bubbles.
They burst . . . And now, beset with troubles,
I lie in a damp and draughty attic;
My head is heavy, my limbs rheumatic;
All of me withered, crippled, and lame,
The once-proud spirit broken with shame.
For each quick pleasure, each joyful vice
I've paid full measure—and often twice.
I've drowned in bitterness, burned in ice,
Been bled by friends and bitten by lice;
I've been attended by blackest sorrow;
I've had to lie, I've had to borrow
From rich young fools and be beholden,
Like a common beggar, to a crusty old 'un.
But now I am tired; I long to sleep
In a new-made bed that's dark and deep.
Farewell. I know, my Christian brother,
In heaven (alas) we will see each other.

SING FOR YOUR SUPPER

Die reichen Leute, die gewinnt

To please your patron, flattery
   Fulsome and flat will do the trick.
Money is flat, so learn from me:
   Lay it on flat, pile it on thick.

Then briskly swing the censer which
   Honors each godlike-golden calf;
Pray in the dust before the rich,
   And don't, my friend, do it by half.

Bread's dear this year, but words are cheap,
Words sweet and warm, freely supplied;
So sing, sing even as you creep,
Maecenas' dog, and fill your hide!

A MEMORY [1]

Dem einen die Perle, dem andern die Truhe

To one life is gray, to another it's pearly—
O Wilhelm Wisetzki, you died too early—
But the kitten, the kitten was rescued.

The board you stood on suddenly broke;
You plunged in the stream; you never spoke—
But the kitten, the kitten was rescued.

We followed the hearse when they took you away;
They buried you under the blossoms of May—
But the kitten, the kitten was rescued.

Oh, you were wise, you found an early
Escape from a world grown old and surly—
But the kitten, the kitten was rescued.

An early haven . . . Oh, you were wise
Not to grow morbid and agonize—
But the kitten, the kitten was rescued.

[1] "It is my fault that little Wilhelm lies there in the churchyard. We were class-mates in the old Düsseldorf Franciscan monastery, and one day as we played on the banks where the Düssel flows between stone walls, I said, 'Wilhelm, save the kitten that has just fallen in.' And Wilhelm cheerfully did it. He climbed the board that spanned the stream, pulled the kitten out of the water, but he fell in. Help came too late—he was dead when they got him out. The kitten lived for a long time." From Heine's *Reisebilder: Das Buch Le Grand.*

Comrade, whenever I think of us two,
My heart is wrung, for I envy you . . .
But the kitten, the kitten was rescued.

THE TEMPERATE ONE

Und ist man todt, so muss man lang

When the end comes and we are dead,
We lie, a long time. I'm afraid,
Yes, I'm afraid the resurrection
Won't come so quickly in this section.

So, once before the veil is dropped,
The light extinguished, the heart stopped,
And life has lost its heady savor,
I would enjoy some woman's favor.

Moreover, it must be a blonde,
With gentle moonlit eyes and fond—
For in the end I've always tired
Of wild brunettes too easily fired.

Young people, fresh and full of life,
Enjoy the tumult, relish strife;
To them your passion is a sport, your
Pain's a delight; they live on torture.

Now not so well and not so young
As I once was, again I long
For all that living, love, and light meant,
And laughter. But without excitement.

MORPHINE

Gross ist die Ähnlichkeit der beiden schönen

Great is the similarity between
These two fair figures, although one appears
Much paler than the other, far more calm;
Fairer and nobler even, I might say,
Than his companion, in whose arms
I lay so warmly. How divine and soft
Were all his smiles, and what a look was his!
It must have been the poppy-wreath he wore
About his brows that touched my throbbing head
And with its magic perfume soothed all pain
And sorrow in my soul. But such sweet balm
Lasts but a little while; I can be cured
Completely only when the other one,
The grave and paler brother, drops his torch.
For Sleep is good, but Death is better still—
The best is never to be born at all.

SOLOMON

Verstummt sind Pauken, Posaunen und Zinken

The trumpets and drums no longer are sounded,
　　Hushed is the dulcimer and flute.
　　King Solomon sleeps, and the night is mute.
He sleeps—by twelve thousand angels surrounded.

They guard his dreams from clamor and cumber.
　　And should he even knit his brow
　　Twelve thousand arms would be lifted now,
Twelve thousand swords would flash through his slumber.

Yet gently now the swords are lying
  Within each scabbard. The night-winds soothe
  The dreamer's dreams and his brow is smooth;
Only his lips are restless, sighing:

"O Shulamite! all people cherish
  My favor, and bring me tributes, and sing;
  I am both Judah's and Israel's king—
But, lacking your love, I wither and perish."

TO THE ANGELS

Das ist der böse Thanatos

Now death comes riding; in despair
I see him striding his pale mare;
I hear the hoof-beats, and I know
That the dark rider will not go
Until he forces me, perhaps tomorrow,
To leave my poor Mathilde engulfed in sorrow.

She was, to me, both child and wife;
And when I take my leave of life
Orphan and widow she will be.
Misery piled on misery,
That wife and child will be not only
Stricken, but comfortless and lonely.

Ye angels, happily on high,
Hark to my pleading, hear my cry:
When I am in the dismal grave,
Protect my poor belovéd, save
The helpless child; strengthen, support, and shield
Your kin, your earthly image, my Mathilde.

By all your pity, all the tears
Ye shed for man throughout the years;
By the dread symbol only named
By priests who shudder when 'tis framed
In words of flame; by the pure power ye wield,
By your own grace and splendor, guard Mathilde.

HELEN

Du hast mich beschworen aus dem Grab

You have called me suddenly out of the grave
    With a magic incantation;
You have warmed me with mortal desire, and now
    You cannot quiet my passion.

Oh, press your mouth upon my mouth,
    With ardor unabated.
I will drain your very soul, for the dead
    Have a lust that cannot be sated.

BAD DREAMS

Im Traume war ich wieder jung und munter

I dreamt that I was young again and care-free—
    The place was the old house that used to stand
High on the mountain near the summit, where, free
    Of kin and custom, we raced hand in hand.

How fine the little figure. How discreetly
    The sea-green eyes changed to a water-sprite's.
How delicate the feet. And how completely
    She seemed the model of the world's delights.

The tone of voice was clear as any linnet;
  The little mouth a rosebud; she was droll.
Yet all she said had so much candor in it
  One could see straight into her very soul.

It was not pain of love that took possession;
  I was controlled; I seemed to understand.
Her presence moved me with a gentler passion,
  And, trembling quietly, I kissed her hand.

And then at last, I think, I plucked a lily
  And gave it, speaking up courageously,
"Oh, marry me and be my wife, Ottilie; [1]
  Let me share all your happy radiancy."

What she replied? How can I ever tell it.
  For suddenly I woke—and I was here;
A sick man lying on a sick man's pallet
  Tortured, as I have been for many a year.

ENFANT PERDU

Verlorner Posten in dem Freiheitskriege

For more than thirty years I've been defending,
  In freedom's struggle, many a desperate post.
I knew the fight was hopeless, never-ending;
  But still I fought, wounded and battle-tossed.

Waking through nights and days, no peaceful slumbers
  Were mine while all the others slept their fill.
(The mighty snoring of these valiant numbers
  Kept me awake when I was tired or ill.)

[1] Discretion, even more than the demands of rhyme, compelled "Ottilie," but Heine meant "Amalie."

In those long nights I have been often frightened,
  For only fools are not afraid of fear,
But I would whistle till the terror lightened,
  And sing my mocking rhymes to give me cheer.

Yes, I have stood, my musket primed and ready,
  On guard; and when some rascal raised his head
I took good aim, my arm was always steady,
  And let him have a bellyful of lead.

And yet those knaves—I may as well admit it—
  Could shoot quite well; the rascals often chose
A splendid mark, and, what is more, they hit it.
  My wounds are gaping . . . and my blood still flows.

One post is vacant! As a bloody token
  I wear my wounds. Another takes my part.
But, though I fall, my sword is still unbroken;
  The only thing that's broken is my heart.

HEBREW MELODIES

HEBREW MELODIES

JEHUDA BEN HALEVY

"Lechzend klebe mir die Zunge"

1

"And if ever I forget thee,
O Jerusalem, may my right hand
Wither and forget its cunning,
May my tongue cleave to the palate—"

And today the words and music
Fill my head with endless echoes,
And I seem to hear men's voices
Singing psalms and celebrations.

With the music there come visions;
Beards dark-shadowed float before me—
Apparitions, which among you
Is Jehuda ben Halevy?

Though they hurry swiftly past me
(For these timid phantoms shrink from
Clumsy human conversation)
Yet I know, I recognize him.

Yes, I know him by the pallid,
Proud and thought-engraven forehead,
By the eyes' intense absorption,
Watching me with searching sadness.

But especially I know him
By the enigmatic curving

Of those rhyme-shaped lips, a feature
That identifies the poet.

Years have come and years have vanished;
Seven hundred years and fifty
Have been numbered since the birthday
Of Jehuda ben Halevy.

He first saw the light of living
In Castile, in old Toledo,
And the music of the Tagus
Was his golden lullaby.

From the start his father strictly
Disciplined his education,
Shaped the unfolding of his spirit
With that godly book, the Torah.[1]

Son and father read the ancient
Text in its true form, the curious
Picturesque and hieroglyphic
Square-cut Old-Chaldean letters,

Which have come down from the childhood
Of the world itself, and therefore
Speak familiarly to children,
Smiling quaintly, confidently.

Faithfully the boy recited
The authentic version daily,
In the ancient, quavering manner,
Known as Tropp, the measured sing-song.

[1] The Torah is the Pentateuch, as revealed by God.

Lovingly the youngster gurgled
Every fat and oily guttural,
And he trilled the open vowels
Like a bird, with the Shalsheleth; [2]

He read Targum Onkelos [3]
Which is written in low-Hebrew,
A half-dialect, half-idiom,
Sometimes known as Aramaic,

And related to the language
Of the prophets as remotely
As the Swabian speech to German.
In this imitation-Hebrew

Young Jehuda made such progress
That he soon acquired the knowledge
To attack that compilation,
That vast work of works, the Talmud. [4]

Yes, his father quickly brought him
To the glories of the Talmud;
There he led the boy, and opened
That great campus, the Halachah, [5]

[2] The Shalsheleth: A chain of associated names, as in a genealogy; a chanted list of prophets, kings, etc.

[3] Targum (Aramaic) Onkelos: An Aramaic translation of the Pentateuch made for the purpose of popular study, and traditionally ascribed to a Greek proselyte by the name of Aquila, Hebraicized as Onkelos.

[4] The Talmud, consisting of two divisions (Halachah and Aggadah), is a monumental piece of exegesis. It is built up by the expositions, interpretations, and sayings of the rabbis and intellectual leaders of the Jews during the first five centuries of the Christian era. It covers the gamut of Jewish life, religious, dietetic, polemical, social, and cultural.

[5] The Halachah, or Oral Law, is that division of The Talmud which concerns itself with the body of custom and traditional practices which grew up around the Written Law. Although avowedly devoted to legislation, the

That great tilting-ground, arena
Where the most accomplished fencers,
Dialectic Babylonians,
Waged their intellectual battles.

Here the youth learned every nuance,
Dialectic and polemic;
And his mastery was proven
When he wrote his own "Cozari." [6]

But high heaven pours upon us
Two varieties of brilliance:
Day's intemperate golden dazzle,
And the mellow glow of moonlight.

So the Talmud sheds a double
Glory, and is thus divided:
The Halachah and Aggadah.[7]
And the first's a school for fencers.

But the second, the Aggadah,
I would like to call a garden,
An immense, fantastic garden,
And resembling such another

Halachah expounds, analyzes, and elaborates the injunctions of the Pentateuch with an extraordinary and sometimes bewildering subtlety. It is a continual combination of skilled hairsplitting, jurisprudence, and dialectical
gymnastics.

[6] "Cozari" or "Kusari" is Halevy's great work, a philosophic defense of
Judaism, written in about 1130.

[7] The Aggadah is that part of the Talmud which reflects the sentiments
and spirit of the Jews in the early centuries of Christianity. It is distinguished from the Halachah by its legendary topics as well as by its popular
tone. Instead of being legal in character and juristic in aspect, it is full of
parables, apologues, and fantasies. Thus the poetic elements of the Aggadah
furnish a strong contrast (and, often, a welcome relief) to the rigorous demands of the study of the Halachah.

Which, arising from the earth, once
Blossomed out of Babylon: the
Garden of Semiramis,
The eighth wonder of the world.

Here the Queen Semiramis
Lived with birds throughout her childhood,
And, therefore, she never lost her
Many bird-like tastes and manners;

Disinclined to walk or wander
On flat earth like beasts of burden
Or like common folk, she planted
A great garden in the air.

High upon colossal pillars
Lordly palm and cypress glittered,
Oranges and marble statues,
Fountains amid beds of flowers,

All so intricately patterned
By a woven web of bridges,
Delicate as hanging creepers,
In which birds were always swinging—

Many-colored birds and solemn,
Serious birds that think in silence,
While the thoughtless little finches
Garrulously flew about them—

And they breathed the balsam-laden
Air like an enchanted perfume,
Unpolluted by the fetid
Smells of earth and common soilure . . .

The Aggadah's such a garden,
Reared by the imagination,
Where the youthful Talmud scholar
Roams whene'er his mind is dusty,

Dusty from the disputations
Of Halachah, of the problem
Of the famous egg delivered
By the hen—or *vice versa.*

Vexed by these and other questions
As perplexing and proverbial,
The poor youth took to his heels, and
Plunged into the bright Aggadah,

Where the lovely legends blossom,
Curious myths, angelic fables,
Secret stories of the martyrs,
Apothegms and holy chorals,

Epigrams, hyperboles,
Farcical but, somehow, fervent,
Faith-inspiring, faith-compelling,
Overflowing with exuberance.

And the boy's enraptured spirit
Soon was captured by the wonder
Of this unforeseen adventure
With its wild, romantic sweetness,

And the legendary terror
Of a world of blessèd secrets,
Of the sudden revelation
That we know as poetry . . .

Thus Jehuda ben Halevy
Grew to be, more than a scholar,
A past-master of poetics,
Grew to be a famous poet.

Yes, a great and famous poet,
Star and beacon of his age,
Light and lantern to his people,
A superb and a resplendent

Flame of song, a fiery pillar,
Burning in the van of Israel's
Endless caravan of sorrow
In the desert wastes of exile.

For his song was like his spirit:
Pure and perfect, without blemish—
When Halevy's soul was fashioned
The Creator kissed it, glowing

With His happy inspiration;
And, distinguished by God's favor,
All the poet's fervent measures
Echo with that kiss forever.

As in life, in art: creation
Is good only with God's favor;
He who has this revelation
Cannot err in prose and verse.

Such a heaven-elected poet
By the grace of God's a genius,
In the realm of thought a monarch,
Proud, accountable to no one.

Only God can call the poet
To account, the people never.
As in life the mob can always
Kill us, but it cannot judge us.

2

"By the waters Babylonian
There we sat and wept for Zion;
And our harps hung on the willows"—
You remember the old burden?

You remember the old ditty
That begins with musing-mournful
Sighs and hums like an old kettle
Slowly boiling on the hearth?

It has boiled in me a thousand
Years or more, a dark affliction;
And Time licks my wounds that fester,
As Job's dog his master's boils.

Thank you, dog, for your endeavors,
But your spittle only cools me
For the moment. Death could heal me—
But, alas, I am immortal.

Years may come and years may vanish—
In the loom the spool is busy,
Flying hither, flying thither,
Though no weaver knows his weaving.

Years may come and years may vanish,
And the tears of men keep trickling
To the earth, and earth receives them
In a long, insatiate silence—

God be praised! The kettle's boiling!
The lid is off! The steam escapes!
Silence after . . . Silence quiets
My West-Oriental spleen.[8]

And my Pegasus is heard now
Whinnying, as if to tell me
He were happy, free of nightmare,
And his eager eyes keep asking:

"Shall we not return to Spain now,
To the little Talmud scholar
Who became the famous poet,
To Jehuda ben Halevy?"

Yes, he grew to be a famous
Magi in the world of fancy;
Lord of dreams and king of spirit,
Crowned as poet by God's favor,

Who, in sacramental numbers,
Madrigals and terza rimas,
Canzonets and strict ghazels,
Poured forth all the quickly burning

Passion of his God-kissed being!
Truly, he was no less moving
Than the best of the enchanting
Lute-players of old Provence,

Of Poitou and of Guienne,
Roussillon and all the other

[8] Heine implies an identification with Halevy. Both were poets; both felt exiled from their spiritual home; both were aware of their Oriental heritage at war with their Occidental environment.

Sweet lands of the golden orange,
Home of Christian gallantry.

Home of Christian gallantry,
Sweet lands of the golden orange!
Shining, ringing, ever fragrant
In the twilight of remembrance.

Happy world of nightingales!
Where the true God was forgotten,
And the Muses and that false God,
Love, were reverently worshiped.

There the clergy, with their tonsures,
Wreathed in roses, kept psalm-singing
In the lively Languedoc; 9
And the noble knights, the laity,

Rode about on haughty chargers,
Quoting gallant rhymes and verses
To the ladies, singing praises
Of the fair who plucked their heart-strings.

No love-songs without the ladies!
And the lyric minnesinger
Minus lady is absurd as
Bread and butter without butter.

Even he, our poem's hero,
Even Jehuda ben Halevy,
Had his heart's belovéd woman;
But his choice was quite uncommon.

9 Languedoc: An old French province, chief state of the Midi, unified in the 13th century.

She, his lady, was no Laura,
Whose bright eyes, those mortal planets,
Kindled the immortal fire
One Good Friday in the Minster—

She was no chateau's fair mistress,
Who, presiding at the tourney,
Blossoming with youth and beauty,
Gave the laurel to the victor—

Not a casuist of kisses,
Not a pretty doctrinaire, who
Lectured in the medieval
Quaint and lively Courts of Love.

She, the Rabbi's central passion,
Was a sad and wretched creature,
Poor and pitiful and ruined,
And her name—Jerusalem.

Even in the days of childhood
All his love was hers completely;
His whole being burned and trembled
At the word "Jerusalem."

And with flaming cheeks the youngster
Stood amid the crowd and listened
When a pilgrim from the Orient
Found his way back to Toledo

And related how polluted
Was the desolated city,
Where the prophets' holy footsteps
Still were seen in trails of light—

Where the very air was perfumed
With the eternal breath of God—
"Oh, the wretched desolation!
Oh, the pity!" cried the pilgrim

With a beard all white and silver,
Save the very tip which darkened
As though trying to recapture,
If it could, its younger days—

Yes, it was a most uncommon
Pilgrim whose dark eyes were peering
From a thousand years of trouble
As he cried "Jerusalem!

"She, the crowded holy city,
Has become a trampled desert,
Where lewd apes, werewolves, and jackals
Live, and roam, and spread pollution.

"Snakes and birds of night are nesting
In abandoned walls and turrets;
From the windows' airy arches
Foxes comfortably ponder.

"Here and there a wandering tribesman,
Rough and ragged from the desert,
Comes to let his hump-backed camel
Pasture on the uncut grasses.

"On the lordly heights of Zion,
Where the golden fortress towered
To the heavens, bearing witness
To a mighty monarch's power,

"There, where only weeds are growing,
Everything's in ashy ruins,
So cast down and so pathetic
That, one thinks, the stones must weep.

"And they do weep on occasion.
Once in every year, on every
Ninth of Ab the stones are mourning.[10]
With my own eyes I beheld them;

"Saw the heavy tear-drops trickling
From thick stones and ruined columns,
And I heard a timeless wailing
Rise from broken temple pillars."

Such reports from pious pilgrims
Woke within the youthful bosom
Of Jehuda ben Halevy
Longing for Jerusalem.

Poet's longing! Vague, foreboding,
And as fraught with unknown dangers
As the fatal dream and yearning
Which pursued the love-sick noble

Messer Geofforey Rudello,[11]
When the knight, upon returning
From his travels in the Orient,
Mid the clashing of the wine-cups,

[10] The ninth of Ab was the date on which Jerusalem fell and the Temple
was destroyed in 70 A.D. Thereafter it became a day of national mourning.
[11] Geofforey Rudello, or Geoffry Rudel of Blaye, has been the central
figure of countless versions of the old romance. The most recent note of the
legend is in Stendhal's On Love; Rostand employed the theme in his play
La Princesse Lointaine.

Heard that lovely Melisanda,
Margravine of Tripoli,
Was the pearl and flower of women,
Symbol of all charms and virtues.

Legend tells us how Rudello
Sighed and suffered for the lady;
How he sang, though without surcease,
And his palace grew too narrow.

How it drove him forth, and longing
Forced him to take ship to Cette;
How he sickened on the journey,
Dying, came to Tripoli;

How, at last, with his own eyes, he
Saw the lovely Melisanda,
Though within the hour his vision
Darkened with death's heavy shadow;

How he sang his final love-song
Dying, dying, at the feet of
His far princess Melisanda,
Margravine of Tripoli . . .

What a curious resemblance
In the fate of both these poets!
Save that one was far from youthful
When his pilgrimage began.

For Jehuda ben Halevy,
He, too, died at his belovéd's
Feet, his worn head resting
On her knees—Jerusalem's.

3

When the mighty Alexander
Swept the field at Arabella,
He was rich in land and loot, he
Took Darius' steeds and beauties.

Horses, harem, crown and scepter,
Elephants and coins—he stuck the
Golden plunder in his swollen
Baggy Macedonian trousers.

In the tent of great Darius,
Who had fled from battle, fearing
To be classed with other booty,
Alexander found a casket,

Found a little golden casket,
Set with miniatures, encrusted
With a wealth of precious jewels,
Cameos, intaglios.

And this chest, itself a treasure
Of incalculable value,
Was the case in which the monarch
Locked his dearest body-jewels.

This, the youthful Alexander
Gave the bravest of his soldiers,
With a smile that men, like children,
Should be pleased with colored pebbles.

Then the finest of the jewels,
Once the signet-ring of Cyrus,

Set into a brooch, became the
Gift he offered to his mother.

In the casket was a necklace,
A great string of glowing pearls,
Which the young impostor Smerdis [12]
Gave to win the Queen Atossa.

But the pearls were real enough—
And the happy conqueror gave them
To a most accomplished dancer,
Thaïs, from the town of Corinth.

Thaïs wore them loosely gathered
In her wild-bacchante tresses
On the night when, madly dancing
At Persepolis, she threw

Torches at the royal fortress,
Adding to the conflagration,
Like a set of flaming pictures
At a carnival of fireworks.

After lovely Thaïs perished
Of a Babylonian illness
In the heart of Babylon,
All the pearls were auctioned off

At a public sale in Memphis,
And a priest of Memphis bought them,
Bringing them to his own Egypt,
Where they found themselves much later

---

[12] Smerdis, the younger son of Cyrus the Great, was murdered and, his death having been kept secret, an impostor calling himself Smerdis, was proclaimed king. The story is narrated by Herodotus.

On Queen Cleopatra's table;
And the best of them was crushed,
Mixed with wine and gaily tossed off,
While Mark Antony frowned and wondered.

Then the last of the Omayads
Brought the necklace into Spain,
Where they twined it in the turban
Of the caliph of Cordova.

Abderam the Third displayed it
On his breast throughout the tourney,
When he plunged his lance through thirty
Gold rings and Zuleima's heart.

When the Moorish rule was over
Christian lords and monarchs claimed it,
And the necklace swelled the treasure
Of the crown-jewels of Castile.

And their Catholic Majesties,
Spanish queens, adorned their bodies
With the pearls at royal dances,
Revels, bull-fights, and processions,

Even at auto-da-fées,
Where, upon their balconies,
They were flattered by the fragrance
Of old Jews that smoked and roasted.

Sometime later, Mendizabel,
Spawn of Satan, pawned the necklace
To repair financial losses,
Covering the deficit.

Finally the string was carried
To the Tuileries; it shimmered
On the bosom of the lady
Solomon, the baroness.

So much for the lovely necklace . . .
Somewhat less adventurous
Is the story of the casket—
Briefly, Alexander kept it.

In it he preserved the poems
Of ambrosial Homer, whom he
Loved beyond all other poets.
Always near him, at his bedside

Stood the casket. And whenever
Alexander slept, the heroes
Rose and shone and took on substance,
Filling Alexander's dreams.

Other times bring other songsters—
I, too, loved the old heroic
Songs of doing and the daring
Of Pelides, of Odysseus.

Then my mood was royal purple,
All my days were turned to sun-gold,
And I wore a crown of vine-leaves,
And I heard the trumpets flourish.

But no more. The triumph's over.
The proud chariot is broken;
Dead the panthers; dead the women,
Who, with drum and cymbal, drew it.

Dead the drum-beats and the dancers,
And, alive but scarcely living,
Here upon the floor I shudder,
Cripple-tortured— But no more.

Let us turn back to the story
Of the casket of Darius;
For I know that if that casket
Ever came in my possession

And financial circumstances
Did not suffer me to sell it,
I would surely lock within it
The great poems by our Rabbi,

By Jehuda ben Halevy.
Songs of triumph, lamentations,
Chants, ghazels, and travel-pictures
Of his pilgrimage. The poems

Would be written by a scholar
On the very purest parchment,
And I'd place the golden poems
In that little, golden casket.

This I'd place upon a table
At my bedside; and when callers
Came and saw the chest and wondered,
Marveling upon its beauty,

Praising all the curious, tiny
Bas-reliefs and their perfection;
Gasping at the great, encrusted
Treasury of precious jewels,

I would merely smile and tell them
This is but the shell, the cover
That contains the finer treasure.
Here, within this little casket

There are diamonds, whose reflections
Sparkle with the light of heaven,
Deeply glowing heart's-blood rubies,
Turquoises without a blemish,

Emeralds of fiery promise,
Pearls impeccable, and purer
Than the string which Queen Atossa
Had from Smerdis, the impostor,

And which, later, decorated
All the most important persons
Of this moon-encircled planet:
Thaïs, sultry Cleopatra,

Priests of Isis, Moorish princes,
Even queens of old Hispania,
And, at last, the most respected
Baroness La Solomon.

For those pearls of universal
Fame and myth are but the illness
Of a poor, benighted oyster
Suffering in some dark sea-bottom.

But the pearls within this casket
Are the growth, the very surplus,
Of a spirit that lies deeper
Than the darkest depth of ocean.

For they are the pearly tear-drops
Of Jehuda ben Halevy,
Tears he wept for the destruction
Of his loved Jerusalem—

Tears like pearls which, bound together,
On a golden thread of music,
Strung with rhyme and fired with vision,
Burned and flashed, a singing poem.

And this song of pearly tears
Is the deathless lamentation
Sung in all the furthest scattered
Tents of Jacob through the world

Every year the ninth of Ab,
Day of universal mourning,
For the downfall and despoiling
Of Jerusalem by Vespasian.

Yes, that is the song of Zion
Which Jehuda ben Halevy,
Dying, sang among the ruins
Of Jerusalem, the holy,

Sitting on a broken fragment
Of a great and shattered column,
Barefoot, clad in pilgrim's sackcloth,
While the thickly tangled hair

Fell below his drooping shoulders,
Framing his fantastic features
With the eyes of some strange spirit,
And the bloodless mask of sorrow.

So he sat and so he sang,
Like a visionary prophet
From the past, like Jeremiah
Risen newly from the grave.

And his song of lamentation
Tamed the wild birds of the ruins,
Even vultures, circling nearer,
Listened to the words with pity.

But along the road a cruel
Heartless Saracen came riding
High upon his saddle, swinging
A white lance in blinding sunlight.

And he hurled the deadly spear
In the breast of that poor singer,
Then he galloped, disappearing
Like an evil, wingéd shadow.

Softly flowed the blood, and softly,
Without faltering, the Rabbi
Sang his last song, and the last word
Was a sigh: "Jerusalem."

Yet there is an ancient legend
Which declared it was no lawless
Saracen intent on evil,
But an earth-translated angel,

Who, descending from the heavens,
Came to rescue God's belovéd
From this earth, and quickly guide him,
Painless, to a happier country.

There, the legend has it, myriads
Met the singer, and received him
With an ardor rarely showered
Upon bards, divine, surprising.

Festive bands of choral angels
Came to welcome him with music;
And the song with which they hailed him
Was his own, the ever-moving

Sabbath-bridal-song, the happy
Hymn of synagogal welcome,
With its sudden rapture-sweeping
Melody and notes of gladness.

Cherubim performed on oboes,
Little seraphs played the fiddles,
Other angels stroked violas,
Rattled drums and struck the cymbals.

And the music grew in volume,
And the sounds increased in beauty
Till the whole of heaven echoed:
Lecho dodi likras kallah.[13]

TRANSLATION OF A HEBREW SABBATH-SONG

Komme, Freund, der Braut entgegen

Come, O friend, to greet the Bride, and let us welcome the Sab-
bath!
With sackbut and psaltery let us praise the one God in one word.
The Lord is one and his name is one; let us honor the Lord.
　　　Come, friend. . . .

[13] *Come, O friend, to greet the bride*—the "bride" being the symbol of the
Sabbath. This is the opening line of the medieval Sabbath-hymn, ascribed to
Halevy.

Up and greet the Sabbath; it is a well of healing, consecrated at
     creation,
The end of labor, and the beginning of meditation.
          Come, friend. . . .

Renew thy youth; lift thyself from the dust, array thyself in
     festive raiment;
The son of Isaiah, the Bethlehemite will bring us freedom.
          Come, friend. . . .

Awake, awake, thy Light has been lit; shine, O Light, awake,
     awake;
Sing hosannah, sing jubilee; the Light of God is kindled.
          Come, friend. . . .

Lift up thy heart; be not ashamed nor bowed down;
The Holy City will be rebuilt, raised from the ruins.
          Come, friend. . . .

Thine enemies will be discomfited, yea, utterly cast down;
Thy God will take joy of thee, as the bridegroom with the bride.
          Come, friend. . . .

Thy seed will spread to the right and to the left;
   O praise God through the children of David.
O the joy! O the jubilee!
          Come, friend. . . .

Come in peace, crown of the bridegroom; in joy and rejuvena-
     tion to the faithful among the chosen people.
Come, O Bride. Come in beauty and benediction;
          Come, O Bride.

LAST POEMS—
POSTHUMOUS POEMS
(1852-1855)

MISCELLANEOUS LYRICS

LONGING FOR PEACE

Lass bluten deine Wunden, lass

Let your wounds bleed, and let your tears
  Flow lavishly without a qualm;
A secret pleasure springs from pain,
  And weeping is a gentle balm.

If others have not wounded you,
  Then lash yourself without restraint;
Pile on the blows, bring on the tears,
  And thank your God without complaint.

The clamor dies; night will arise,
  Her long veils trailing in the west.
Go, take your rest; no blustering fool
  Will dare disturb you on her breast.

Here you are safe from music's din;
  Here the piano shrieks no more;
Here even opera is hushed,
  And the bravura's long uproar.

The grave's a simple Paradise
  For ears that hate the mob's loud call.
Yes, death is good, but better 'tis
  Never to have to live at all.

BODY AND SOUL

Die arme Seele spricht zum Leibe

The poor soul to the body spoke:
"I cling to you; in double yoke
We two are paired. When you go down
To nothingness then I will drown
In death, then only will I die.
My second self, my other I,
Surrounding you with love, I cleave
Fast as a gown of finest weave.
Alas! Abstract and naked now,
Lacking a body, I must go,
A sacred nothing, taking flight
Through cold celestial leagues of light,
Or drooping in the halls of sky,
While dumb eternities go by
And yawn at me, and never lose
The echo of their leaden shoes—
A ghastly-grim eternity.
O well-loved body, stay with me!"

To the poor soul the body said:
"Compose yourself; be comforted,
Our fate is hard, our ills increase,
But we can bear them. Be at peace.
I was the wick and am consumed;
But you, the spirit, never doomed,
Will burn eternally and clear
In a far purer atmosphere.
I am but matter, crumbling trash,
Trivial and temporary ash,

And I go down, devoid of flame,
To the dead earth from which I came.
Console yourself, and so good-by!
Perhaps 'tis livelier there on high
Than you expect. And if, up there,
You meet with Ursa, the Great Bear
(Not Meyer-Beer!), dazzling and free,
Greet him a thousand times for me.

BABYLONIAN SORROW

Mich ruft der Tod—Ich wollt', o Süsse

Death calls me.—Sweet, 'twere almost good
To leave thee in some lonely wood,
In some dark, pine-enshrouded forest
Where wolves and all that thou abhorrest
Howl through the night, and the wild boar
Calls to his mate with grunt and roar.

Death calls me.—Dear, 'twere but devotion
To leave thee on the raging ocean.
My child, my wife, 'twere better far
To leave thee where the northwinds are
Lashing the waves, stirring the deeps,
Where horrors breed and nothing sleeps,
Where the gray shark shoots out to kill
And crocodiles are never still—
Trust me, Mathilde, my wife, my child,
Nothing on earth is half as wild,
No spot so fierce and terror-driven,
As this, the very place we live in.
Frightful though wolf and vulture be,
And shark, the terror of the sea,

No beasts more terrible can roam
Than those grim brutes which make their home
In this abode of song and mirth,
Paris, the show-place of the earth.
Paris, where light and laughter dwell,
Fiend's paradise and angel's hell.
That dying, I leave thee behind
In such a place is one more kind
Of torture for this tortured mind.

Black flies are settling on me now.
With spiteful buzzing round my brow,
Mocking my fears with cheap grimaces—
And most of them have human faces,
And black prehensile trunks as odd
As Hindustan's great elephant-god.
My brain is sick with fearful knocks,
As though it were a beaten box,
And—would, alas, it were not true—
My mind will go before I do.

THIS VALE OF TEARS

Der Nachtwind durch die Luken pfeift

The windows shake, the whistling gale
   Tries panes loose and unleaded;
And in the attic, poor and pale,
   Two freezing souls are bedded.

One speaks: "These are but vain alarms.
   What though the world is stormy,
Your mouth on mine is sweet, your arms
   Are all I need to warm me."

The other, whispering, replies:
  "Such moments make us stronger;
For when I look into your eyes
  There is no cold nor hunger."

They laugh and hold each other fast,
  Their kisses have no number;
They weep and sing, and then at last
  Fall into wordless slumber.

Next day there came the coroner
  And, doctor, widely cherished;
And both of them agreed 'twas clear
  That the poor souls had perished.

"An empty stomach," they averred,
  "Combined with bitter weather
Hastened the death which here occurred,
  Or caused it altogether.

"When cold sets in one must withstand
  The weather; we've discovered
It's best to be well-nourished, and
  To lie in bed well-covered."

GOOD ADVICE

Lass dein Grämen und dein Schämen

Walk erect you win respect, you
  Take life boldly in your stride;
Thus no man will dare neglect you,
  And you'll carry home the bride.

Give the devil due precédence;
　Pay the fiddler, have your dance.
Though you wish them all good riddance,
　Court your cousins, kiss your aunts.

Praise each prince, as may be lawful;
　Praise the burgher and his frau;
Do not minimize the offal
　When you're slaughtering the sow.

Do you hate the church? Then faster
　Run to worship at each shrine.
Take your hat off to the pastor;
　Send the priest a flask of wine.

Do you itch, it seems, by inches?
　Scratch yourself till it is gone.
If the shoe you're wearing pinches
　Draw the old house-slippers on.

If the soup is salty, snarling
　Won't improve it; overlook
Such a fault and murmur, "Darling,
　What a soup! And what a cook!"

If your wife mopes and grimaces
　For a shawl, why, get her two.
After spangles, silks, and laces,
　Jewels probably will do.

If, my friend, these freely given
　Rules are kept for all they're worth,
You will surely win to heaven
　And enjoy your peace on earth.

THE SONG OF SONGS

Des Weibes Leib ist ein Gedicht

Woman's white body is a song,
  And God Himself's the author;
In the eternal book of life
  He put the lines together.

It was a thrilling hour; the Lord
  Felt suddenly inspired;
Within his brain the stubborn stuff
  Was mastered, fused, and fired.

Truly, the Song of Songs is this,
  The greatest of his trophies:
This living poem where soft limbs
  Are a rare pair of strophes.

Oh, what a heavenly masterpiece
  That neck and its relation
To the fair head, like an idea
  Crowned with imagination.

In pointed epigrams, the breasts
  Rise under teasing rallies;
And a caesura lies between,
  The loveliest of valleys.

He published the sweet parallel
  Of thighs—what joy to be there!
The fig-leaf grotto joining them
  Is not a bad place either.

It is no cold, conceptual verse,
  No patterned abstract study!
This poem sings with rhyming lips,
  With sweet bones and warm body.

Here breathes the deepest poetry!
  Beauty in every motion!
Upon its brow it bears the stamp
  Of His complete devotion.

Here in the dust, I praise Thee, Lord.
  We are—and well I know it—
Rank amateurs, compared to Thee:
  Heaven's first major poet!

I'll dedicate myself to learn
  This song, the lyric body;
With ardor and with energy
  All day—and night—I'll study!

Yes, day and night, I'll never lack
  For constant application;
And though the task may break my back
  I'll ask for no vacation!

SONG OF THE VIVANDIÈRE

Und die Husaren lieb' ich sehr

The gay hussars—I love them all—
  They are such splendid fellows;
The thin and small, the large and tall,
  The blue ones and the yellows.

And then I love the musketeers—
  I love them without penance;
The shy recruits, the grizzled boots,
  The privates and lieutenants.

The cavalry and the infantry
  Have furnished many a lover,
And often the old artillery
  Has kept me under cover.

I love the Welsh, I love the Dutch,
  The Swedes, the French, the Germans;
I serve them all whate'er befall
  Th' upstanding and infirm 'uns.

I do not care what flag they bear;
  Whether they're poor or wealthy;
I do not care what faith they swear,
  As long as they are healthy.

Faith and the Fatherland! These are
  The shreds of outworn clothing!
Without his clothes a woman knows
  If man's a man—or nothing.

Woman and man are greater than
  Religion and its raiment!
So strip and be at one with me—
  Forget about the payment.

Laughter and youth surround my booth;
  Heaven declares good weather;
The *Malvoisie* today is free.
  Come, let's be drunk together!

THE ONE METHOD

Du bist begeistert; du hast Mut

You are inspired to hardihood—
Ah, that is good!
Yet inspiration's not sufficient;
Remember, evil is omniscient.

The foe, I grant you, does not fight
For light or right.
But he is armed whatever happens;
His always are the heavier weapons.

So arm yourself, steady your hand,
And take your stand.
Aim well; and if the shot should carry,
Rejoice and let your heart make merry.

PALACE OF AFFRONT

Die Zeit verfliesst, jedoch das Schloss

Time passes; yet the battlements,
   The walls and turrets of that palace,
And all its dull inhabitants—
   I can't forget them, crude and callous.

I still can see the weathercock
   Lording it o'er the whole dominion;
The good folk took a timid look
   Before they dared risk an opinion.

Whoever wished to speak, required
   Leave of the wind, the all-censorious,
Or it would blow him undesired
   And furious buffetings by Boreas.

The wise ones held their tongues; they heard
  There was an echo in that palace,
An echo that would twist each word
  Into its opposite with malice.

A fountain made of sphinxes rose
  In the dead center of the garden;
Tears had been shed there, but it was
  Drier than stones and hearts that harden.

Accursèd garden! There was not
  A foot but held some wretched token;
Here I had wept—here on this spot—
  And here my sick heart had been broken.

There was, in fact, no single tree
  Whose listening leaves had never fluttered
With insults and with calumny
  Crudely or delicately uttered.

The toad, that gossip in the grass,
  Informed the rats what they were missing;
They told their aunt what came to pass,
  And she, the snake, went blithely hissing

And told it to her brother-in-law,
  The frog, who spread it through the country,
Till the least vermin's wagging jaw
  Was foul with venomous effront'ry.

The roses had the richest bloom;
  But suddenly a poison settled
Deep in their hearts, and a quick doom
  Found each rose withered and unpetaled.

And he who rhapsodized the rose,
 The nightingale, that noble scion,
Still singing in his desperate throes,
 Found the same poisoned thorn to die on.

Accurséd garden! Yes, that place
 Suffered a curse, an evil essence;
Even into the sunniest days
 There seemed to creep a ghostly presence.

A grinning spook lived near the house;
 He mocked me with his ghastly sneering,
While darkened yews stretched forth their boughs
 To sounds half-sighing and half-jeering.

A terrace marked the garden's end,
 And there the North Sea crashed like thunder;
And there the great tides would descend,
 As though to tear the stones asunder.

There you could look far out to sea;
 And there I often dreamed at gloaming,
Full of the ocean's surge: in me
 The tide came tossing, raging, foaming.

A tossing, raging, foaming tide
 That smote the rocks and stormed at heaven,
As vainly as the waves that died
 Feebly though proudly they were driven.

Bright ships sailed on to happier lands;
 I saw them in an envious vision.—
Yet I was bound with curséd bands
 In that dark palace of derision.

TO MY RELATIONS

Sie küssten mich mit ihren falschen Lippen

They kissed me with false lips; they pledged potations
  With the sweet, sparkling juices of the vine,
  And then they poured black poison in the wine—
For this I am obliged to my relations.

They robbed me of my youth; with defamations
  They stripped my flesh from me. Now I repine,
  A pack of meager bones and weakened spine—
For this I am obliged to my relations.

The records show I am a Christian, and
  Therefore I must forgive them all, and pray
    Devoutly for their souls and wish them well;
But there are times I would I could command
  A hearty curse. Oh, how I long to say,
    "God damn your souls and may you rot in hell."

APPENDIX TO "LAZARUS"

Lass die heil'gen Parabolen

Put aside all dialectics;
  Parables provoke impatience.
Facing the accurséd questions,
  Let's have truth with no evasions.

Why must good men bear the burden
  Of the cross, reviled and driven,
While the wicked ride proud horses,
  Conquering with consent of Heaven?

Where's the blame? Has God no power
   Over wrong? Does He plan evil?
Is He less than All-Embracing?
   Then He might well be the devil.

Thus we probe and press for truthful
   Answers until something jealous
Stops us with an earthy mouthful.
   But is that an answer, tell us!

Wie langsam kriechet sie dahin

How slowly Time, the frightful snail,
   Crawls to the corner that I lie in;
While I, who cannot move at all,
   Watch from the place that I must die in.

Here in my darkened cell no hope
   Enters and breaks the gloom asunder;
I know I shall not leave this room
   Except for one that's six feet under.

Perhaps I have been dead some time;
   Perhaps my bright and whirling fancies
Are only ghosts that, in my head,
   Keep up their wild, nocturnal dances.

They well might be a pack of ghosts,
   Some sort of pagan gods or devils;
And a dead poet's skull is just
   The place they'd choose to have their revels!

Those orgies, furious and sweet,
   Come suddenly, without a warning . . .
And then the poet's cold, dead hand
   Attempts to write them down next morning.

Mitteralterliche Roheit

Medievalism's crudeness
Has been softened by the fine arts.
And our modern culture's climax
Is, I'm sure, the grand piano.

Railways, also, are a splendid
Influence on our way of living;
For they lighten half the sorrow
When we part from our relations.

'Tis a pity the consumption
Of my spine makes it seem doubtful
That I shall remain much longer
In a world so swift with progress.

Wer ein Herz hat und im Herzen

Who has a heart, and who, within it,
   Carries love is half-defeated.
So is it with me: I lie here,
   Gagged and bound, betrayed and cheated.

When I die, my tongue will soon be
   Severed from me—never doubt it—
For they fear I'll dare to come back
   From the grave, and talk about it.

Dark and silent, slowly rotting,
   In my coffin I'll be staying;
And no word of all my suffering
   This poor tongue will be betraying.

EPILOG

Unser Grab erwärmt der Ruhm

"Glory warms us in the grave."
Nonsense. That's a silly stave.
There's a better warmth than this
Found in any cow-girl's kiss,
Though she be a thick-lipped flirt,
Though she reek of dung and dirt.
And a better warmth, I'm thinking,
Every man has found in drinking;
Lapping wine, the lucky dog,
Punch or even common grog;
Sprawling over filthy benches
With the vilest thieves and wenches
That have yet deserved a hanging;
Yes, but—living and haranguing—
Worth more envy, every one,
Than fair Thetis' noble son.

Old Pelides spoke the truth:
Richer is the poorest youth
Who's alive, than lords and ladies
And the greatest kings in Hades
Praised in many a classic tome, or
All the heroes sung by Homer!

THESE LITTLE SONGS

Ich mache die kleinen Lieder

I make these songs that, singing
    With all a lover's art,

Fly straight to reach you, winging
   Themselves into your heart.

Your husband's children rally
   (No shadows, it is true)
From meadow, wood, and valley;
   They also run to you.

The world rewards its songsters
   With smiles and sighs and tears;
But when they hear your youngsters,
   People must hold their ears.

And yet—though maybe wrong stirs
   This body that burns and longs—
I'd rather have made your youngsters
   Than any and all of my songs.

THE LETTER

Ein Wetterstrahl, beleuchtend plötzlich

Suddenly, out of the dark, your letter
   (Lightning revealing night's abyss)
   With its cold brightness showed me this:
How deep is my despair, how bitter.

You even showed a spark of pity,
   You, who have mocked this hot-head fool,
   You, marble-fair and marble-cool,
Standing aloof, so prim and pretty!

O God, what anguish must control me
   That even she is moved to speak!
   If tears should warm that polished cheek
The stones may next try to console me!

If such a heart can stoop to crying,
 Dear God, you can afford to send
 One quick relenting flash, and end
This spun-out tragic farce of dying.

SPHINX

Die Gestalt der wahren Sphinx

There is really little difference
 Between the Sphinx and any woman:
The sharp claws, the cat-like body,
 And the rest of it is common.

Dark as death the Sphinx's riddle,
 Everyone on earth confessed it;
Even Jocasta's son and husband
 Never, never could have guessed it.

Luckily, for mankind, woman
 Does not comprehend her mystery;
Were the answer ever uttered
 There would be an end to history.

DOMESTIC END

Es geht am End', es ist kein Zweifel

This is the end—and just as well—
Passion has swept itself to hell.
Free of love's turmoil, pain, and din,
At last the better days begin
As domesticity comes in.
At last one can enjoy one's self
With just the proper touch of pelf;

Pamper the stomach with delight;
No longer turn and toss at night
With feverish love, but slumber warm
On a consoling wifely arm.

POTATIONS

Geleert hab' ich nach Herzenswunsch

Though it was often wild and risky,
  I gratified my heart's desire—
  A drink as full of heady fire
As a hot punch of burning whisky.

But older now, I bend the knee
  To friendship that no passion fouls,
  Friendship that warms the heart and bowels,
Like a domestic cup of tea.

ETERNITY

Ewigkeit wie bist du lang

Eternity, it now appears,
  Outlasts a thousand years and one;
I have broiled these thousand years
  And yet, it seems, I am not done.

Eternity, alas, is long,
  Long as a thousand years of care.
And then the devil comes along
  And eats me, head and hide and hair.

PAIN

Stunden, Tage, Ewigkeiten

Hours, days, eternities
Seem to crawl on hands and knees,
Or like gray, gigantic snails,
Making slow and slimy trails.

Sometimes in the misty void
A brief beacon has destroyed
My heart's darkness, like her eyes
With their sudden gold surprise.

But a moment later, all
Is dark again; beyond recall
Every promise. There remain
These eternities of pain.

FINIS

Es kommt der Tod; jetzt will ich sagen

Death brings the end; and, though I dread it,
  My tight-lipped pride is ended, too,
  And I can say: "For you, for you,
My heart has beat." There—I have said it.

The grave is dug; prepared the coffin;
  And I will slumber without rue.
  But you will weep; yes, even you
Will dream of me, remembering often.

Comfort yourself. No use pretending
  This doesn't happen everywhere.
  Whatever's good, and great, and fair,
Always will have a shabby ending.

HYMN

Ich bin das Schwert, ich bin die Flamme

I am the Sword, I am the Flame.

I have lit you through the darkness; and when the battle began, I fought in the first rank and led you on. . . .

Round about me lie the bodies of my friends, but we have triumphed. We have triumphed—but round about me lie the bodies of my friends. Amid the jubilant songs of victory the dirge of the funeral is heard. But we have neither time for rejoicing nor for sorrow. The trumpets are sounding again. There shall be new and holier battles. . . .

I am the Sword, I am the Flame.

FIRES OF LOVE

Die Liebesgluten, die so lodernd flammten

The fires of love so passionately burning,
  Where do they go when they have lost their flame?
To where, upon their spits, the damned are turning;
  To the same curséd hell from which they came.

IN A LADY'S ALBUM

Hände küssen, Hüte rücken

To kiss the hand, and doff the hat,
And make a curtsey—what of that!
That, my child, is mere pretense.
The wise heart has far more sense.

IN THE CATHEDRAL

Des Oberkirchners Töchterlein

The sexton's daughter showed me all
    Of which the church was proud.
Around her neck she wore a shawl
    As closely as a shroud.

For a few coins I saw the cross,
    Candles, and burying-place,
Softened with age, fingered by moss—
    Then I saw Elspeth's face.

The pictures glowed with more than paint;
    The incense was enhanced;
The monstrance burned, and every saint
    In every window danced.

The sexton's daughter guided me
    Wherever I cared to go;
And in her clear eyes I could see
    More than the church could show.

Pure eyes they were, without a fleck;
    But I was not misled.
The shawl had fallen from her neck
    And, oh, her mouth was red!

BERTHA

Sie tat so fromm, sie tat so gut

She was so good it seemed I wooed
    An angel hour by hour;

She wrote the loveliest notes to me,
   And wouldn't harm a flower.

The wedding day grew near, and gay
   Were we; my love grew bolder.
But Bertha's aunts detested me—
   And she did what they told her.

She broke the oath that pledged our troth,
   Yet I forgive her gladly;
Had we been wed we would have led
   Lives that had ended badly.

Yet faithless, she was more to me
   Than confidante and neighbor;
Therefore I pray at least she may
   Come safely through her labor.

A PRETTY PAIR

Derweilen auf dem Lotterbette

While in her arms I lay enfolded
   With Laura on the couch, that fox,
   Her husband, rummaged through my box
And took a roll of bills, and bolted.

My pockets empty, I must smile at
   Her lie as one who understands.
   And what is Truth? Washing his hands,
The question first was asked by Pilate.

Soon I shall leave this glib, deceiving
   Worst of all worlds without regret,

For I observe when you're in debt
And out of funds you're scarcely living.

Spirits above, beyond all feeling,
    Even (it may be) beyond thought,
    I envy you. You need for naught,
And so you never think of stealing.

DUELS

Zwei Ochsen disputierten sich

Two oxen argued long and loud
Within a barnyard. Both were proud,
Impetuous, and stubborn brutes;
And in the heat of their disputes,
Matters reached such a furious pass
One called the other ox an ass,
(Which is an insult to an ox)
And so the beasts began to box.

At the same time, in the same yard,
Two asses fought; the words were hard
As blows (you know what asses are)
Till one wild long-ear went too far.
Hee-hawing high he raised his hocks
And called the other ass an ox.
This was a thing he could not pass,
("Ox" is an insult to an ass!)
So one ass fell upon his brother—
In short, they nearly killed each other.

The moral's this: Occasions vary,
But it is always necessary

That students fight to prove the truth
When one is called a stupid youth.

ADVICE

Gib ihren wahren Namen immer

Give the true names in all your tales,
   For if you don't it's always worse;
Fools see themselves—it never fails—
   In every chapter, every verse.
They cry, "Whenever X appears
   It's meant for me. That asinine
Look is my own! Those are my ears!
   That beastly braying noise is mine!
And though the name does not disclose me
Everyone in the country knows me!"

Yes, though you satirize yourself,
The portrait will be claimed by twelve.

WARNING

Verletze nicht durch kalten Ton

Do not affront this youth with slight.
   The needy stranger whom you scorn
   May be (who knows?) divinely born,
A god, a very child of light.

When next you see him he may wear
   An aureole about his head,
   And from his eyes there may be shed
A look you cannot hope to bear.

FOR "LA MOUCHE"

Es träumte mir von einer Sommernacht

I dreamed a dream: It was a summer night.
  Pale and uncertain in a vague moon's glances
Structures arose of Renaissance delight,
  Frail, legendary ruins of romances.

And here and there, as though with fixed intent,
  A stern and solitary Doric column
Seemed challenging the lowered firmament,
  Defying thunder, delicate but solemn.

Everywhere broken sculpture lay about:
  Doors, portals, roofs, and many a shattered gable,
Centaur and sphinx, chimeras, and a rout
  Of beasts and satyrs from the Age of Fable.

There, in an open, carved sarcophagus,
  Preserved among the parts of scattered creatures,
Intact, where everything was ruinous,
  A dead man lay with mild and suffering features.

Strong caryatides with stress and strain
  Upheld the tomb, their stony necks uprearing;
Carven upon the sides one saw a train
  Of curious figures curiously appearing.

Here the lewd pagan gods all seemed to leave
  Olympus gladly as they hotly hastened;
And here was Adam standing with his Eve,
  In fig-leaf aprons, obviously chastened.

Troy flamed again and fell in ashes; here
  Were Helen and young Paris who possessed her;
Moses and Aaron, too, were strangely near
  With Judith, Holofernes, Haman, Esther.

Phoebus Apollo rose, and one could see
  Vulcan, and Cupid, with his mother, Venus,
Pluto, and Proserpine, and Mercury,
  God Bacchus, and Priapus, and Silenus.

Beside them stood poor Balaam and his ass,
  About to speak. There, direst of all slaughters,
Abraham held young Isaac, and, alas,
  Lot came carousing with his drunken daughters.

Here you saw Salome, who danced so well,
  Bearing the Baptist's head so lewdly given;
Here was King Satan with the hosts of hell,
  And here was Peter with the keys of heaven.

Then, with a change of scene, you looked upon
  Jove's lustihood and his lascivious power,
Seducing Leda as a regal swan,
  And wooing Danae with a golden shower.

Wildly Diana and her hunt went by.
  Heroic Hercules, discarding his staff,
Dressed like a woman, made the spindle fly,
  The while his brawny muscles held the distaff.

Here Sinai raised its summit, and here smiled
  Israel with his oxen, sleek and ample.
And here you saw God as a little child
  Disputing with the scholars in the Temple.

The contrast deepened, grew ironical
  With Greek light-heartedness and the God-yearning
Judaic spirit—and about them all
  The ivy tendrils' arabesques were turning.

Then as the whirling pictures filled my head,
  And the whole dream grew rich and riotous . . .
Then, suddenly, I knew that I was dead;
  I was the man in the sarcophagus.

Guarding my resting-place there grew
  A tall strange flower, a flower without its fellow,
Modest, and yet its power was amorous, too;
  Its fleshy petals blue and sulphur-yellow.

The passion-flower they call it, and they say
  When Christ was crucified, from his fair bosom
The precious drops of martyrdom that lay
  Upon the earth became this mystic blossom.

Blood-witness, so they claim; for here one sees
  The marks when, driven out of Pilate's palace,
The torturers increased His agonies—
  All, all are in the flower's perfumed chalice.

Yes, all the Passion's properties adorn
  This bloom so innocent of pain and clamor:
The scourge, the binding rope, the crown of thorn,
  The cross, the cup, the nails, the very hammer.

Such was the flower that grew upon my grave
  And bent above my body in its coffer,
And kissed my brow and eyes, and, somehow, gave
  The healing grief that mourning women offer.

Then, like a magic vision, all things grew
  Clear and the yellow flower itself grew clearest;
For now I saw, at last, that it was you—
  You were the passion-flower; you, my dearest.

You were the flower, you, belovéd child;
  That kiss was all I needed to inform me.
No flower-lips could ever be so mild,
  No flower-tears so passionate and stormy.

My eyes were closed, but still I saw your face.
  The moon was baffling; but my spirit captured
The very gestures of your ghostly grace
  As you bent over me, intense, enraptured.

We did not speak, yet I felt every thought
  Your chaste and silent tenderness could fashion—
The spoken word is shameless, good-for-naught,
  But silence is the very flower of passion.

Soundless communion! Ecstasy supreme!
  Never was there a swifter hour, a rarer
Intimate conversation in a dream
  As in that night, woven of joy and terror.

And what we spoke of? Never ask the theme.
  What do the glow-worms glimmer to the grasses?
What are the small waves lisping to the stream?
  What does the west-wind whisper as it passes?

What makes the carbuncle and ruby burn?
  What is the reason for the scents that hover
Over the roses? What's the strange concern
  The passion-flower has for the buried lover?

I do not know how long my soul enjoyed
   That marble chest, that slumber-cooled security;
I only know that something dark destroyed
   The dream that was all peacefulness and purity.

Death, with your silent grave, you give the best
   Of endless pleasure, lavish in your giving;
Life only offers yearning without rest,
   Raw passion and the silly lust for living.

But woe is me! My peace was put to rout,
   As from without there came an overpowering
Clamor and stamping, strident shout on shout;
   I saw my timid blossom bent and cowering.

Yes, from without I heard the hateful brawl
   Of voices scolding, arguing, and jangling;
And suddenly I recognized them all—
   The figures on my marble tomb were wrangling!

Must superstitions haunt me even here?
   Must marble argue among phantom roses?
Does pagan Pan utter his shriek of fear,
   Wild with the harsh anathemas of Moses?

Oh, the same fight will rage forevermore;
   The Beautiful and Good will be at variance.
Mankind will split itself, as heretofore,
   Into two parties: Hellenes and Barbarians.

Endless their oaths and shouts—a pretty pass—
   The wind of argument made heavy weather;
The controversy grew, as Balaam's ass
   Triumphed and brayed down gods and saints together.

And while the vile hee-hawing still increased,
   All hope of peace or further sleep denying,
In sheer despair against the stupid beast,
   I, too, cried out—and woke myself with crying.

LOTUS-FLOWER

(FOR "LA MOUCHE")

Wahrhaftig wir beide bilden

Truly, the two of us offer
   A pretty picture to frame.
The one has lumbago to suffer,
   The other is chronically lame.

She is an ailing kitten,
   He is as sick as a dog;
Their brains have become somewhat addled,
   And both of them live in a fog.

She thinks she's a lotus-blossom
   Whose cup will be opened soon;
And he, because of his pallor,
   Fancies that he is the moon.[1]

The lotus-blossom uncovers
   Her being the whole night long;
But all she conceives for her trouble
   Is a metaphor and a song.

See the poem on pages 72-73.

UNWILLING PLATONIST

Worte, Worte! Keine Taten!

Words, words, words, but never action!
   Wit is all that I can boast!
Poor dear, there's small satisfaction
   In a sauce without the roast!

But the stubborn loin's effusive
   Strength is sadly checked this year;
And, perhaps, it's not conducive
   For your delicate health, my dear.

Yes, these orgies of embracing
   Wear the body out, I hear;
Cupid's reckless steeple-chasing
   Is too much for you, I fear.

It is best for you, this ember
   Of a man (a man indeed!)
Who can scarcely lift a member.
   Here's the lover that you need.

Take the impulse. Make a sport of
   Continence and our despair.
Thus we shall enjoy a sort of
   Pure and healthy love-affair.

DYING

Erstorben ist in meiner Brust

Now from the chambers of my heart
The pleasures of the world depart.

Flesh has become an irksome weight;
I leave what's evil to its fate,
Being too dead to love or hate.
To grieve now is to waste good breath
When all that lives in me is death.

Curtain. The last lines have been said.
And, yawning on the way to bed,
My dear old German public drools.
Those worthy people are not fools,
They do not plague themselves with thought,
But drink and gossip, as they ought.

Old Homer's hero had it pat:
The poorest burgher on the Neckar
Who lives for little more than liquor
Is far more blesséd doing that
Than I, the toast of all the ladies,
The hero dead, the prince Pelides,
Lord of a shadowy host in Hades.

IN THE MORNING

Meine gute, liebe Frau

My beloved and loving wife,
My most kind and liberal lady,
Has prepared the early breakfast:
Rich, brown coffee; cream like satin.

And, behold the way she serves it,
Smiling, teasing, singing, tempting.
In the whole of Christendom
Never a mouth can smile so sweetly.

And her flute-like voice is heard
Only now and then from angels
Or, at all events, among the
Very choicest nightingales.

FOR MATHILDE

Ich war, o Lamm, als Hirt bestellt

O little lamb, take comfort; see,
I am the shepherd meant for thee.
My bread was shared with thee; I'd bring
Sweet water from the clearest spring.
When the fierce winter-storms alarmed
Here in my bosom thou wert warmed,
Sheltered against each dread occurrence.
And when the rain came down in torrents
And wolf and stream and evil weather
Howled in the rocky gorge together,
Thou didst not tremble, nothing mattered.
Even when sudden lightning shattered
The tallest pine, thou still wouldst rest
Sleeping securely on my breast.

My arm grows weak, my anxious soul
Feels the approach of death. My rôle
As pastoral-guardian, shepherd-lover
Is done, alas. The play is over.
O God, I put back in Thy hands
The shepherd's crook, with no demands
But this: When I am laid away
Watch o'er my lamb lest she should stray
In briars and her fleece be torn.
Protect her, Lord, from every thorn

And every bog with treacherous mire.
Beneath those feet before they tire
Let the new green be quickly spread
With a blue heaven overhead;
And let her sleep, when she is fed,
Serene as when she took her rest
Sleeping securely on my breast.

ANNUAL MOURNING

Keine Messe wird man singen

There will be no whispered masses,
    There will be no songs nor crying,
None will rise to say a *Kaddish*
    On the day that I lay dying.

But the day may be a fair one.
    Then (the thought is most consoling)
With Pauline upon Montmartre
    My Mathilda will go strolling.

And perhaps she'll carry flowers,
    Immortelles, dead-white and yellow;
And her pretty eyes will moisten,
    And she'll say (in French), "Poor fellow."

I'll be living far too high
    Up in heaven (how it rankles!)
To invite her to sit down
    And relieve her tired ankles.

Oh, my plump and breathless pigeon,
    Walking's quite unnecessary.
See—the carriages are standing
    Just outside the cemetery.

IT GOES OUT

Der Vorhang fällt, das Stück ist aus

The curtain falls; the play is done;
Ladies and gentlemen one by one
Go home at last. How was the play?
I heard applause as I came away.
A much-respected audience
Praised the author beyond a doubt;
But now that they have all gone hence
The house is silent, the lights are out.

But wait! A sound is heard within,
Feeble but fairly near the stage;
Perhaps the string of a violin
Has suddenly broken down with age.
Peevishly in the dark parterre
The restless rats run here and there,
And the place smells of rancid oil.
All things grow musty; all things spoil;
The last lamp tries to stem the rout.
Then, with a sputter and sigh of doubt,
The light (that was my soul) goes out.

WHERE?

Wo wird einst des Wandermüden

Where will I, the wander-wearied,
  Find a haven and a shrine?
Under palms will I be buried?
  Under lindens on the Rhine?

Will I lie in desert reaches,
  Buried by a stranger's hand?
Or upon the well-loved beaches,
  Covered by the friendly sand?

Well, what matter! God has given
  Wider spaces there than here.
And the stars that swing in heaven
  Will be lamps above my bier.

INDEX OF FIRST LINES
IN GERMAN

INDEX OF FIRST LINES
IN GERMAN

BOOKS BY MR. UNTERMEYER

POETRY

FIRST LOVE
CHALLENGE
THESE TIMES
THE NEW ADAM

ROAST LEVIATHAN
BURNING BUSH
ADIRONDACK CYCLE
FOOD AND DRINK

SELECTED POEMS AND PARODIES

PARODIES

THE YOUNGER QUIRE
—AND OTHER POETS

INCLUDING HORACE
HEAVENS

COLLECTED PARODIES

TALES AND TRAVEL

MOSES
THE DONKEY OF GOD

CHIP: MY LIFE AND TIMES
BLUE RHINE—BLACK FOREST

TRANSLATIONS AND ADAPTATIONS

THE POEMS OF HEINRICH HEINE; 325 LYRICS
THE FAT OF THE CAT (*after Gottfried Keller*)
THE LAST PIRATE (*after W. S. Gilbert*)
MAN AND THE MASSES (*Toller's Masse Mensch*)

ESSAYS

AMERICAN POETRY SINCE 1900

CRITICAL COLLECTIONS

AMERICAN POETRY: FROM THE BEGINNING TO WHITMAN
MODERN AMERICAN POETRY   MODERN BRITISH POETRY
THE FORMS OF POETRY: A POCKET DICTIONARY

ANTHOLOGIES

THE BOOK OF LIVING VERSE
THIS SINGING WORLD

YESTERDAY AND TODAY
RAINBOW IN THE SKY

COLLABORATIONS

POETRY: ITS APPRECIATION AND ENJOYMENT
(*with Carter Davidson*)
NEW SONGS FOR NEW VOICES (*with Clara and David Mannes*)

INTRODUCTIONS

to Joseph Moncure March's *The Wild Party,* Maxwell Bodenheim's *Minna
and Myself,* Anna Wickham's *The Contemplative Quarry,* Charles Rezni-
koff's *By the Waters of Manhattan,* James Branch Cabell's *Gallantry,*
Robert Nathan's *A Cedar Box,* Merrill Moore's *Six Sides to a Man,* The
Modern Library's edition of *The Canterbury Tales,* and *Walt Whitman,
Emily Dickinson,* and *Conrad Aiken* in The Pamphlet Poets.